manifesto of fragility

Edited by Sam Bardaouil and Till Fellrath

The many lives *and* deaths *of* Louise Brunet

SilvanaEditoriale

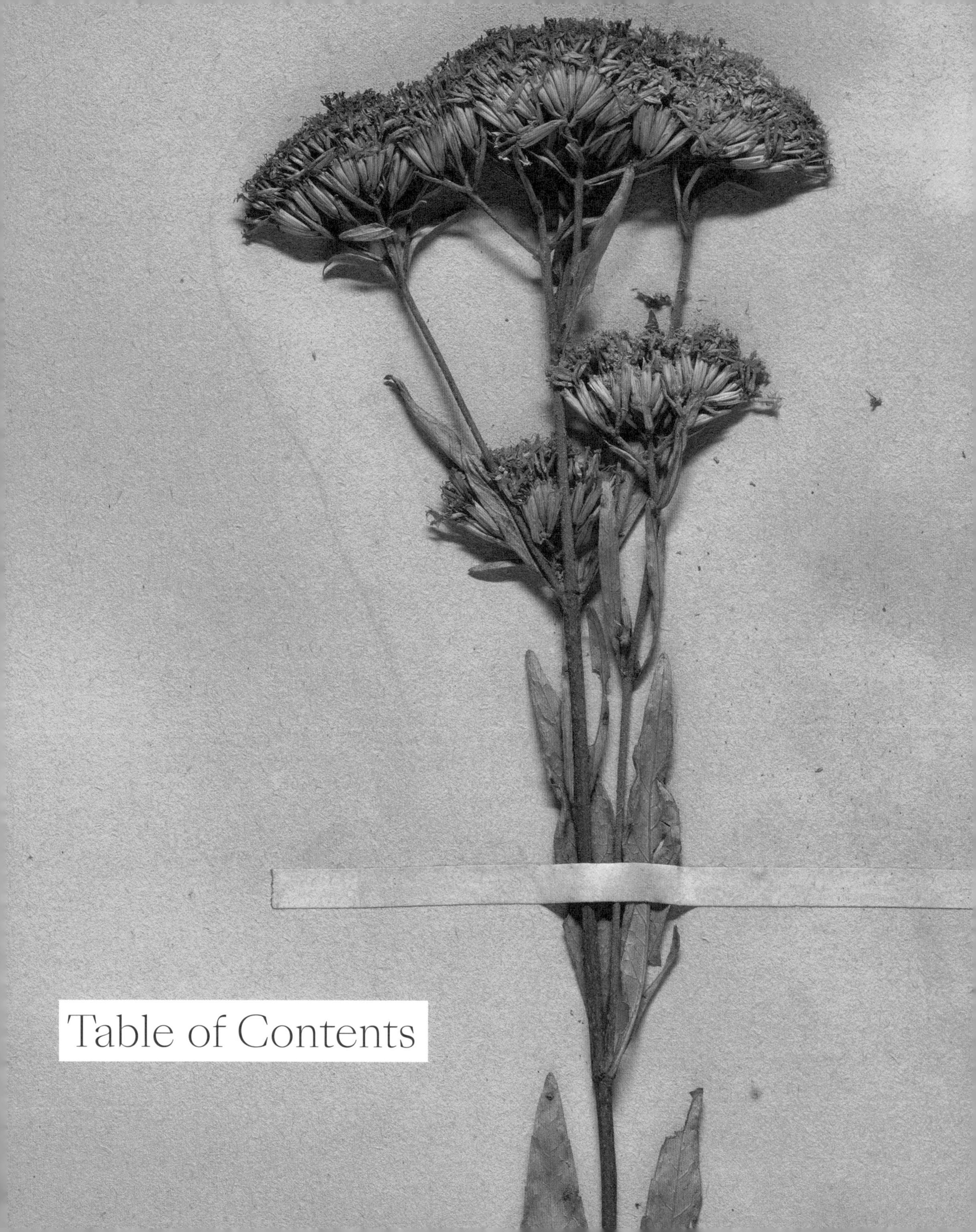

Table of Contents

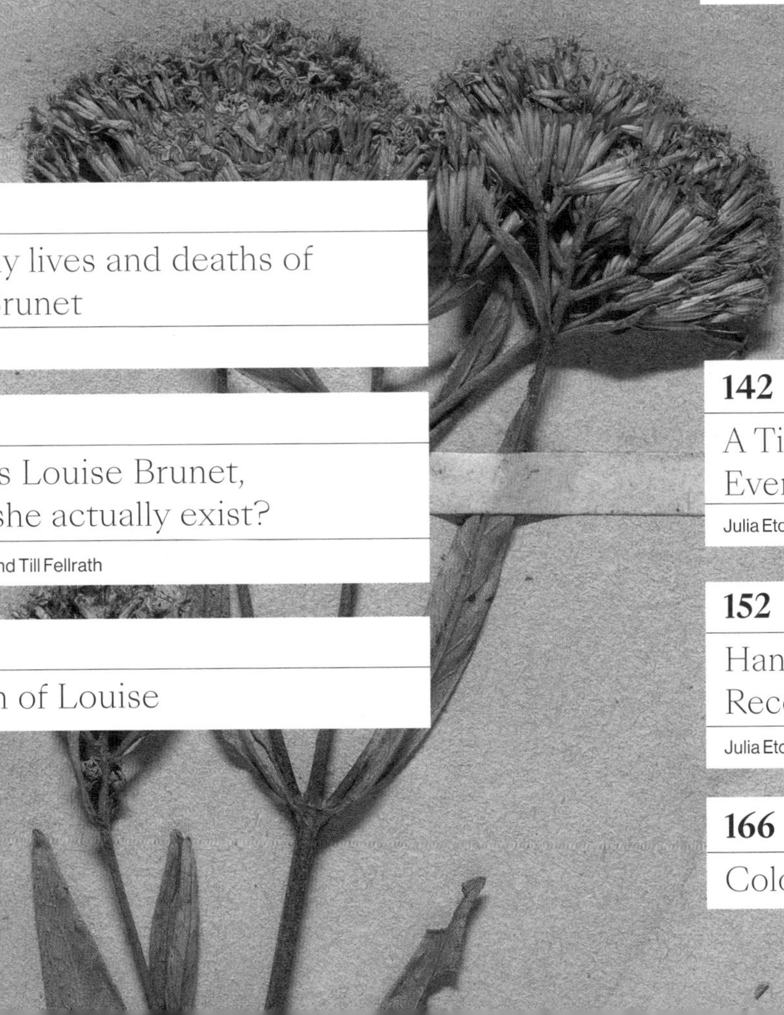

List of Artists

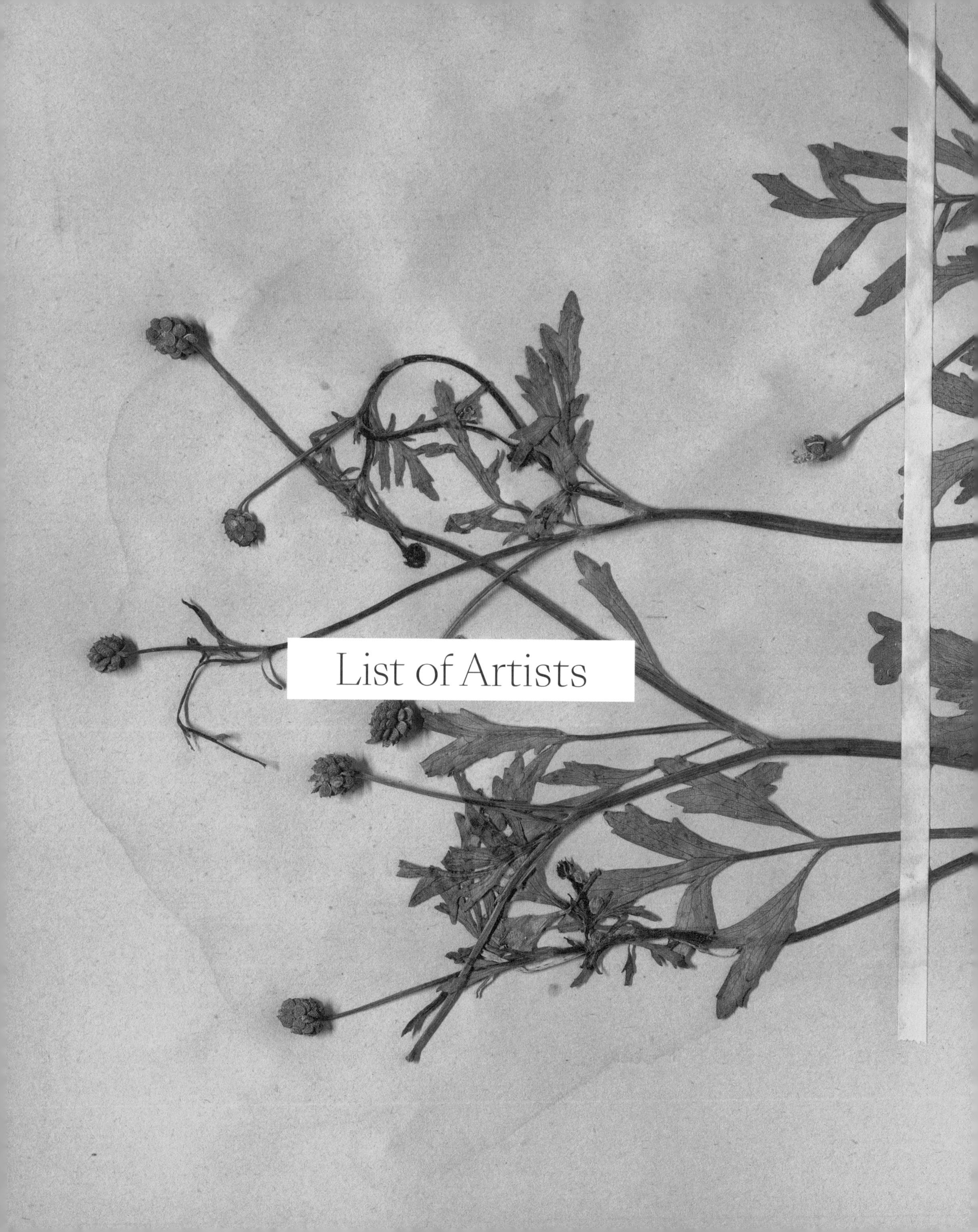

Mohamad Abdouni
Gabriel Abrantes
Ann Agee
Julio Anaya Cabanding
Giulia Andreani
Ayné
Joachim Bandau
Jean-Adolphe Beaucé
Semiha Berksoy
Phoebe Boswell
Louis Boulanger
Louis Bouquet
Sarah Brahim
Georges Brunet-Mahuet
E. Caryocost
Jean-Baptiste Charlier
Jean Claracq
J.P. Clerc
Pierre Combet-Descombes
Antoine Coysevox
Nicolas Daubanes
Alexandre-François Desportes
Devambez
Michael Zeno Diemer
Etienne Dinet
Johann Ludwig Rudolph Durheim
Buck Ellison
Léo Fourdrinier
Rafael França
Jean-Baptiste Frénet
Tony Garnier
J.E. Goossens
Nicki Green
Hudinilson Jr.
Peter Hujar
Auguste Jahandier (after Victor Grilat)
Lucien Jonas
Mohammed Kazem
Philippe de Lassalle
Richard Learoyd
Hannah Levy
Lucy McRae
Jesse Mockrin
Jean-Baptiste Monnoyer
Morelan
Ailbhe Ní Bhriain
William de Niewkerque
Joanna Piotrowska
Charles Plessard
Carlo Portelli
Christina Quarles
Erin M. Riley
Ugo Schiavi
Markus Schinwald
Sylvie Selig
Jeremy Shaw
Kim Simonsson
Francisco Tamagno
David Teniers the Younger
Augustin Thierriat
Salman Toor
Underwood & Underwood Publishers
Vachon-Imbert
Abraham van der Eyck
Alessandro Varotari called Il Padovanino
Émile Vernet-Lecomte (after)
Munem Wasif
Zhang Yunyao

And several anonymous artists…

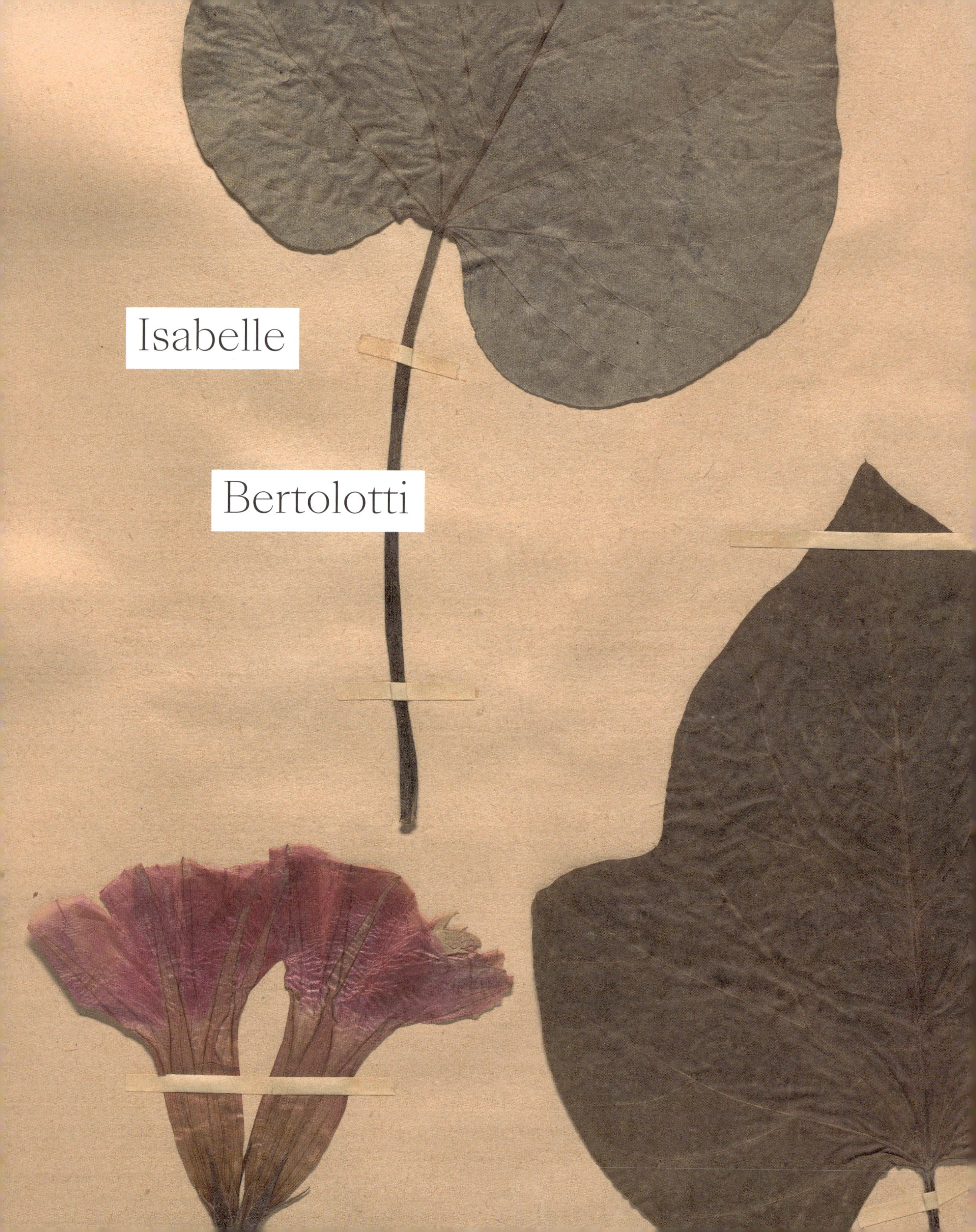
Isabelle
Bertolotti

Foreword

Director's Note

Bringing transhistorical works
together with contemporary works,
the 16th edition of the Lyon Biennale
encourages the public to
contemplate the continuous
ebbs and flows of prosperity
and decline that make up the cycles
of global history. It also presents
an opportunity to seek new
forms of inclusivity not
based on difference but rather on
the only truly universal quality
that binds us all:
the inevitability of our frail humanity.

Created in 1991, the Lyon Biennale asserts itself today after more than thirty years of existence as the most important event in France devoted to contemporary art and a highlight on the global agenda of major events. Firmly established in the region and endowed with innovative methods of mediation, it fosters dialogue and exchange by addressing an ever-wider audience.

While the Biennale has previously used the particular geography of Lyon as a starting point to open up reflections on contemporary ecosystems, this 16th edition borrows more particularly from history and the close links it maintains with the history of art. By unearthing events that have had local impact in the past, it also lifts the veil on unsuspected international repercussions on the political, economic or social level as well as on artistic creation, proving definitively how much art bears witness to its time.

The two guest curators invited to the 16th Lyon Biennale, Sam Bardaouil and Till Fellrath, have put together a *manifesto of fragility* in three stories based on their in-depth research in public and private archives; numerous visits to monuments and unusual sites; and numerous encounters with researchers, curators, scientists and directors of Lyon-based and international institutions, among others. The 16th Lyon Biennale invokes these numerous influences to inform an exploration of fragility that searches for connections beyond the limits of geography and time.

One local account marks the first of the three points of entry into the Biennale's exploration of fragility. This part of the exhibition, titled *The Many Lives and Deaths of Louise Brunet,* takes inspiration from the story of Louise Brunet, a young woman who took part in the revolution of Lyon's *canuts* (silkweavers) in 1834. As a symbol of resistance, she is manifested in multiple incarnations throughout the history of art, from antiquity to the present day. Through the connections discovered between Lyon and Lebanon, the second part of the exhibition, titled *Beirut and the Golden Sixties*, explores fragility and resistance in the Beirut art scene of the mid-20th century as an example of resilience in the face of unfathomable hardship. And finally in the third part, *A World of Endless Promise,* the invited artists from all over the world find – through their expressive sensitivity – strategies of resistance in a world beset by crises like disease, war, the climate emergency and so many other upheavals.

Bringing transhistorical works together with contemporary works, the 16th edition of the Lyon Biennale encourages the public to contemplate the continuous ebbs and flows of prosperity and decline that make up the cycles of global history. It also presents an opportunity to seek new forms of inclusivity not based on difference but rather on the only truly universal quality that binds us all: the inevitability of our frail humanity.

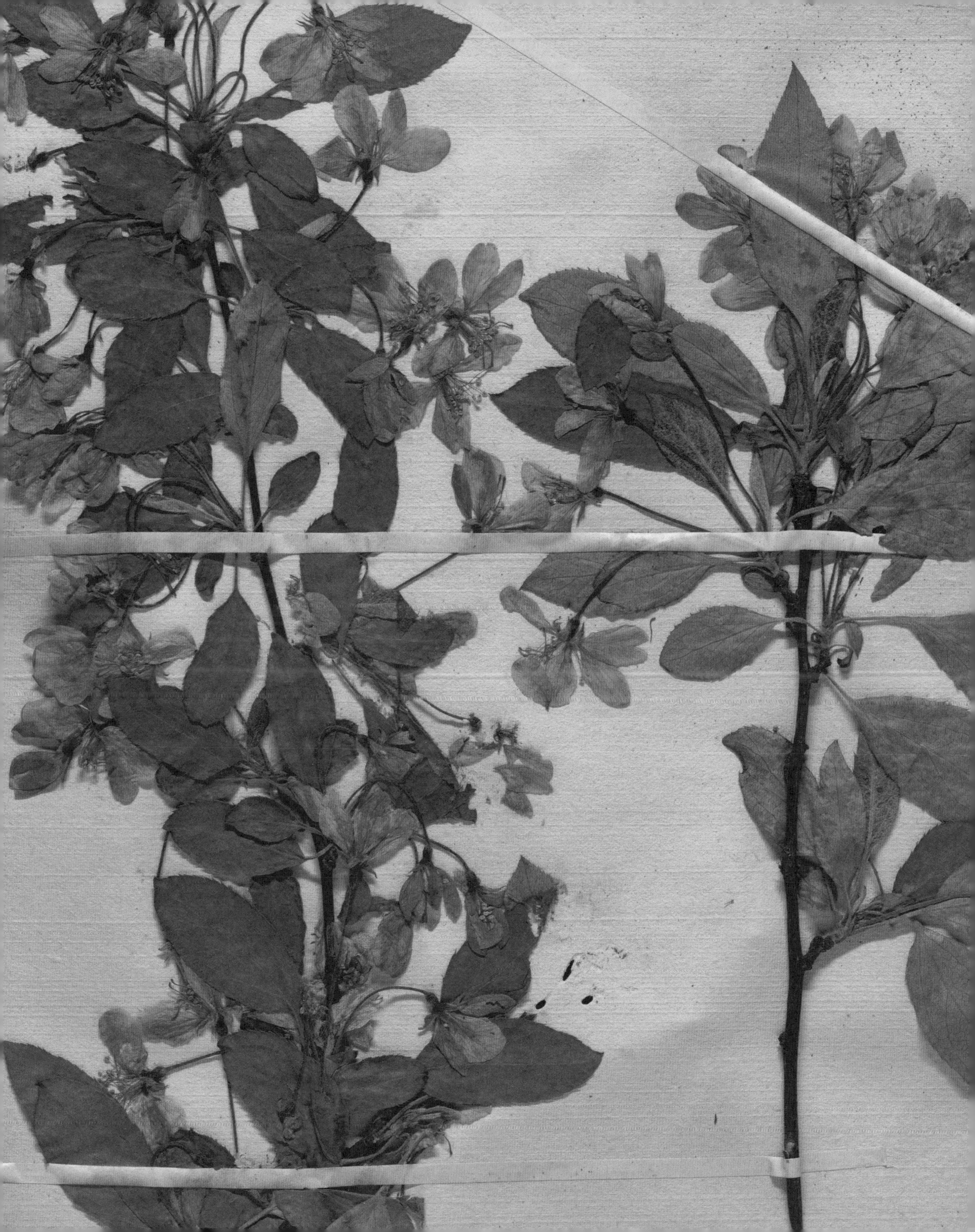

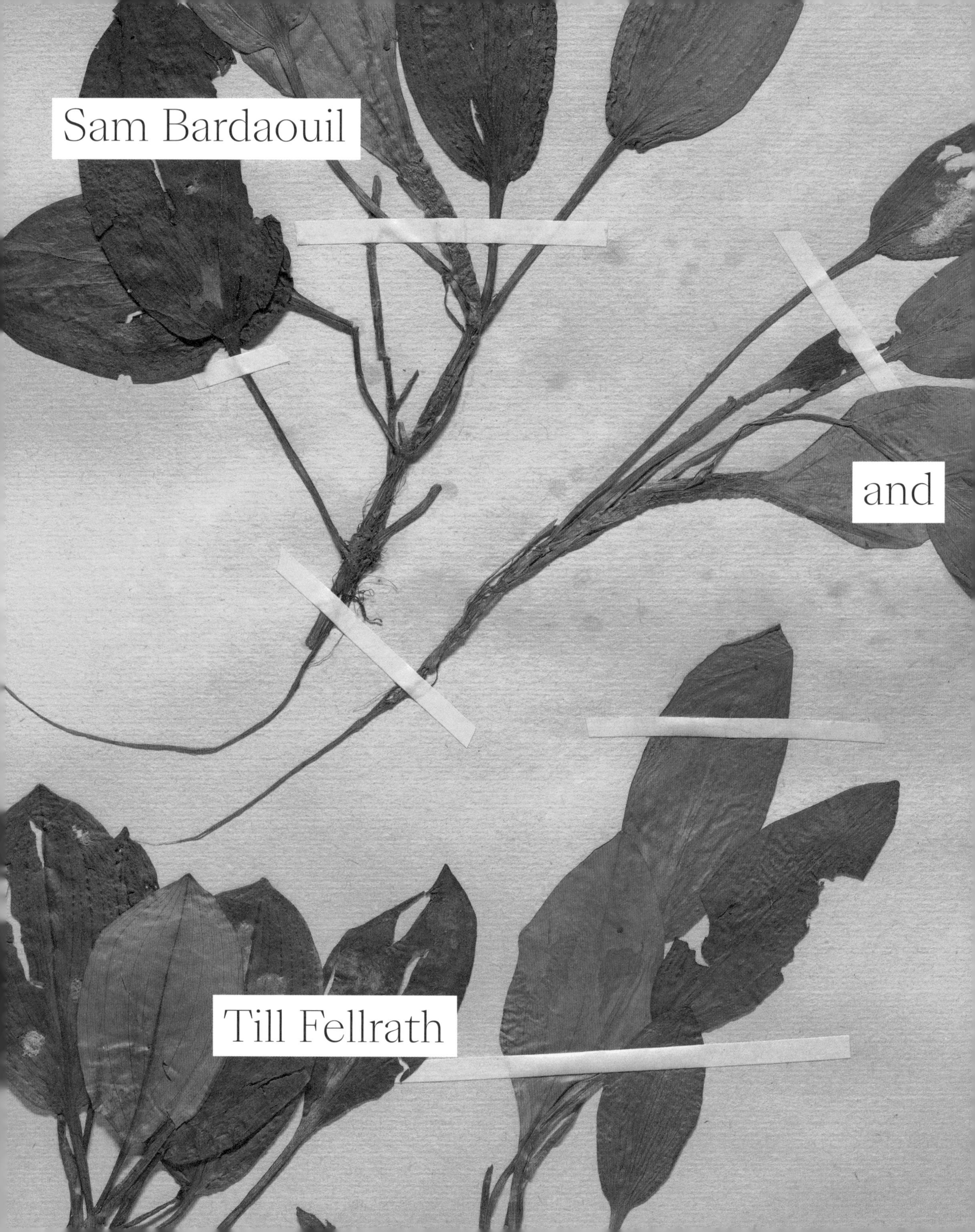

Sam Bardaouil

and

Till Fellrath

manifesto of fragility

Curators' Foreword

The 16th Lyon Biennale:
manifesto of fragility
is a sobering invitation
to ponder the fallibility of the
human condition, the ephemerality
of existence and the precariousness
of the entire planet.
By acknowledging the transience
of worldly experience in all its forms,
we open ourselves to the possibility
of fragility's emancipatory
power as a way towards new forms
of collective resilience: grounded
in an acceptance of our common
vulnerability, harnessing the
incredible potential
found in leaning on each other
and sharing the burden of
pushing forward.

The 16th Lyon Biennale: *manifesto of fragility* positions fragility at the heart of a generative form of resistance that is emboldened by the past, responsive to the present and primed for the future. It imagines a world where vulnerability is actively engaged as a foundation for empowerment rather than shunned as a sign of weakness. Conceived as a collective statement, it is buttressed by a plurality of resilient voices thriving on tenderness and flourishing in adversity. With words, images, sounds and movements, it calls communities together to draft a manifesto for a world that is blamelessly fragile.

Our interest in exploring strategies of change that could find inspiration in this revised outlook on fragility took off almost three years ago as we began to immerse ourselves in Lyon and its untold histories. Rising from the foundations of Lugdunum, on the echoes of Napoleon's declaration of love to the *Lyonnais,* and out of the flickering images of the Lumière brothers' *actualités,* the destiny of Lyon is marked by the particularities of its people, and the traces of their experiences that enrich the lives of those who come to know the city today.

The many lives and deaths of Louise Brunet

The Biennale is structured around three concentric layers that function as focused points of entry into the topic at hand. The first layer, titled *The Many Lives and Deaths of Louise Brunet,* presents an exploration of fragility that is centred around the obscure tale of one individual, Louise Brunet, a young woman who was sent to prison for taking part in the revolution of Lyon's *canuts* (silkweavers) in 1834, only to find herself a few years later on a perilous journey from Lyon to the silk factories of Mount Lebanon. This micro-narrative serves as the foundation for an innovative exploration of fragility where the real, historical Louise Brunet is reimagined as different protagonists living in different times and places. Fiction and reality converge in a rewriting of this forgotten woman's story, which becomes an opportunity to delve into various experiences of fragility through the lenses of race, gender, mortality and economy, among many other considerations.

Out of the micro-narrative of this individual *Lyonnaise,* the Biennale expands outward into its second layer, broadening its scope to explore fragility through the example of the city where Louise Brunet arrived sometime around 1838: Beirut. Titled *Beirut and the Golden Sixties,* this section of the Biennale alights on a fascinating yet lesser-known period of prolific artistic production and political engagement in Beirut. This focus on Beirut acquires added poignancy in Lyon given the two cities historical entanglements, particularly through the 19th century silk trade and during the French Mandate era in Lebanon from 1920 until 1943, which set the stage for the 1950s to 1970s period of central concern to this layer of the Biennale.

Beirut and the Golden Sixties

From Beirut, the Biennale looks into the complexities of fragility and resistance in the rest of the world through an expansive survey of artworks by known and anonymous artists and creators spanning three millennia. Titled *A World of Endless Promise,* this section of the Biennale collapses the axis of time to build a nuanced patchwork of narratives illuminating moments of resilience in the face of social, political and environmental upheaval. Spread across several locations around the city, *A World of Endless Promise* brings visitors face-to-face with the architectural richness of Lyon, a remarkable configuration of historical treasures showcasing ancient Roman amphitheatres, mediaeval quarantine districts, Renaissance palazzos, brutalist modern architecture and 1970s industrial sites. The artworks displayed in these unique locations respond to the specificity of their environments. The assembled artists invoke various aspects of fragility both in the topics they address and the materials they use. Together they present a timeless panorama which, through the abundance of its contributors, uplifts a globalised perspective of past and present accounts of

A World of Endless Promise

perseverance in the face of adversity to propose future modes of thriving in a challenging world.

The 16th Lyon Biennale: *manifesto of fragility* is a sobering invitation to ponder the fallibility of the human condition, the ephemerality of existence and the precariousness of the entire planet. By acknowledging the transience of worldly experience in all its forms, we open ourselves to the possibility of fragility's emancipatory power as a way towards new forms of collective resilience: grounded in an acceptance of our common vulnerability, harnessing the incredible potential found in leaning on each other and sharing the burden of pushing forward.

manifesto

of

fragility

manifesto of fragility: The many lives and deaths of Louise Brunet

Prologue

Conceived as a focused exploration of the fragility of one individual, ***The Many Lives and Deaths of Louise Brunet*** starts with a search for a young silk weaver and revolutionary who went by the name of Louise Brunet and lived in Lyon in the early decades of the 19th century. It quickly turns into a fictional retelling of the story of several individuals whose struggles, like those of Louise Brunet, have been undermined and forgotten.

Blurring the boundaries between fact and fiction with an investigative approach, this part of ***manifesto of fragility*** is more like an artistic installation than a curated exhibition. A wide plethora of artworks and archival materials spanning two millennia come together as parts of an unfinished puzzle. Alongside the works on display are several short stories that have been conceived as literary extensions of the exhibition's fictional narrative. They serve as clues from a larger body of evidence through which traces of several Louise Brunets begin to appear. From a Senegalese woman fleeing the colonial exhibition of Lyon in 1894, to a gay artist dying of AIDS at St. Vincent's Hospital in New York in 1992, the turbulent lives of these people hover between reality and imagination. They serve as gateways into distinct forms of fragility and resistance as experienced through the lens of the body, race, gender, labour, desire or colonial struggle. ***The Many Lives and Deaths of Louise Brunet*** begin to emerge.

Who was Louise Brunet, and did she actually exist?

A note from Sam Bardaouil and Till Fellrath

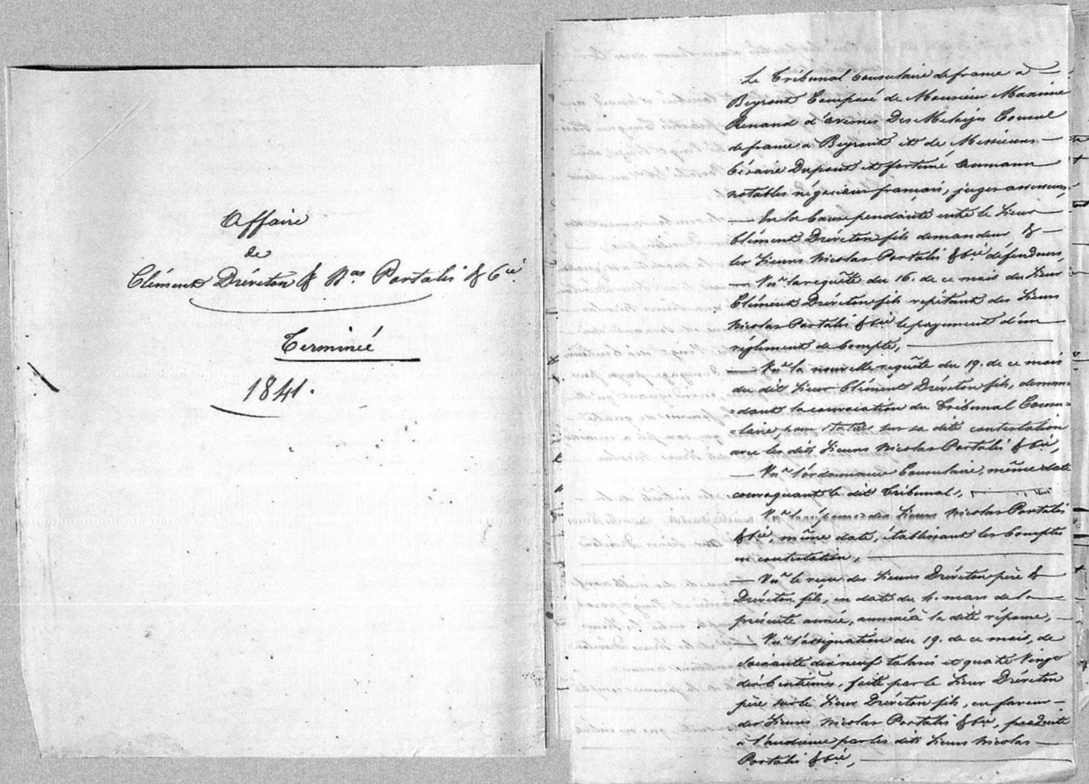

Documents in the archives of the French Consulate in Lebanon, 1841. Photo: Julia Etournay-Lemay.

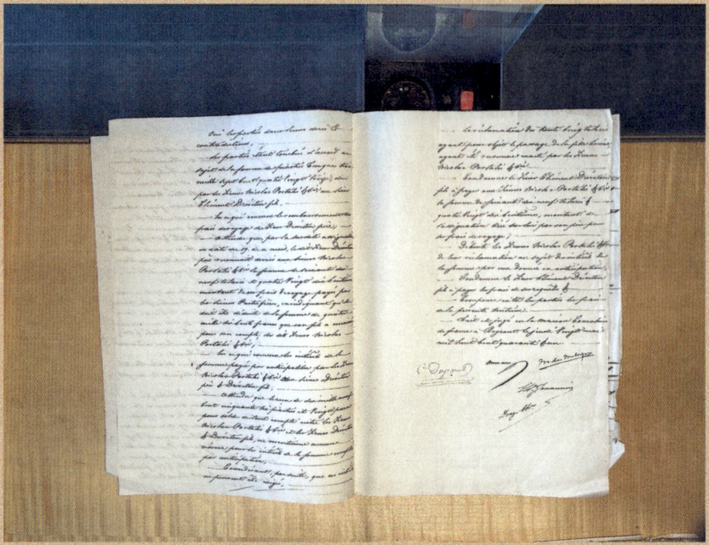

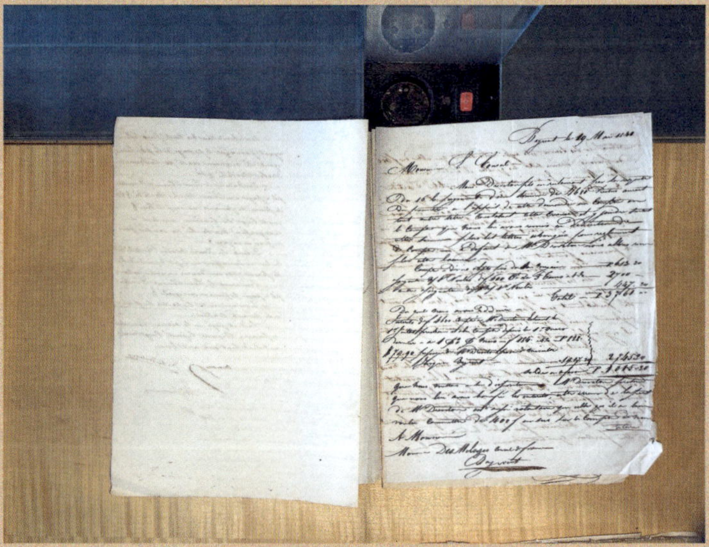

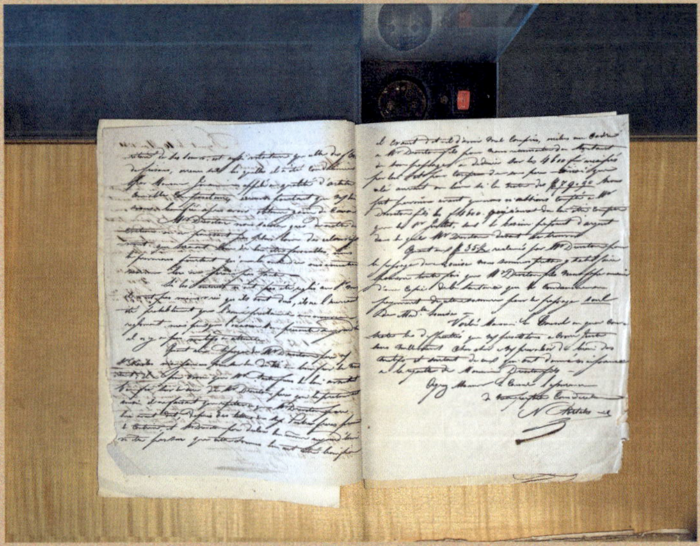

Documents in the archives of the French Consulate in Lebanon, 1841. Photo: Julia Etournay-Lemay.

A few letters and some official documents buried in the archives of the French Ministry of Foreign Affairs in Paris and Nantes indicate that there was once a young woman who went by this name. These classified files show that Louise Brunet was someone who rebelled against the established orders and fought for a better life alongside Lyon's silk workers in the famous Canuts revolt of 1834. But is this the same Louise that you are about to encounter here? Yes and no.

Yes, because you will come face to face with obscure remnants that we have assembled from the turbulent life of one Louise Brunet. No, because, as you will discover, the world is full of countless Louise Brunets whose stories, deemed far too insignificant for the grand annals of history, have been swept into the far corners of oblivion. The little evidence that you shall examine next, despite some of its dubious nature, reveals the existence of many Louise Brunets.

Our search for Louise Brunet begins with a faded, handwritten letter found in the private archive of the descendants of a notable Lyonnaise silk dynasty. Dated 9 March 1840, it was addressed from Louise in Beirut, where she was working in a Mount Lebanon silk factory owned by a Lyon-based entrepreneur, to her sister in Lyon. How this letter ended up in this archive only to be rediscovered some 180 years later remains a mystery.

The revelation of this first correspondence is corroborated through additional personal letters, visual fragments and long-lost relics, many of which are presented here. As our investigation advances, a common thread begins to develop, and two things in particular stand out. Though originating from different times and places, each object embodies, in tangible form, the existence of a person seeking to liberate themselves from the circumstances into which they were born. The second shared peculiarity: these individuals almost always disappear, vanishing from existence under conspicuous circumstances. The mass of collected evidence presents a picture of individual struggles from these seemingly unrelated cases that are unequivocally related to these subjects' bodies.

Racialised, gendered, colonised or depleted by unjust power structures, the body is the first of many thresholds where conflict rages and resolves, illness festers and abates, and life in all of its complexity, at least in some sense, begins and ends. Across concepts of race, nationality and gender, among other determining factors, the fragile yet resilient lives that emerge from the gathered materials bear such an uncanny resemblance to Louise Brunet, the silk weaver from Lyon, that one has to wonder whether they are in fact different manifestations of the same being appearing in various guises in unknown iterations. Could it be that this being only surfaces in history at pivotal junctures, called upon to perform a certain role, and then moves on to another time and place to continue the same eternal battle?

It is possible that if one considers this hypothesis – which many will likely dismiss as madness – it might start to make sense and the many lives and deaths of Louise Brunet will emerge. Here you shall encounter some of them and get a glimpse of the ways in which fragility was harnessed as a generative form of resistance. But the investigation is far from over. Many Louise Brunets might be waiting to be revealed, including the one that may be residing within us: rising to the fore, seemingly disappearing, but somehow lingering on underneath time's thick skin, dormant yet not gone, silent but never silenced.

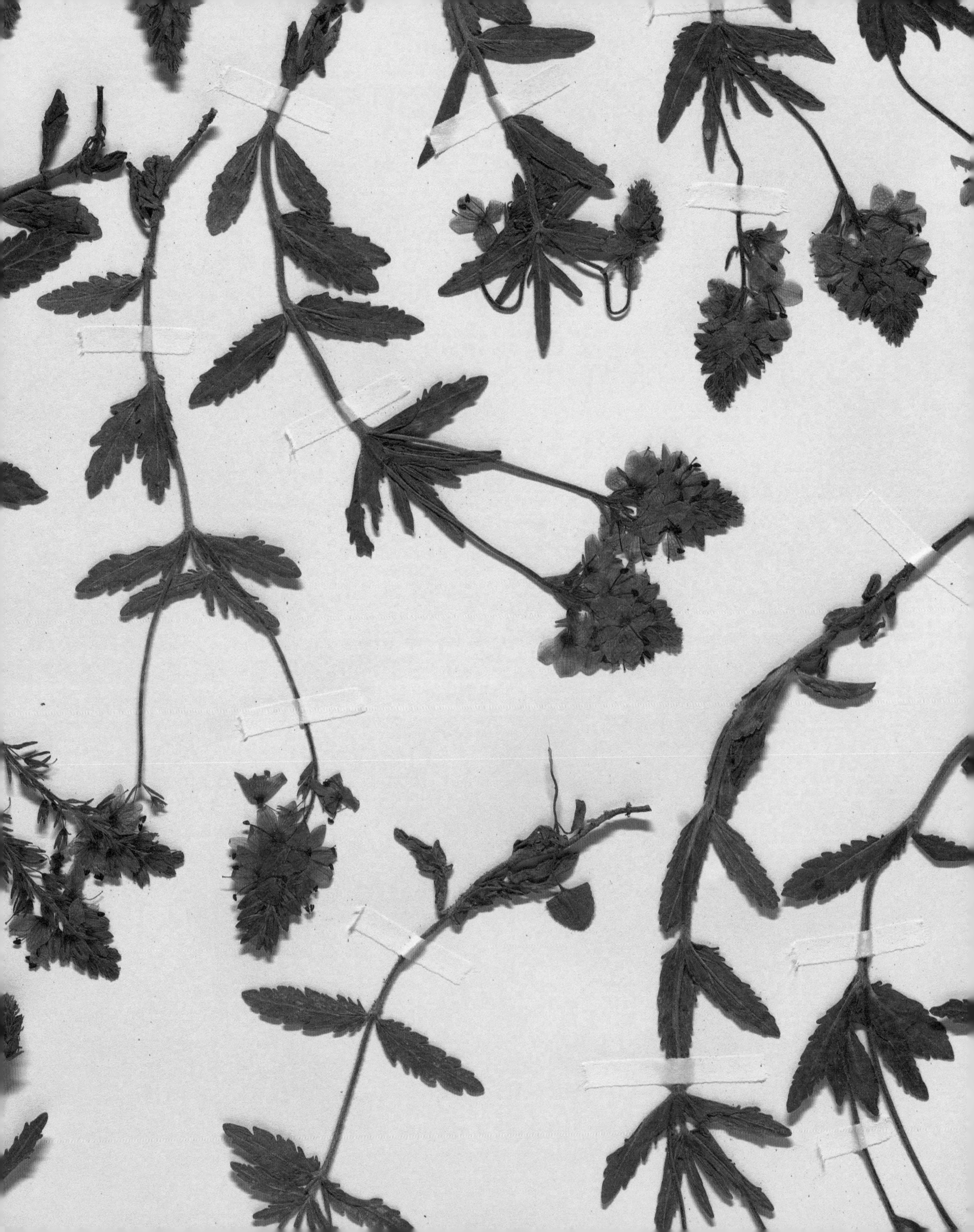

In Search of Louise

For every Louise Brunet in existence, there are countless people who seek to bring her down. Louise walks in this world not quite a part of it. The world holds her back and asks her to conform. Louise is free, dignified and daring. Yet in the eyes of the world, she is childish, arrogant and mad. While she is determined to carve her own path, the world is set on breaking her down with lies. Everyone insists that she must take heed of the finger showing the way. Louise refuses to obey. She stands up. She speaks out. This is the finger that told scholars that the Earth is flat, betrayed the rebellious prophet in the garden, forced the oppressed to renounce their gods and punished the innocent boy for wanting to be a girl. Louise fights back. And the world retaliates. Frightened by difference, oppressors reach for the bullet and the knife. They threaten, lie, preach and kill. The world points its finger still. Louise resists. At times she falters, but her patient truth leads the way.

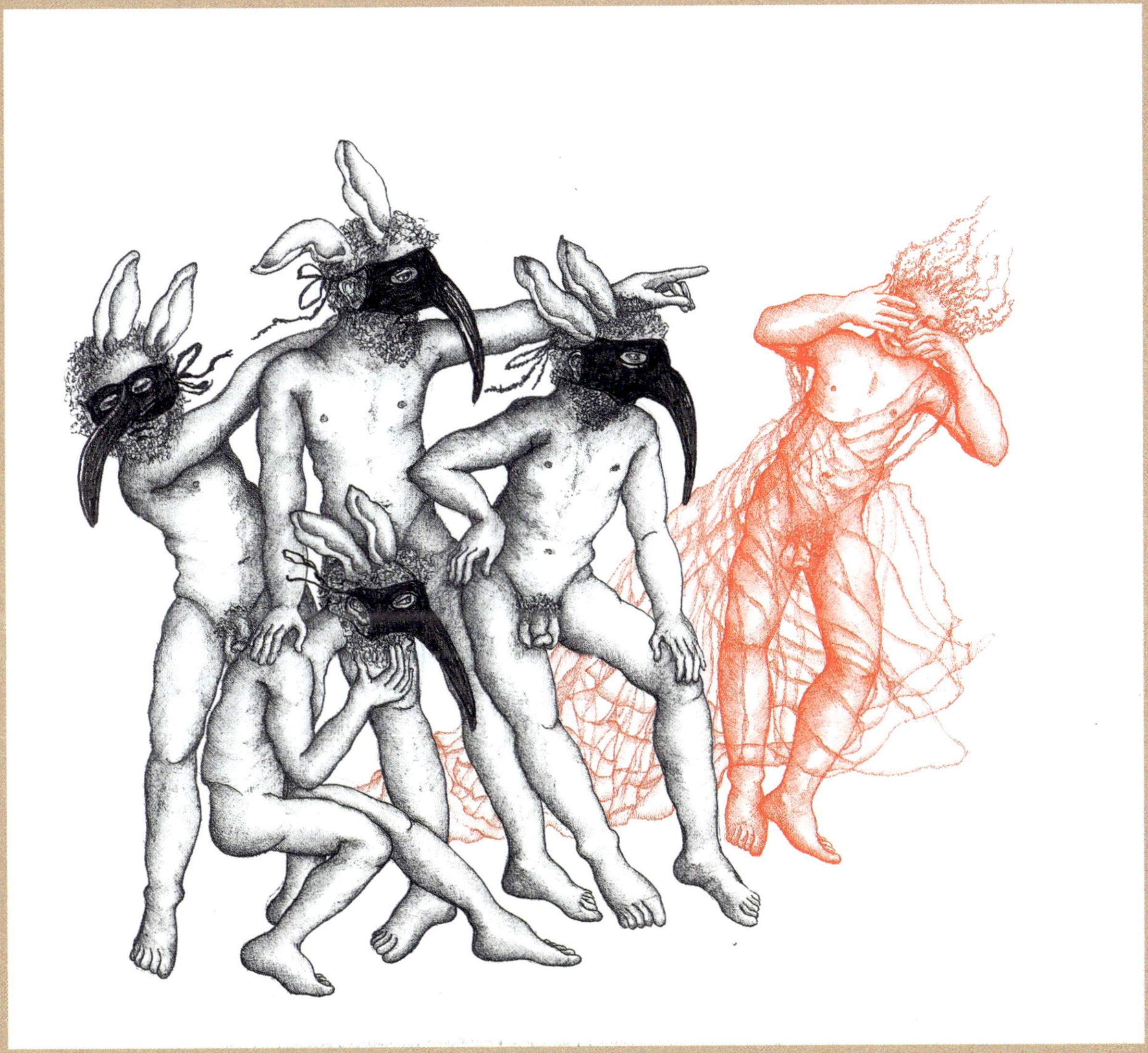

Sylvie Selig, *Boys Don't Cry*, 2019, 125.5 x 138 cm. Courtesy of the artist.

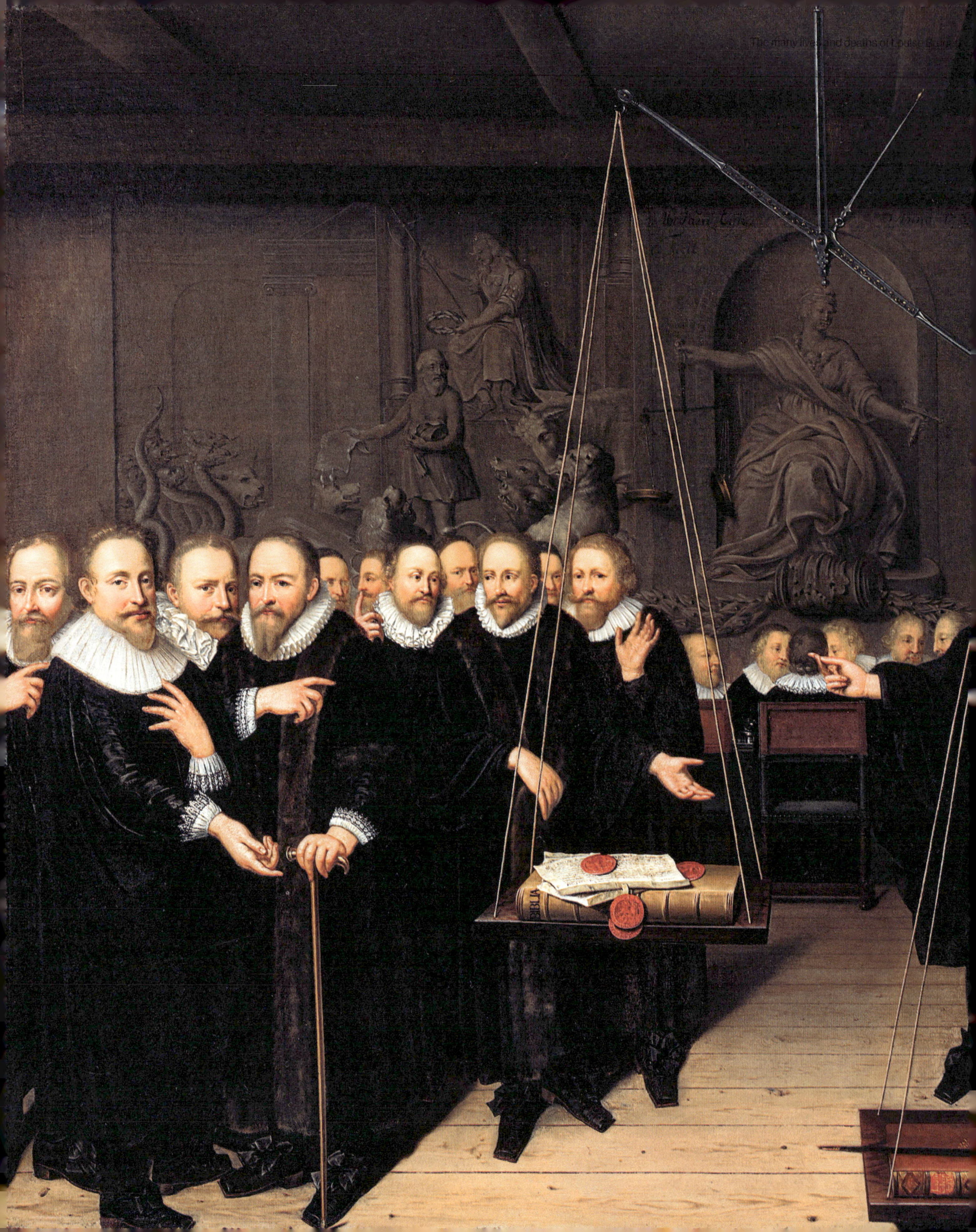

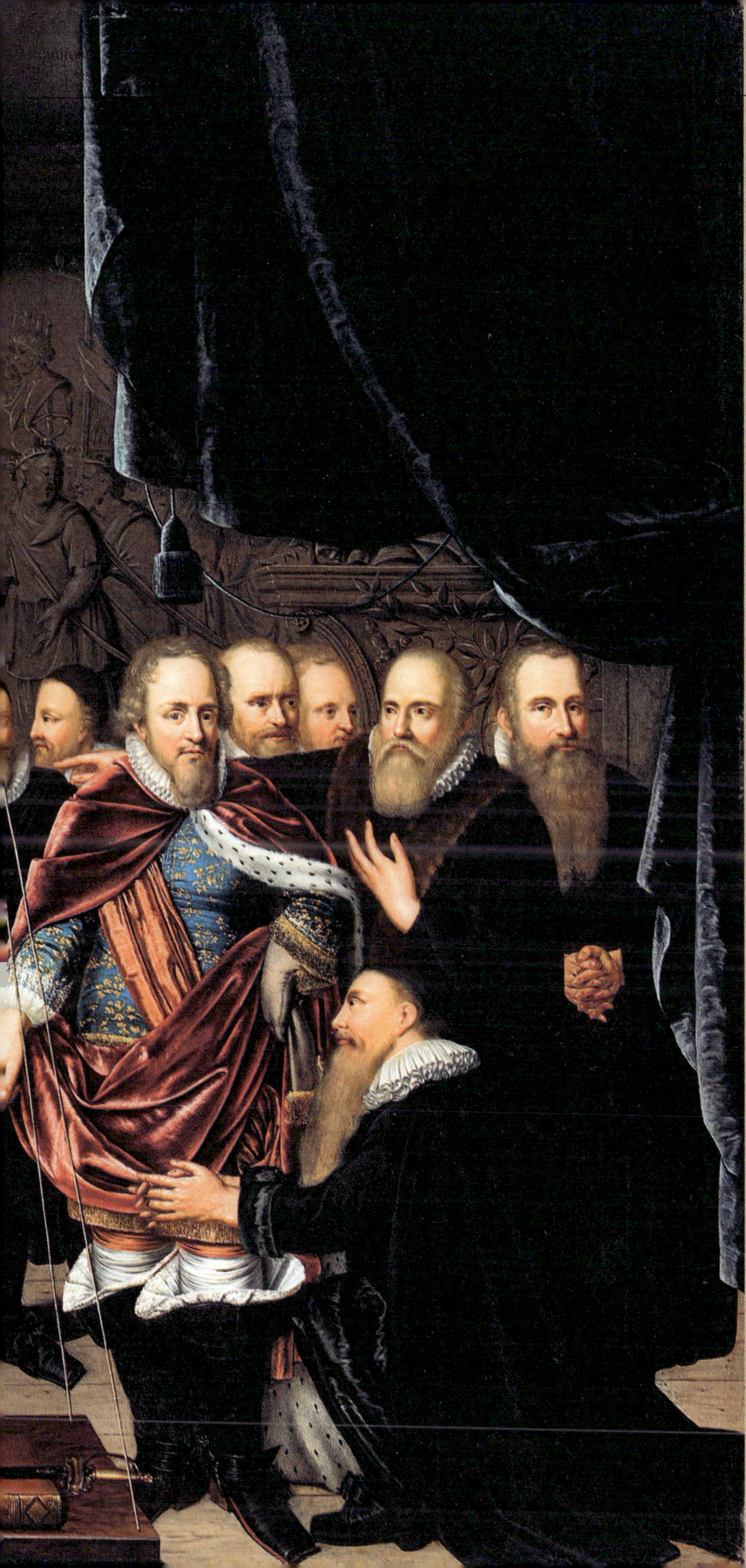

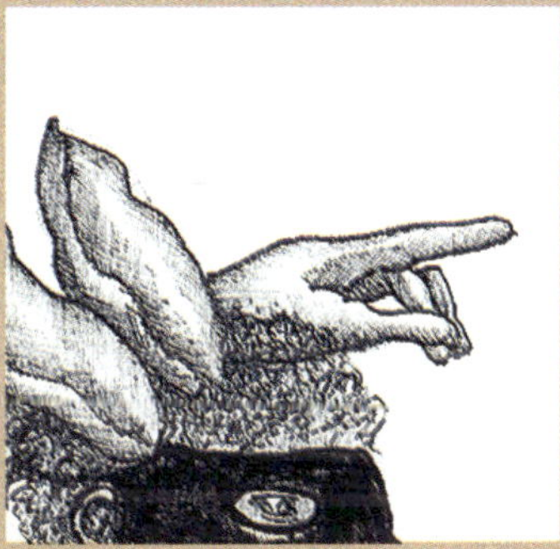

Left Abraham van der Eyk, *Allegory on the Disputes of the Remontrants and the Counter-Remontrants 1721*, 17th–18th centuries, 66,8 x 86 cm (framed), inv. H1151.
Musée des Beaux-Arts, Lyon. Photo: Martial Couderette.

Right Sylvie Selig, *Boys Don't Cry* (detail), 2019, 125.5 x 138 cm. Courtesy of the artist.

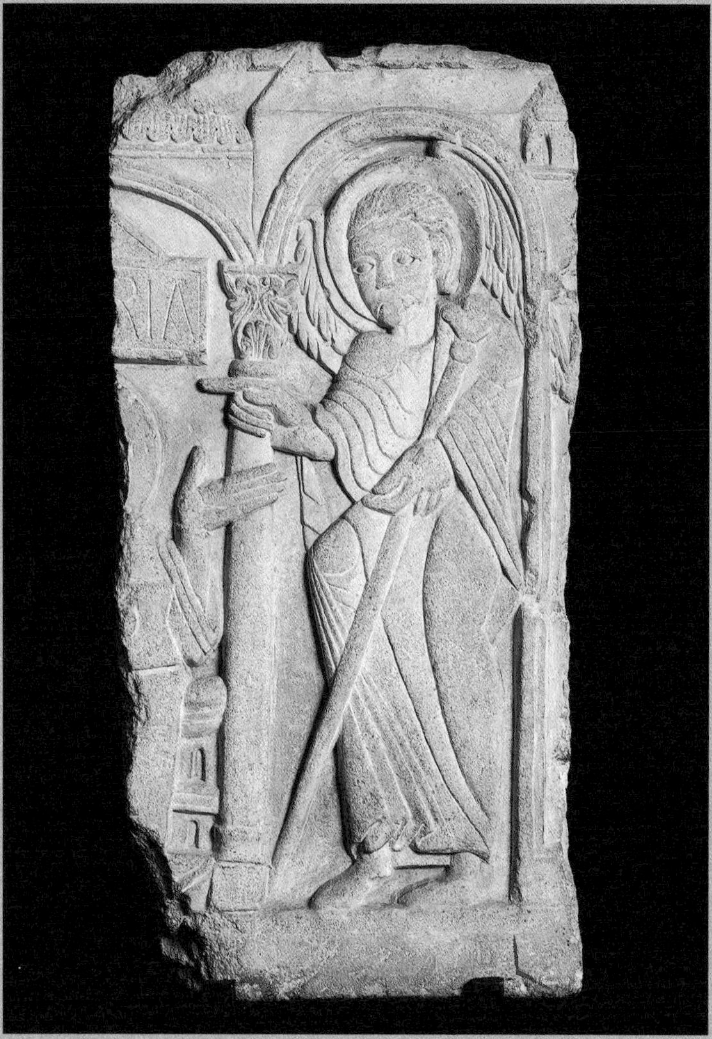

The Annunciation, 11th–12th centuries, limestone fragment from l'Île Barbe, inv. G 40.411. © Musée d'Histoire de Lyon - Gadagne. Photo: Jérôme Pantalacci.

The Annunciation

This relief, which came from the abbey on the Île Barbe, a river island just north of Lyon, depicts a scene from the Annunciation. The Archangel Gabriel, knees slightly bent, turns to Mary and tells her of Jesus's forthcoming birth. After a long period of prosperity up to the 14th century, the abbey on the Île Barbe went into slow decline. It was ravaged during the Wars of Religion and left deserted in 1782 before being sold as state property in 1793. Its religious buildings were dismantled and served as a quarry for the construction of new residential blocks in the Vaise district of Lyon.

Visit the Missionary Exhibition

Missionary exhibitions enjoyed great success in the 19th and 20th centuries. The Catholic orders embarked on conversion missions all over the world. On their travels, the prelates gathered artefacts of the converted cultures, which were displayed in France in these exhibitions. In Lyon, the Œuvre de la Propagation de la Foi, a missionary society founded by Pauline Jaricot, held the largest exhibitions.

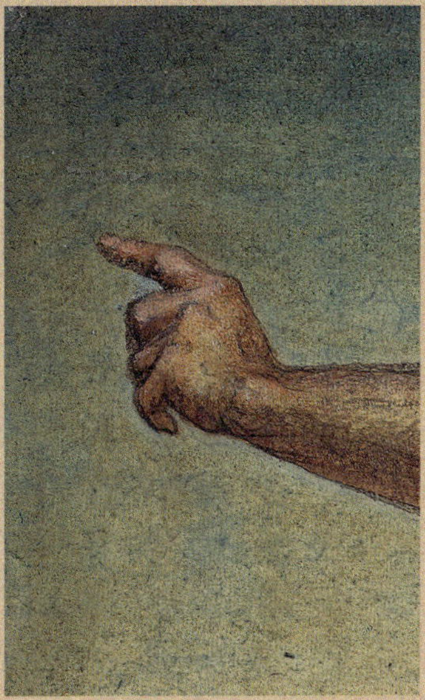

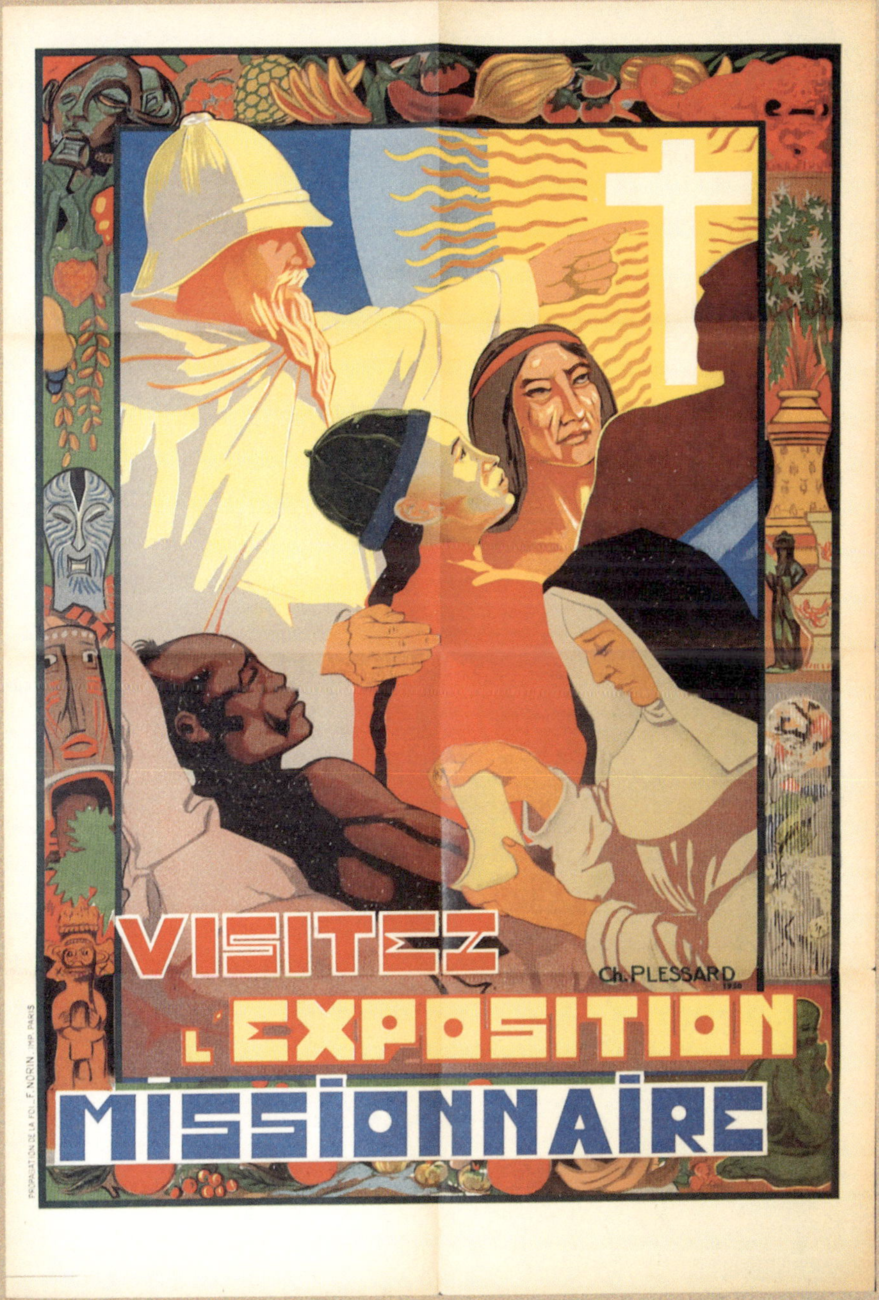

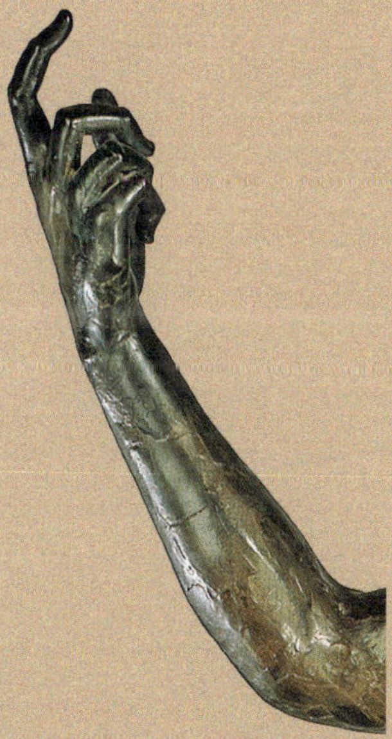

Top Jean-Baptiste Frénet, *Nude Self-Portrait* (detail), ca. 1850 – 1860, oil, gouache, charcoal and pastel on carton, 85 x 64.8 cm (framed), inv. 2016.8.1. Musée des Beaux-Arts, Lyon. Acquisition with the support of the state and the Auvergne-Rhône-Alpes region as part of the regional museum acquisition fund (FRAM), 2016.

Bottom Anonymous, Statue of the God Mars of Coligny (detail), 2nd half of the 1st century BCE, bronze. © Lugdunum Musée et théâtres romains. Photo: Jean-Michel Degueule - Christian Thioc.

Charles Plessard, *Visit the Missionary Exhibition*, The 1931 Missionary Week, Imprimerie F. Norin, Paris, 1930, poster. © Archives des O.P.M.

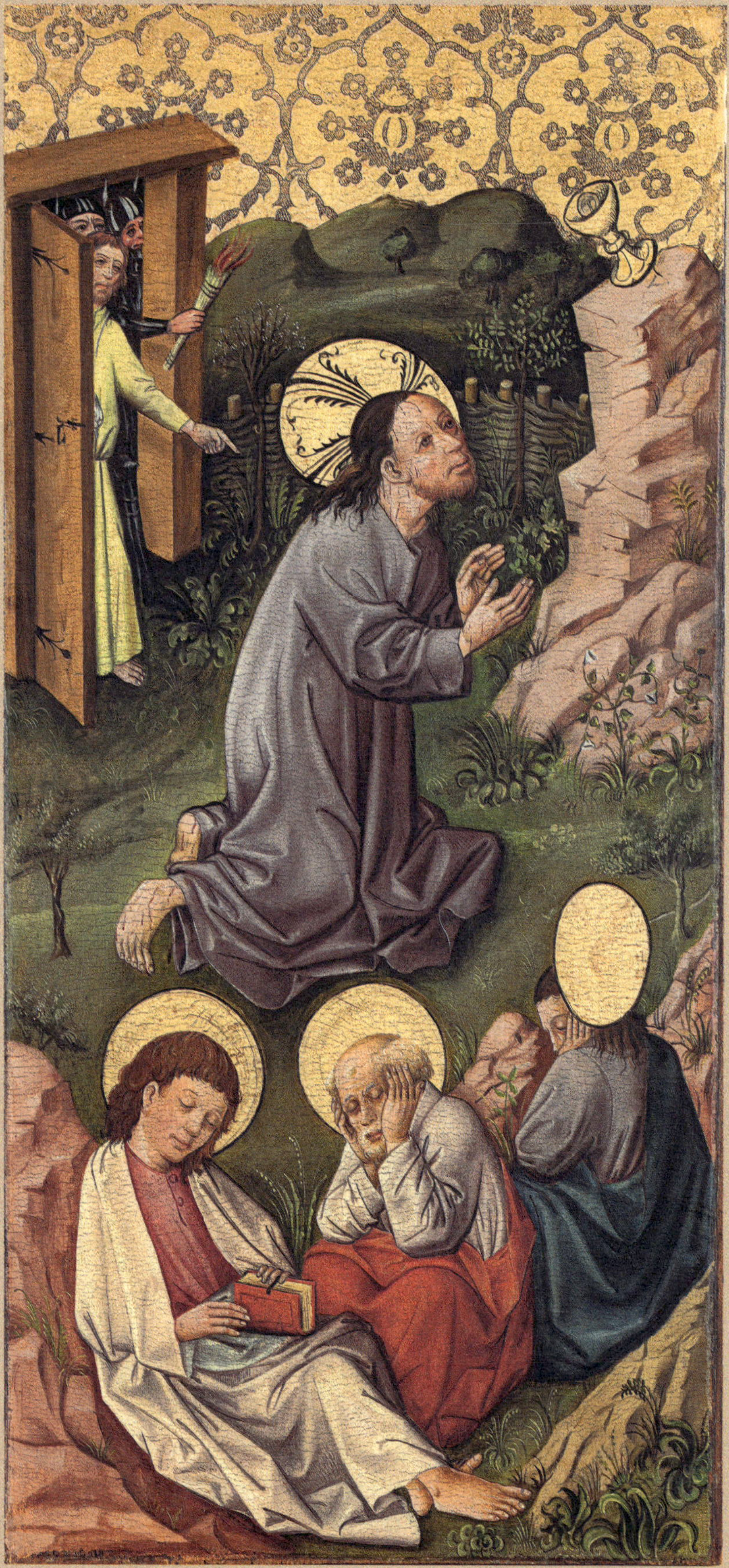

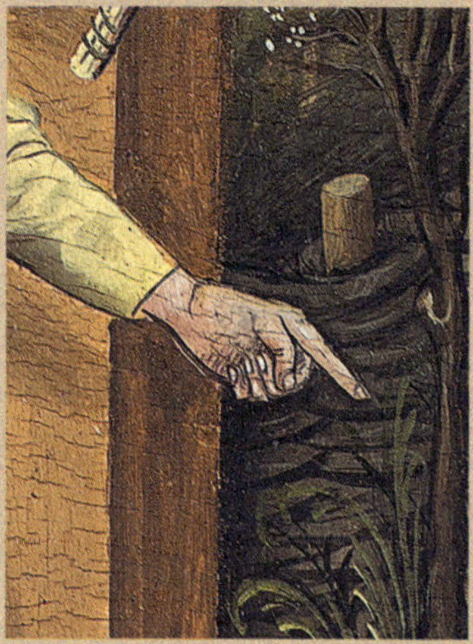

Left Lac de Constance, *Christ in the Olive Gardens*, ca. 1460, tempera on wood, 108 x 52.4 cm, inv. H 641. Musée des Beaux-Arts, Lyon. Photo: Martial Couderette.

Right Lac de Constance, *Christ in the Olive Gardens* (detail), ca. 1460, tempera on wood, 108 x 52.4 cm, inv. H 641. Musée des Beaux-Arts, Lyon. Photo: Martial Couderette.

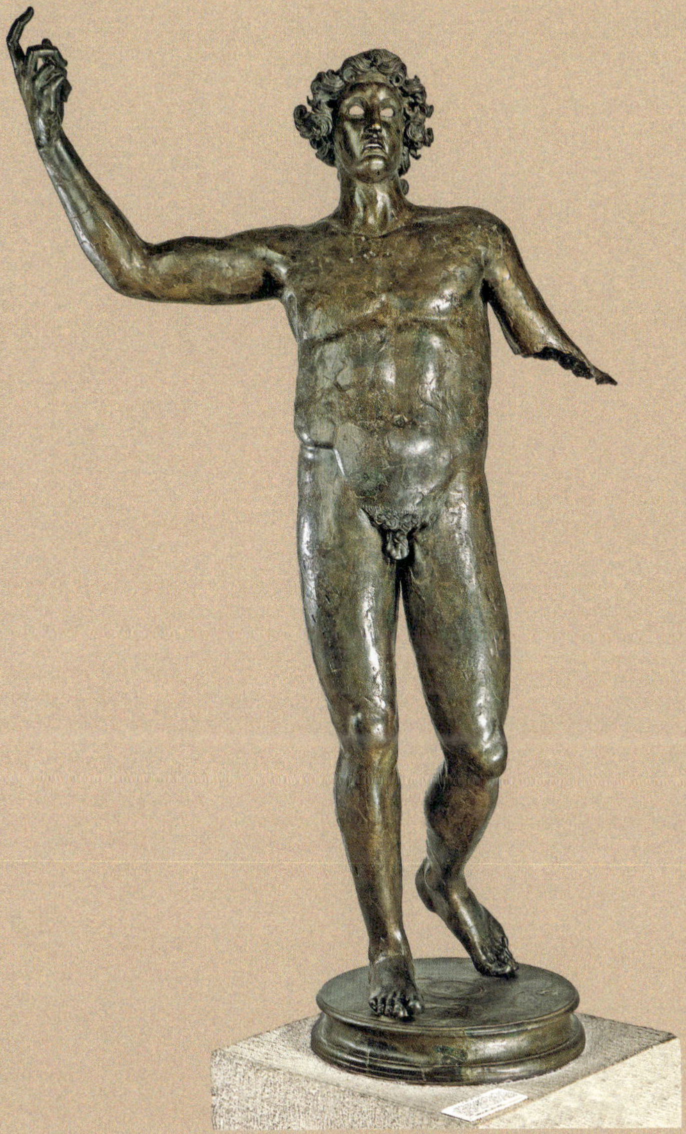

Anonymous, Statue of the God Mars of Coligny, 2nd half of the 1st century BCE, bronze. © Lugdunum Musée et théâtres romains. Photo: Jean-Michel Degueule - Christian Thioc.

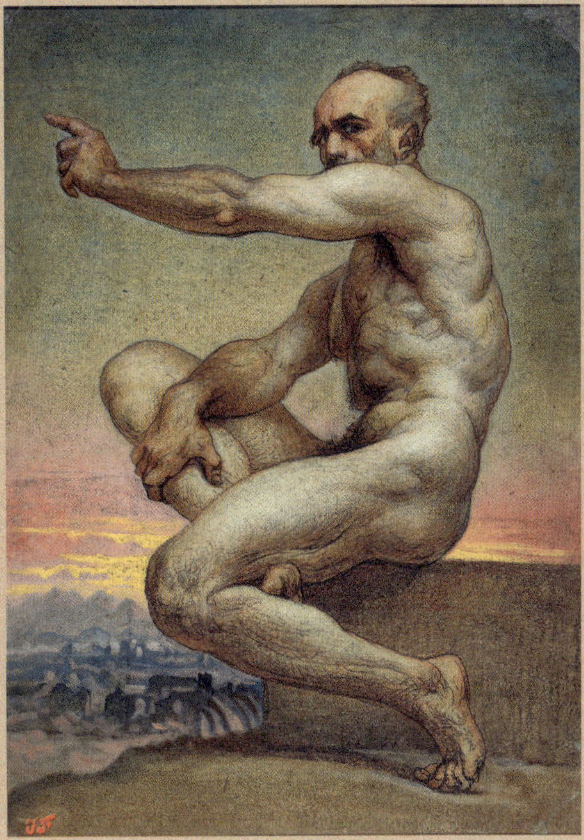

Naked Self-Portrait

Having decided to give up painting following fierce criticism of his decoration for the Saint-Blandine crypt in the Basilica of Saint Martin d'Ainay in Lyon, Jean-Baptiste Frénet produced this strange self-portrait in the 1850s–1860s. Breaking away from the traditional grammar of the genre, the artist readily displays his naked body for the spectator. Pointing to the left with his index finger, he is perhaps referencing the injustice he suffered when his decoration was destroyed, as if castigating those responsible.

Jean-Baptiste Frénet, *Nude Self-Portrait*, ca. 1850 – 1860, oil, gouache, charcoal and pastel on carton, 85 x 64.8 cm (framed), inv. 2016.8.1. Musée des Beaux-Arts, Lyon. Acquisition with the support of the state and the Auvergne-Rhône-Alpes region as part of the regional museum acquisition fund (FRAM), 2016.

Fragile Bodies

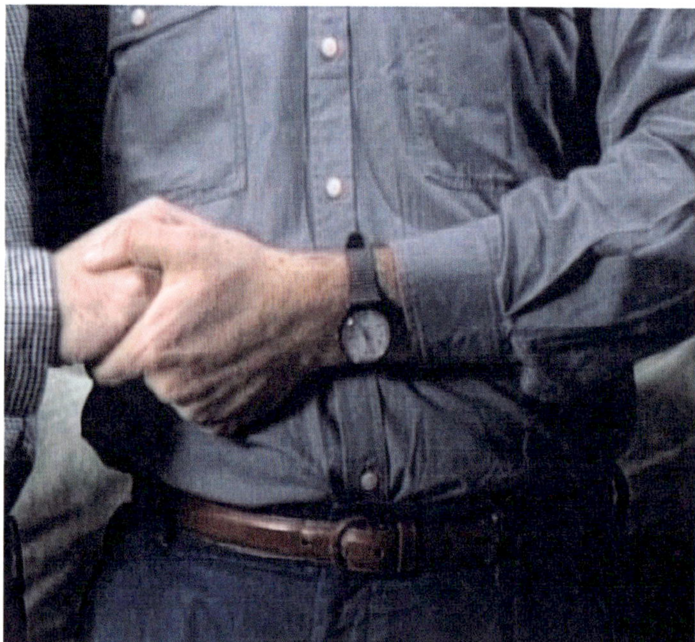

Preludio de Uma Morte Anunciada

Rafael França's final work, Prelúdio de Uma Morte Anunciada *(*A Prelude to an Announced Death*), which he made just days before his death, shows the artist and his partner Geraldo Rivello caressing and kissing each other. While Brazilian soprano Bidu Sayão sings* La Traviata, *the names of França's friends who died from AIDS appear on the screen. The video ends with the text: "Above all, they had no fear of vertigo".*

Louise Brunet 01

It is a sweltering mid-July day in 1992. Louise Brunet is a faded presence. He is curled up in this unfamiliar bed where he has been for several weeks, growing weaker by the day: moving less, eating less and not speaking much. An advance copy of his latest book *Memories That Smell Like Gasoline* lies next to him, open to the last page. A few lines are marked with a faltering line: "I am waving my hands. I am disappearing. I am disappearing but not fast enough."

Louise had arrived in New York in the late 1970s and lived there ever since. He quickly established himself as a prolific visual artist, writer and gay rights activist. His daring art and critical writing captured the voice of the stigmatised gay community. New York had been attracting a swarm of defiant artists like Louise who were drawn to the irresistible blend of cheap rent, ample space and risk-taking spirit that permeated the city at the time. Young and hungry, they immersed themselves in the city, the East Village in particular. Amidst the crumbling blocks of one of New York's most notorious neighbourhoods, these misfits started making new art that echoed the politically-charged cultural landscape of their generation. Artists and curators were turning their flats into exhibition spaces showing unconventional work with photography, collage, DIY sculpture, graffiti and performance art taking centre stage. Concurrently, the music scene was bursting at the seams with newly exploded forms like punk and hip-hop. The parties had been legendary. Yet while all these free souls had been dancing their nights away, a sinister shadow had begun to fall upon the city.

Rafael França, *Prelúdio de Uma Morto Anunciada* (*A Prelude to an Announced Death*), 1991, video. Courtesy of Galeria Jaqueline Martins, Brussels.

The AIDS epidemic had hit New York hard. Rumours of a so-called gay plague had begun circulating as early as 1981. Because AIDS first emerged among marginal communities like sex workers, drug users and queer people, the official response to the disease was uneven and underfunded. Conservative forces demonised the communities most affected. As late as 1986, the Reagan administration had continued its course of inaction by saying that HIV/AIDS almost exclusively affected gay men and intravenous drug users.

Louise is coughing. He gasps for air. A flashback of an image of a smiling boy wearing a patterned shirt and suspenders races through his mind. Louise had used a photocopy of this image in a collage two years earlier. A short text he had written around the image comes back to him. His lips murmur the ominous words from this illegible scribble: "One day, this kid will do something that causes men who wear the uniforms of priests and rabbis, men who inhabit certain stone buildings, to call for his death." The original photograph was a picture of Louise as a little boy. The words hint at the desires he had gradually discovered in himself "to place his naked body on the naked body of another boy."

It is almost midnight at Saint Vincent's Hospital in New York's Greenwich Village – the place twenty-something kids go to die. Louise is struggling. His friend has been staying up with him all night, which has begun to turn into a tortuously early morning. Louise's friend is afraid that if he sleeps, he will not be there with Louise at the moment of his passing. He puts the book aside, dims the bedside lamp and crawls into the narrow hospital bed with him. He tells him that he will be right there, that he will make sure he keeps breathing. He promises him that nothing bad will happen to him while he sleeps. Finally, Louise closes his eyes.

* In memory of artists Nicolas Moufarrege (1947–1985), Rafael França (1957–1991), David Wojnarowicz (1954–1992) and many other whose lives were cut short by the AIDS epidemic

* This text is inspired by testimonials from the AIDS Memorial Instagram account @theaidsmemorial

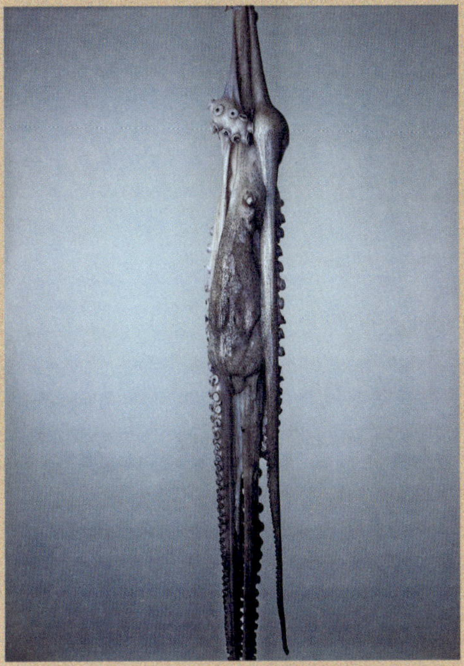

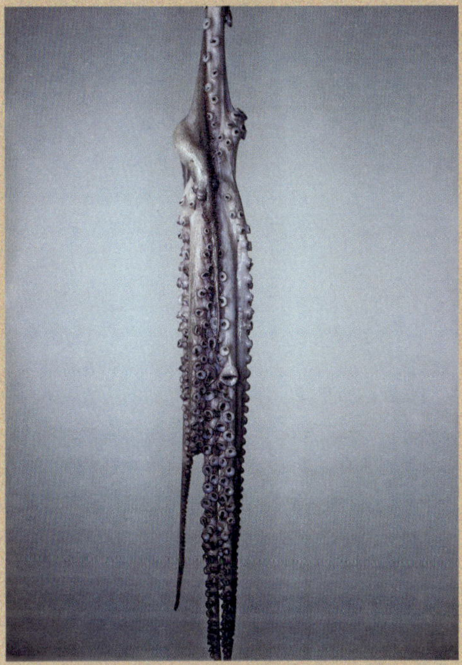

Octopus triptych

Richard Learoyd creates his large-scale photographs using a complex technical process. His self-made bespoke camera obscura comprises two room-like chambers separated by a lens, through which the image is projected directly onto the opposing mirror surface. With this age-old device, Learoyd crafts unique direct-positive images without negatives or digital technology.

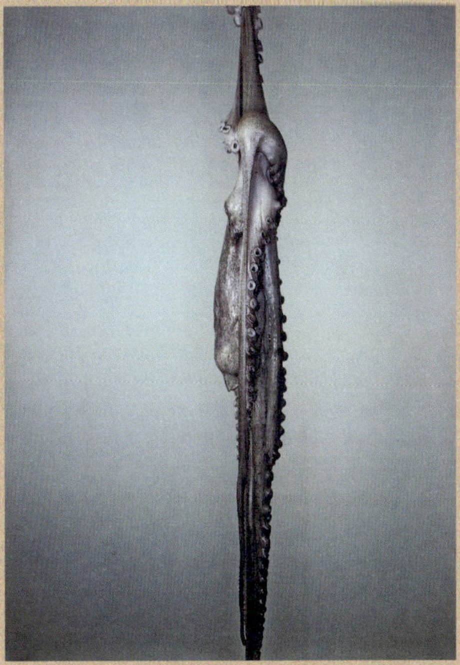

Richard Learoyd, *Octopus triptych*, 2007, unique Ilfochrome photographs, 172.7 x 121.9 cm (each). Courtesy of the artist, Pace Gallery and Fraenkel Gallery.

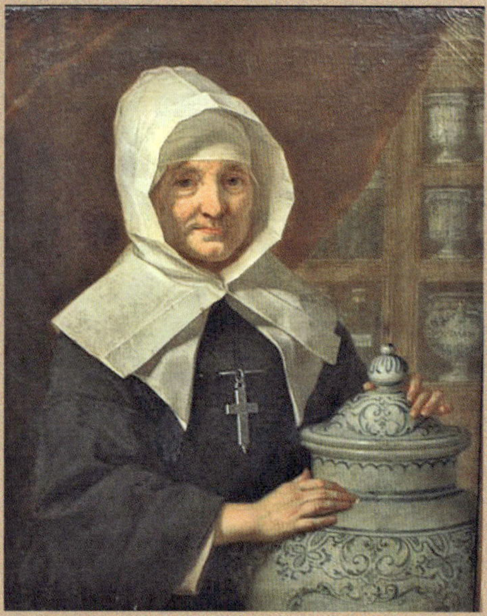

Anonymous, *Portrait of Sister Catherine Giroud*, oil on canvas, 100 x 82 cm. © Musée d'Histoire de Lyon - Gadagne. Photo: Xavier Schwebel.

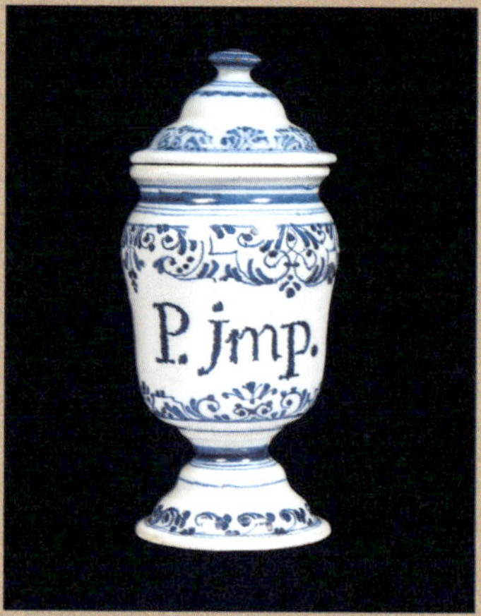

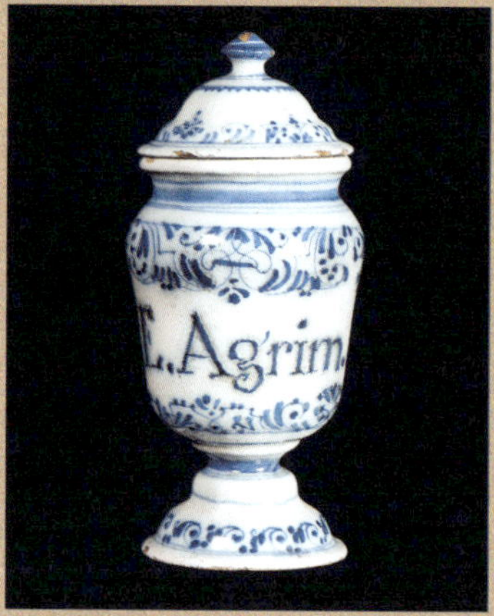

Top Moorish (Morelan) apothecary vase, earthenware, on loan from Musée des Beaux-Arts de Lyon, inv. 39.48.3. © Musée d'Histoire de Lyon - Gadagne. Photo: Xavier Schwebel.

Bottom Moorish (Morelan) apothecary vase, earthenware, on loan from Musée des Beaux-Arts de Lyon, inv. 39.48.1. © Musée d'Histoire de Lyon - Gadagne. Photo: Xavier Schwebel.

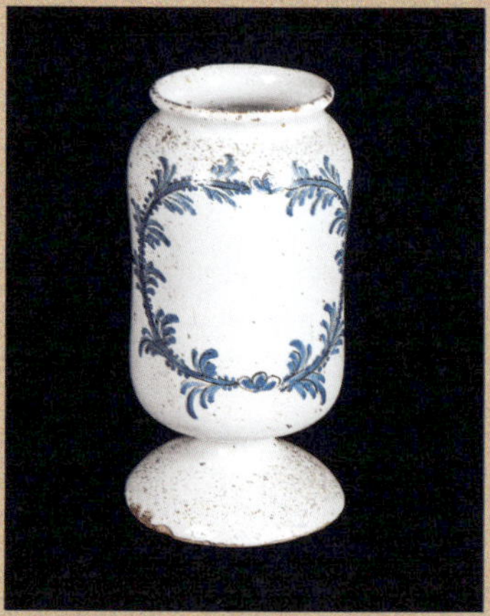

Apothecary vase, earthenware, inv. 41.260. © Musée d'Histoire de Lyon - Gadagne. Photo: Xavier Schwebel.

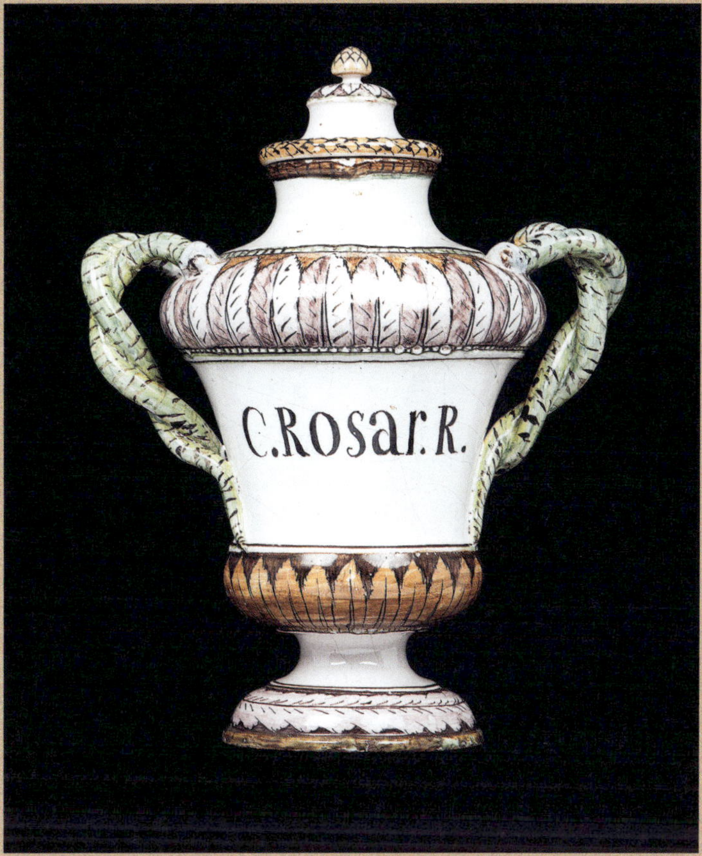

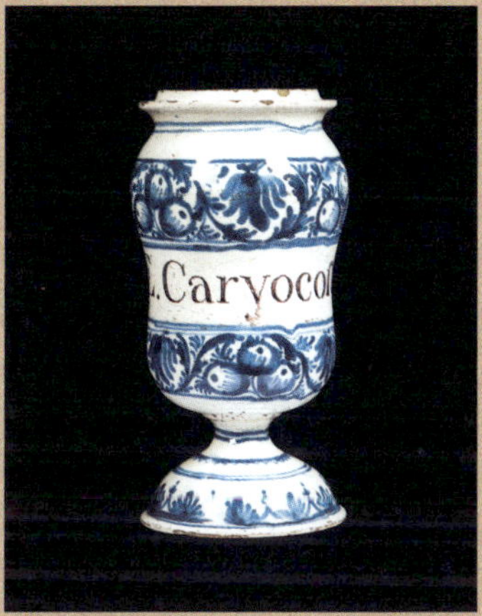

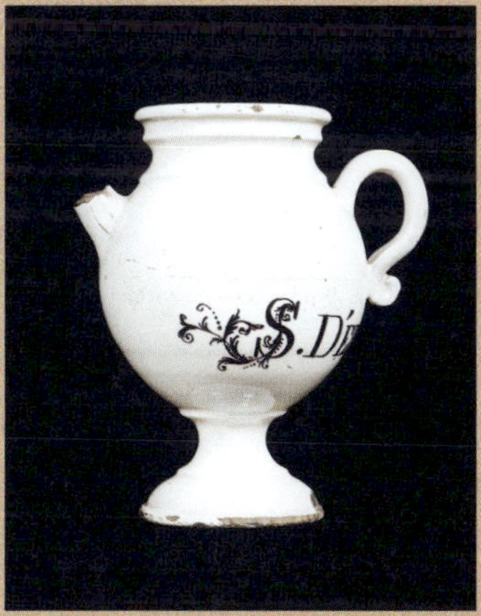

Apothecary vases

Dating from the 16th to 18th centuries, these apothecary vases – which once contained unguents, pomades, potions, elixirs and decoctions – suggest the imagination of the apothecary, heir to the priests of the ancient world and ancestor of modern-day pharmacists. For instance, in 1552 the physician and astrologer Nostradamus published his Traité des fardements et des confitures *(*Treatise on Cosmetics and Conserves*) in Lyon; in it, he gives recipes for numerous remedies. The cracks and chips on these jars underscore their fragility while also testifying to their long history.*

Top Apothecary vase, earthenware, E. Caryocost, Lyon, on loan from Musée des Beaux-Arts de Lyon, inv. 42.214.2. © Musée d'Histoire de Lyon - Gadagne. Photo: Xavier Schwebel.

Bottom Apothecary vase, 19th century, earthenware, inv. 592.2. © Musée d'Histoire de Lyon - Gadagne. Photo: Xavier Schwebel.

Apothecary vase, also referred to as "Monster" vase, 18th century, earthenware, inv. 013.1.1.1. © Musée d'Histoire de Lyon - Gadagne. Photo: Xavier Schwebel.

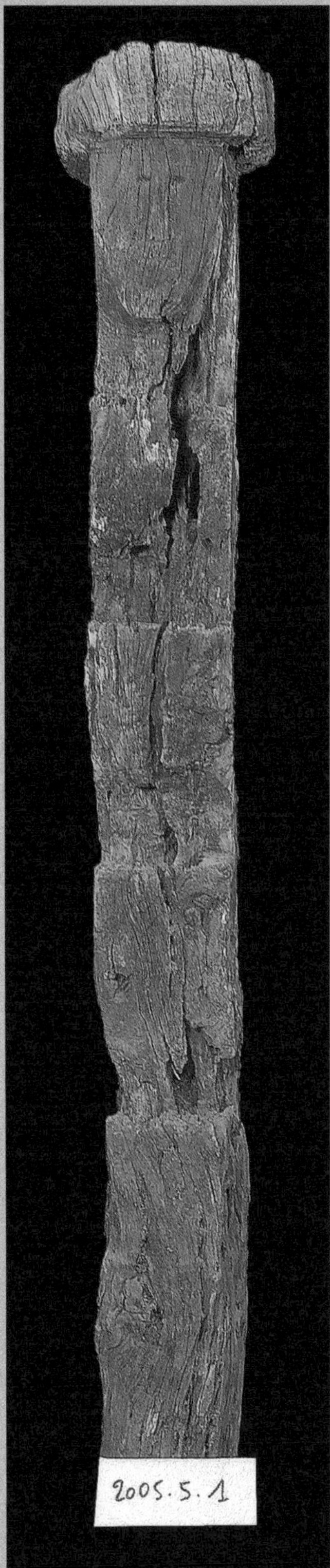

Mapuche culture (Chile), ceremonial pole, 20th century, inv. 2005.5.1. © Musée des Confluences, Lyon.

Ceremonial pillar of the Mapuche culture

The machi *(shaman), who is often a woman, is the intermediary between their people and the land of the gods. The symbol of their condition is the* Rewe, *or sacred ladder, carved out of hardwood, the top of which is sculpted in the form of a human head. The Rewe comes into service on the machi's initiation day, and vanishes on the day they die, when it returns to nature, desacralised and abandoned in a river or a forest. The Rewe is placed in the ground near the* Ruka, *the machi's hut; it can rest against the sacred tree El Canelo, and/or surrounded by the tree's branches. During ceremonies, the machi climbs the steps of the Rewe while beating their* Kultrum *(drum).*

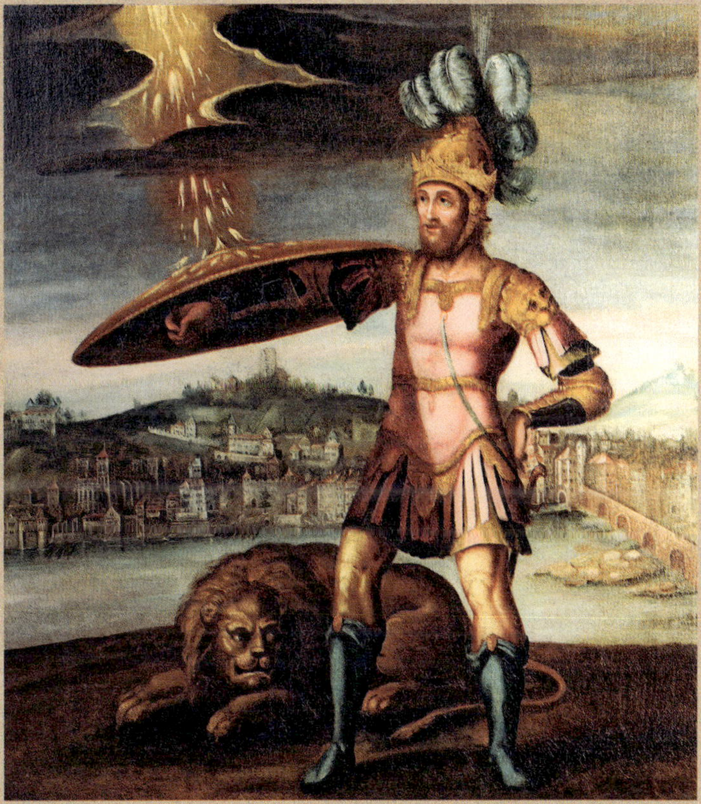

The City of Lyon Saved from the Plague

In 1720, the last major outbreak of bubonic plague struck France, wreaking havoc in Marseille. Lyon, which traded heavily with the Mediterranean port, feared it would be laid low by the disease in due course. Following a series of ordinances issued by the municipal health office that expelled beggars and market stallholders; ordered street cleaning and stricter monitoring at the city gates; and quarantined certain goods, the plague was stopped in 1723 – the year this work was likely created. It portrays a warrior – perhaps Camille Perichon, the city's provost of merchants from 1730–1740 – protecting the lion at his feet with his shield and saving his city from the divine scourge.

Anonymous, The city of Lyon kept from the plague, oil on canvas, inv. 173. Musée d'Histoire de Lyon - Gadagne. Photo: Xavier Schwebel.

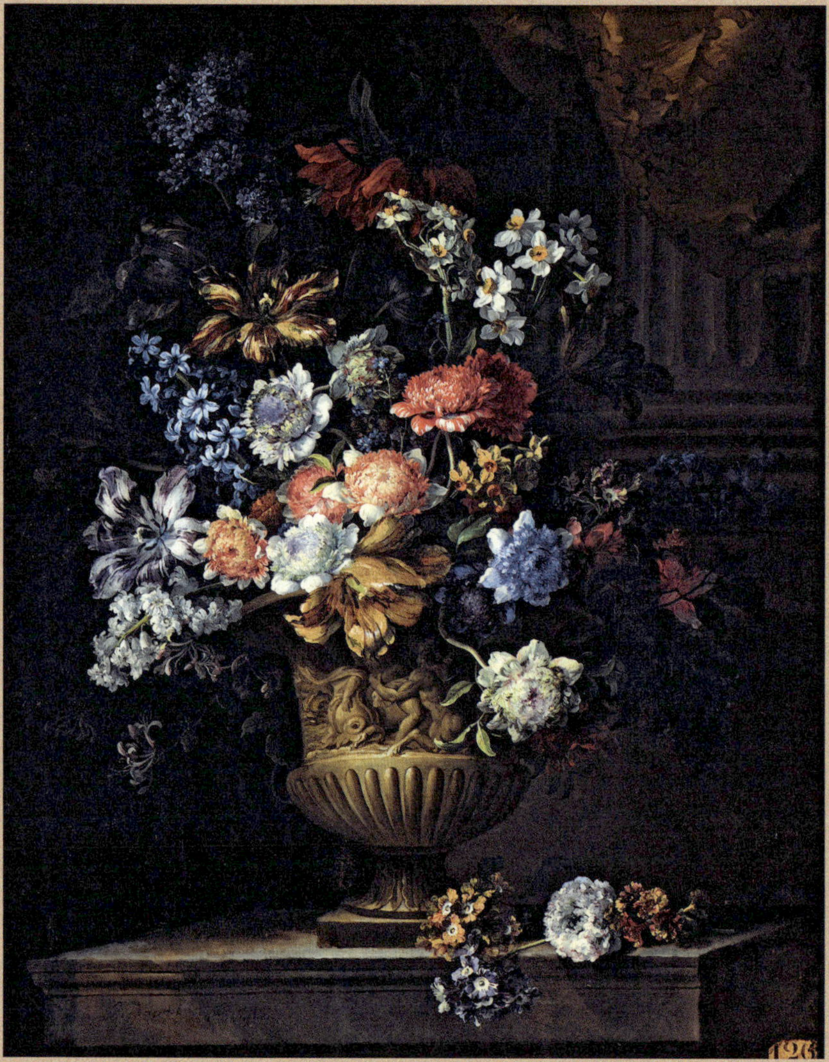

Flowers in a Vase

Placed on a table in front of a curtain, a stone vase decorated with antique bas-reliefs contains a plentiful bouquet of flowers. By dint of its complex composition, the painting bears witness to the evolution of the still-life genre, which had rivalled history painting and portraiture since entering France's Académie royale de peinture et de sculpture. The artist is thus seeking to demonstrate his virtuoso skill with a sophisticated, monumental arrangement.

Jean-Baptiste Monnoyer, *Flowers in a vase*, 1680–1690, oil on canvas, 122.5 x 102.5 cm, inv. B686. Musée des Beaux-Art, Lyon.

Still Life at the Trellis

The spoils of the hunt – a partridge, hanging by its foot, and a hare – are surrounded by peaches and a basket of plums and placed on the ledge of an arched, stone window frame, through which a wooded landscape is visible. The science of the composition, with the vine trellis frame; the decorative intent; the arrangement of the various, skilfully lit props; and the touch of understated refinement, all typify the art of Alexandre-François Desportes.

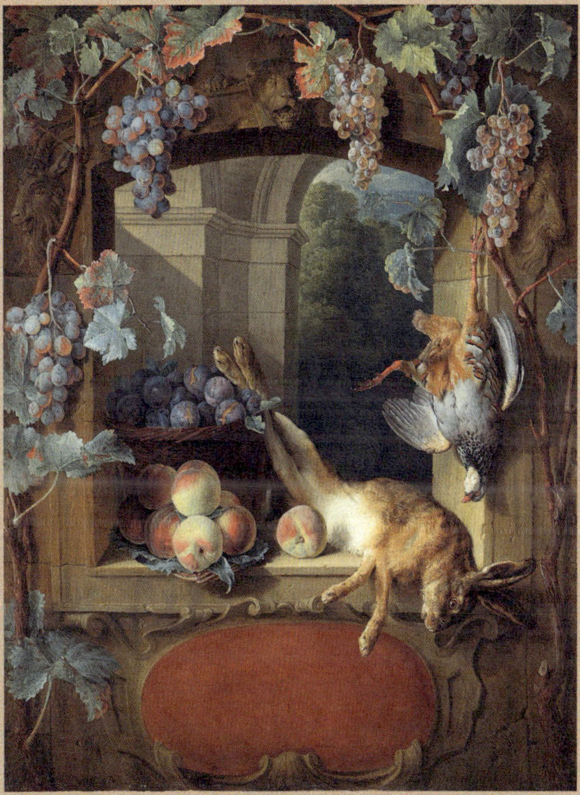

Alexandre-François Desportes, *Still life at the trellis*, 1730–1735, oil on canvas, 147 x 121 cm, inv. A172. Musée des Beaux-Art, Lyon.

Statuette of two figures

This wood sculpture was collected in Tanzania by the Missionaries of the Œuvre de la Propagation de la Foi. The former kingdom of Dahomey is well known for its representations of twins, which were generally made to honour the dead. The indestructible bond between the two figures is reflected in the one-piece form of the sculpture: attached by their abdomen, the twins share their lower limbs like ischiopagus Siamese twins.

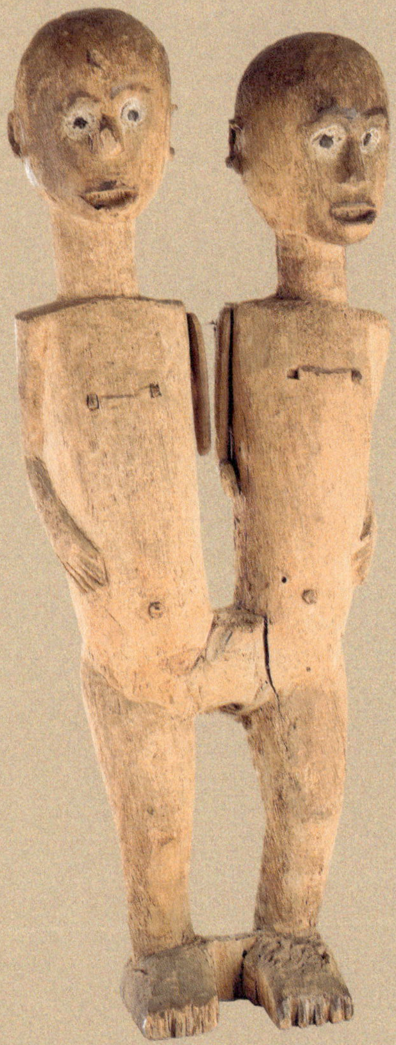

Sukuma or Nyamwezi culture (Tanzania), Statuette of two figures, 2nd half of 19th century, inv. D979-3-754, on loan from Œuvres Pontificales Missionnaires – 1979. Musée des Confluences, Lyon.

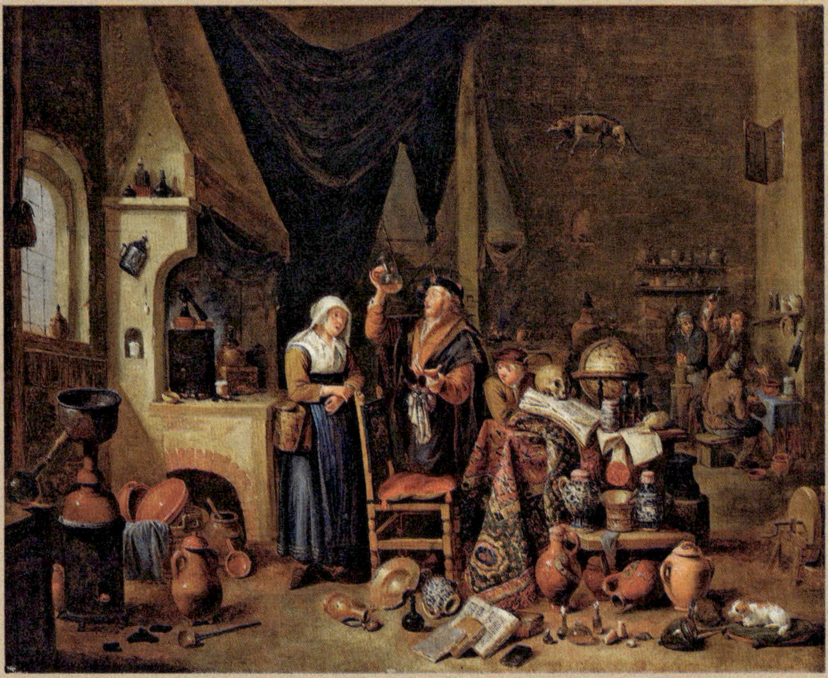

David Teniers the Younger, *An Alchemist / The Medical Consultation*, ca. 1630-1690, oil on canvas, 69.2 x 87.6cm, inv. H1152. Musée des Beaux-Art, Lyon.

David Teniers the Younger

Amid the clutter of vials, retorts and books of spells in his workshop, an alchemist examines his patient's urine to detect a possible pregnancy. Assembling as much knowledge as possible, the alchemist strived to unlock the secrets of matter and obtain the formula of the elixir of life. Depicted many times by David Teniers the Younger, the figure of the alchemist embodies a senseless and ungodly quest that leads him astray from the Christian faith.

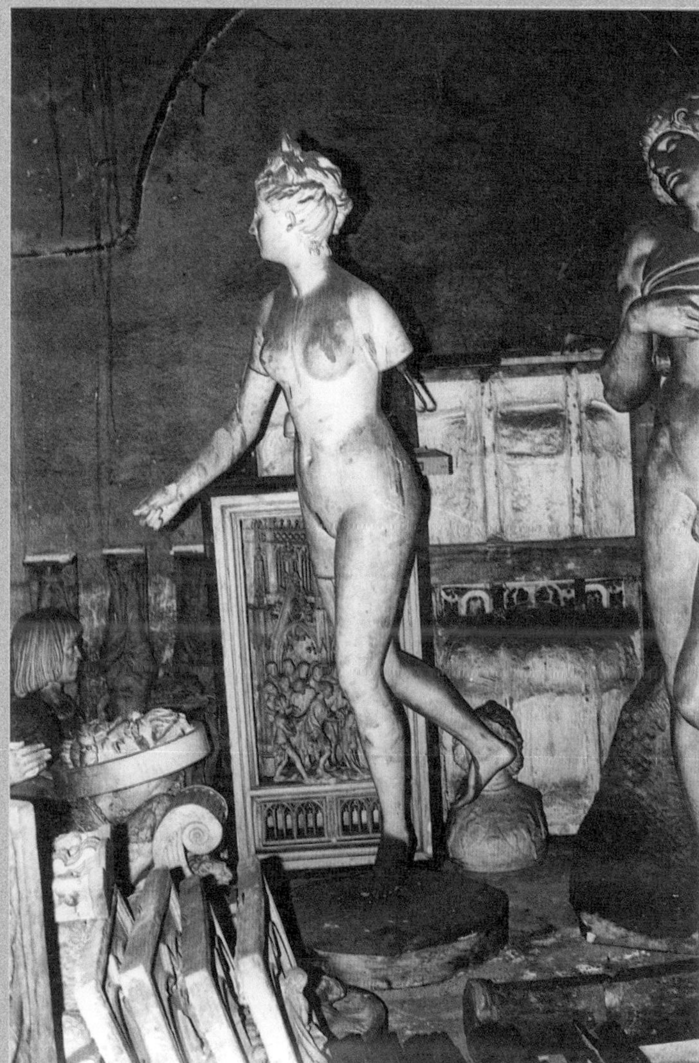

Cast of *Diane the Huntress* in the cellars, 18 quai Claude Bernard, 1974, Musée des Moulages, Lyon. Photo: © G. Chomer and C. Franck.

Großes weißes Tor

Dating to the late 1960s and early 1970s, Joachim Bandau's monumental sculptures are made with glass fibre, covered in polyester and lacquered with monochrome paint. With their rounded and sinuous forms, these structures are equally reminiscent of medical devices and funeral sarcophagi. With its two arches, Großes weißes Tor *(The Great White Gate) represents a portal whose openings are deliberately too small, protecting bodies but constraining them too.*

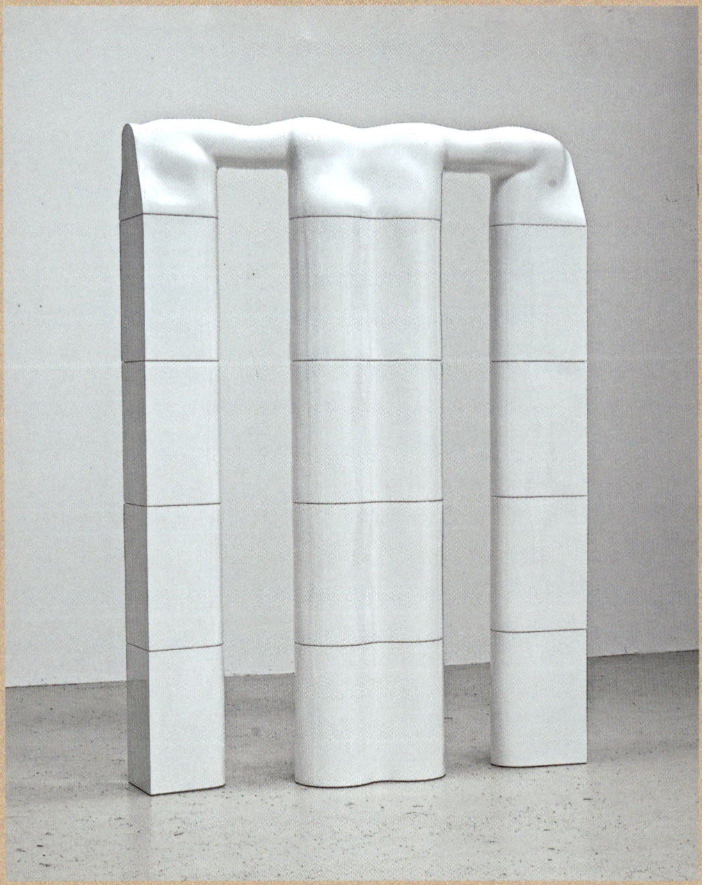

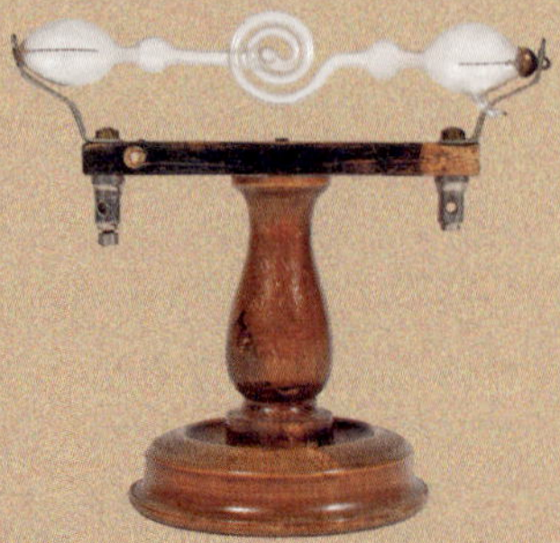

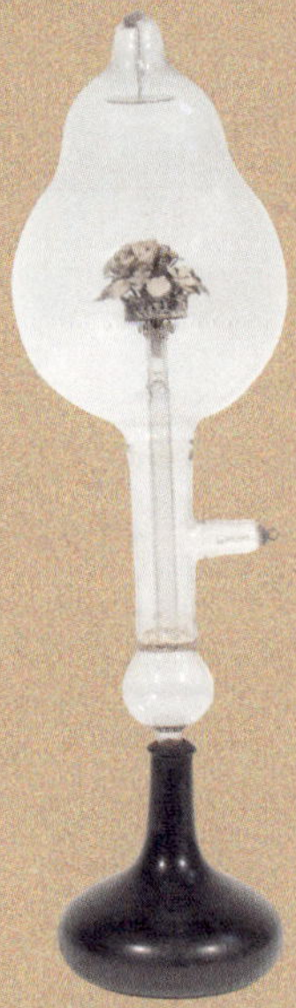

Joachim Bandau, *Großes weißes Tor*, 1969, glass, reinforced polyester, car lacquer. Courtesy of Galerie Maubert, Paris / Atelier de Joachim Bandau, Aix-la-Chapelle.

Top Crookes Tube, radiology tube, inv. 2007.0.8052.M_01. Musée des Hospices Civils, Lyon.

Bottom Johann Wilhelm Hittorf, Rarefied Gas Tube by J. Hittorf, radiology tube, inv. 2007.0.8054.M_01. Musée des Hospices Civils, Lyon.

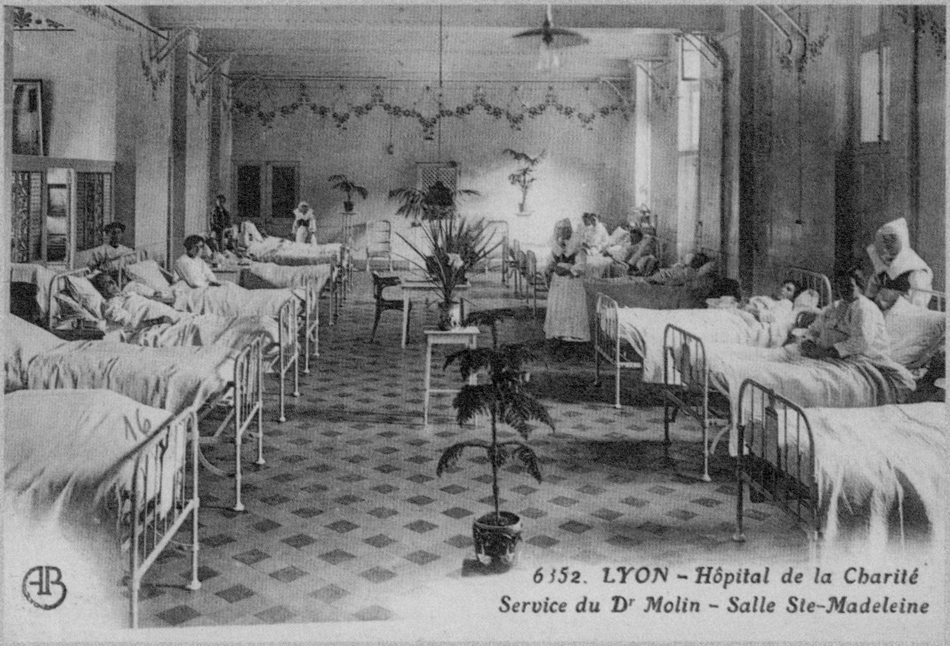

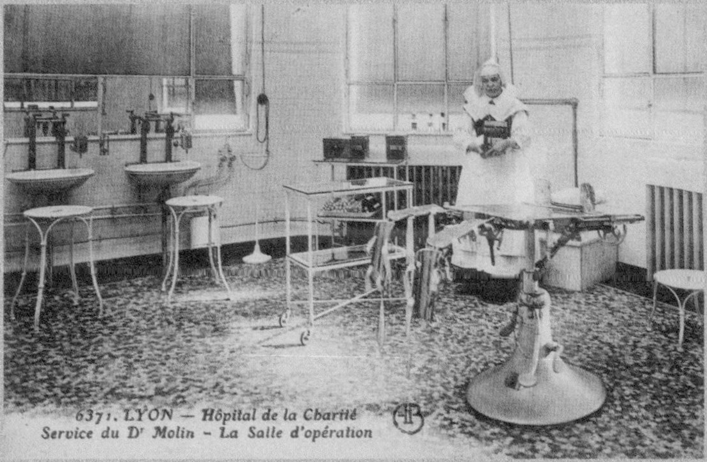

Hôpital de la Charité

Hôpital de la Charité de Lyon was established in the early 17th century. Initially used to accommodate Lyon's poor orphans, it soon added the medical functions performed by modern-day hospitals. It was demolished in 1934 when the new Hôpital Edouard Herriot Hospital was built. The only remaining part is its belltower, which today still dominates Place Antonin Poncet. These anonymous photographs show Dr. Molin's department in 1922.

Hôpital de la Charité, department of Dr. Molin, postcard, A.B. editions, inv. 004.12.78
© Musée d'Histoire de Lyon – Gadagne.

Hôpital de la Charité, department of Dr. Molin, postcard, A.B. editions, inv. 004.12.79.
© Musée d'Histoire de Lyon – Gadagne.

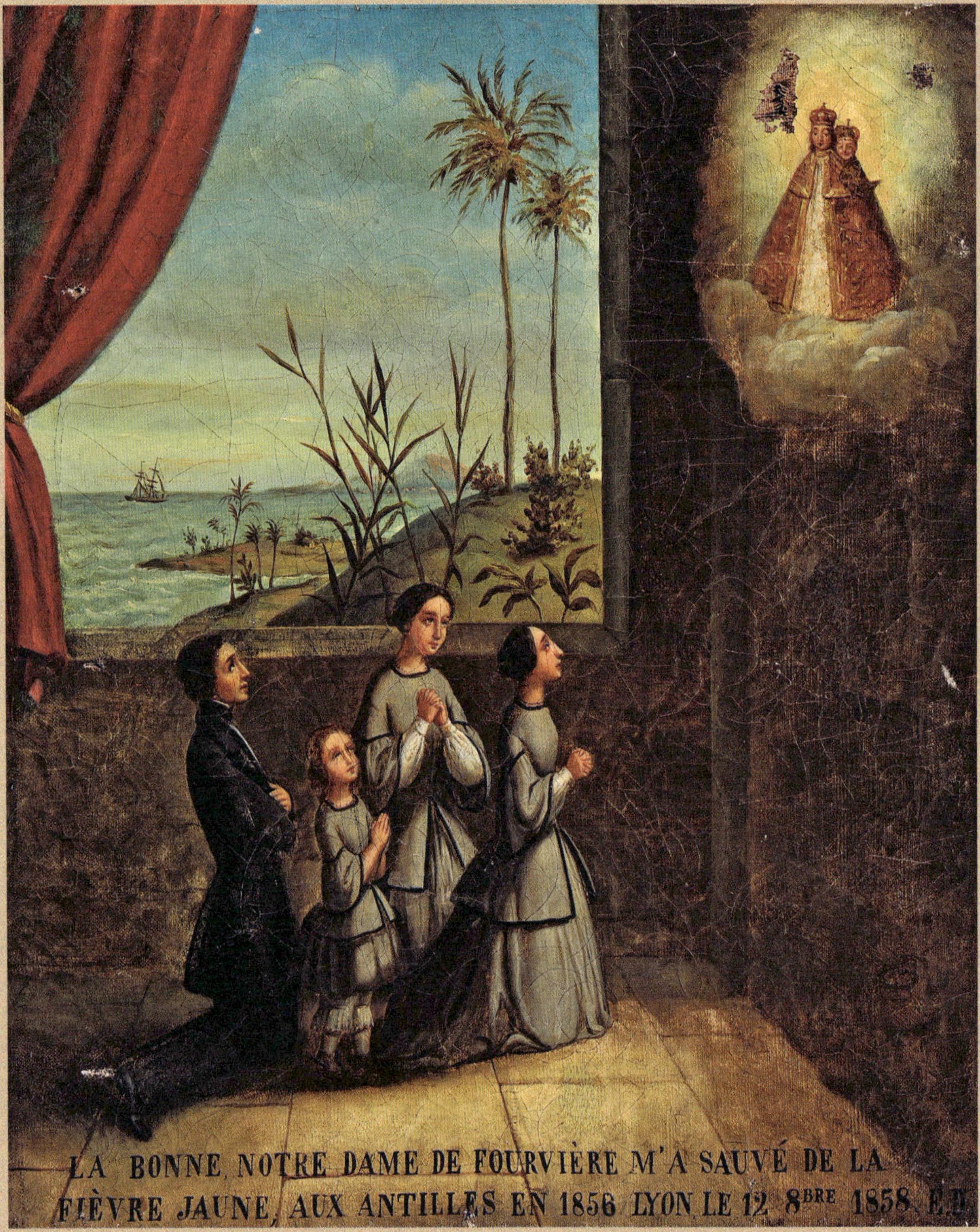

Anonymous, *The Good Lady of Fourvière saved me from yellow fever in the West Indies in 1858, on 12 August 1858 EB*, 1858, oil on canvas, 54 x 43 cm, inv. P3. Fondation Fourvière / Fourvière Museum Lyon. Photo: G. Gambier.

Gratitude to our beloved mother for having saved our whole family from cholera in 1854

Cholera epidemics struck France in 1832 and 1854. To drive the scourge away, the city's inhabitants prayed fervently to the Virgin of the Basilique de Fourvière. One family, having escaped the disease, gifted this ex-voto to the basilica; it depicts them kneeling and gazing up to Mary who is crushing the serpent, a symbol of the "dreadful malady", with her feet.

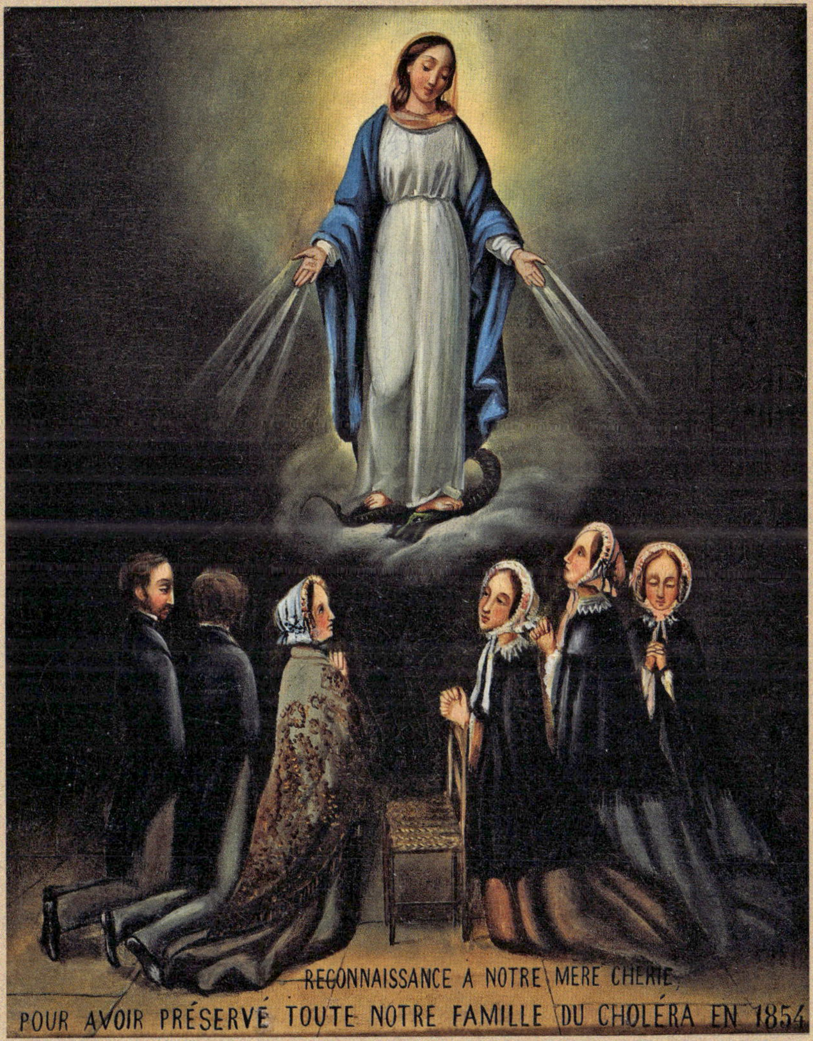

Anonymous, *Gratitude to our beloved mother for saving our whole family from cholera in 1854*, oil on canvas, 48 x 37 cm, inv. P162. Fondation Fourvière / Fourvière Museum Lyon. Photo: G. Gambier.

Fragile Labours

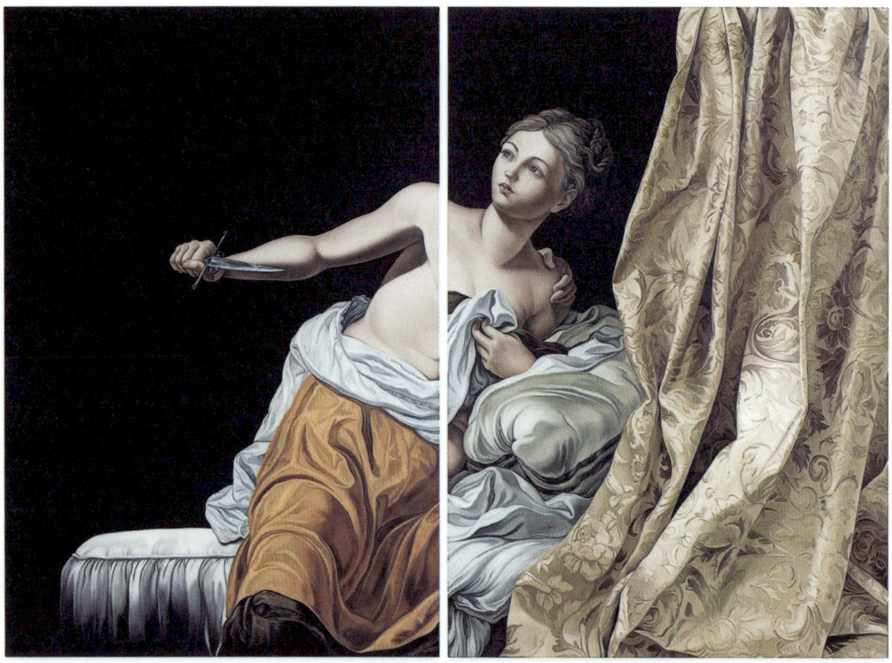

Louise Brunet 02

Louise Brunet is only 18 years old when she is recruited by a henchman of the great silk merchant Nicolas Portalis upon her release from prison in the Drôme region south of Lyon. On an icy cold morning in 1839 with few better alternatives, she embarks on the *Heliopolis* from Marseille to try her luck in Lebanon. Eighteen other women all seeking the better life promised to them by this merchant of great repute also join the voyage. To the dismay of Portalis' recruiter, some appear with their children. The additional cost of accommodating these unexpected extra travellers will become a matter of financial contention a few months later.

Portalis had recently hatched the idea of "importing" experienced spinners to launch his business: a major silk factory in the village of Btetir in Mount Lebanon. Lyon was an ideal breeding ground for this high quality workforce, but the city's history of revolts would not make it easy for him. In April 1834 , in the hope of improving their living conditions, the silk workers, known locally in Lyon as canuts, had thrown the capital of Gauls into chaos during the second Canut revolt. The civil unrest became so widespread that the French state was forced to intervene, sending armed troops from Paris to reestablish order, which they had already done in 1831 and would do again in 1848. The Brunet household – built by a spinner to provide housing for his workers and who most likely was related to Louise – became a stronghold for the canuts. The revolt was ultimately suppressed by force. Louise Brunet was imprisoned along with over 10,000 other participants in the revolt. However, as her story proves, the seed of her resolve against the established order was deeply rooted.

Jesse Mockrin, *Between Desire and Dread*, 2019, oil on cotton, 157 x 121.9 cm. Courtesy of the artist. Photo: Marten Adler.

At some point during the voyage to Lebanon, the captain deviously suggests he no longer wants to deliver Louise and the other spinners to Portalis. Louise is forced to submit to him sexually in order to reach her final destination. A few months later, she writes to her sister to tell her about the hell of her daily life. "It is a blessing that some of these women perished due to the cholera pandemic that had swept across Beirut upon our arrival," Brunet laments. She tells her sister how she has taught young Lebanese women not to put their health at risk in spinning mills. Many of these women are actually six-year-old children. They were recruited from Jesuit and Lazarist orphanages financed by the affluent Lyon Silk merchants who own the factories. The most notorious among them are the spinning factories of Mourgue d'Algue in 'Ayn Hamadé, Palluat and Testenoire et Cie in Al Qrayyé, which will eventually be bought by Veuve Guérin et Fils. The latter, whose factories are the largest with 558 basins spread over four buildings, are infamous for their collaboration with the sisters of the Filles de la Charité.

The working conditions are so bad that Louise foments a revolution with some of her peers and eventually flees. She is captured and once again finds herself imprisoned. Louise's name appears once more in a letter addressed from Portalis to Nicolas Prosper Bourée, the newly installed French Consul General in Beirut. In the letter, Portalis refuses to pay for her expatriation. In one ambiguous passage from this correspondence, which can be found in the classified archives of the French Ministry of Foreign Affairs as file number 92PO_A_28, Portalis' strongman Clément Dreveton proposes paying for Louise's trip to the neighbouring island of Cyprus but declines to finance her travels any further. Beyond this letter, Louise disappears. Resistant at heart, the image of the young woman dipping her skilled hands every day in bubbling chemicals to pull out thin threads of silk is still haunting. Almost two hundred years later, is it not imaginable that Louise Brunets around the world continue to be depleted by the skewed economic structures that exploit them?

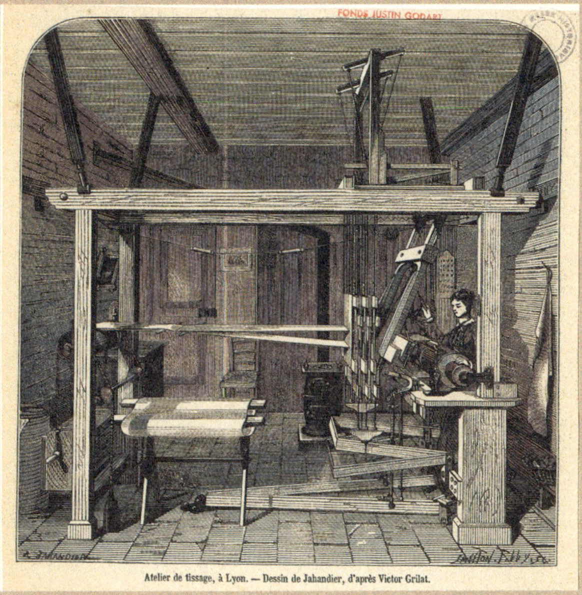

The Old Spinster

First shown in an exhibition held at Lyon City Hall in 1827 in aid of unemployed workers, this picture by Augustin Thierriat portrays an old woman spinning on the top floor of a house with her cat beside her. Through its meticulous execution, descriptive precision and sense of detail – notably the hole in the waxed paper used instead of glass – this genre scene reflects the taste for paintings from the Dutch Golden Age, a feature of the Lyon art scene in the early 19th century.

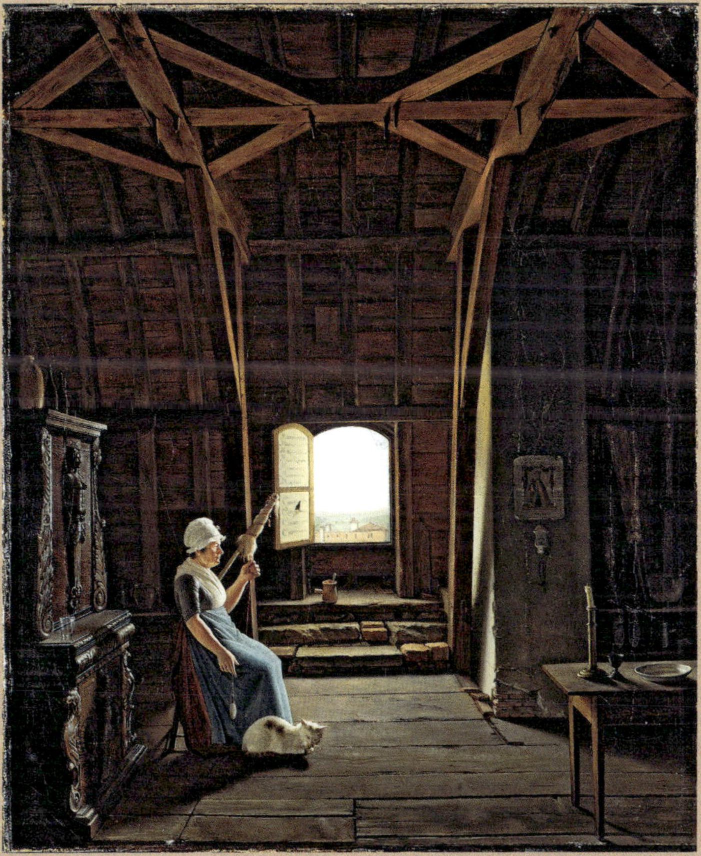

Auguste Jahandier (after Victor Grilat), *Weaving workshop in Lyon*, lithograph, Justin Godart Fund, inv. FG 93.05. © Musée d'Histoire de Lyon - Gadagne.

Augustin Thierriat, *The Old Spinster*, 1815, oil on canvas, 66.3 x 58.4 cm, inv. 2006-2. Courtesy Musée des Beaux-Arts Lyon. Acquired in 2006.

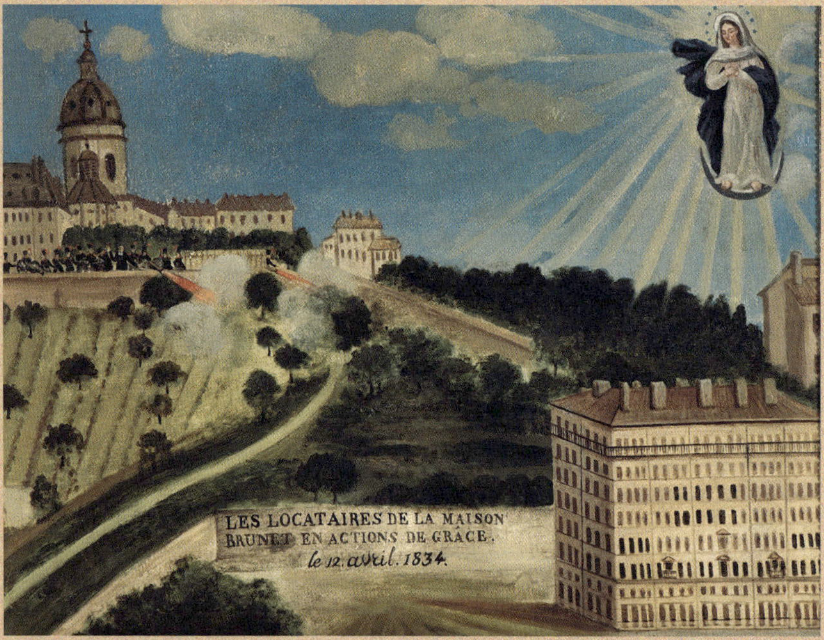

Anonymous, *The Tenants of the Brunet Residence Saying Grace, 12 April 1834*, 1834, gouache on carton, 68 x 89 cm. G. Gambier – Fondation Fourvière / Musée de Fourvière.

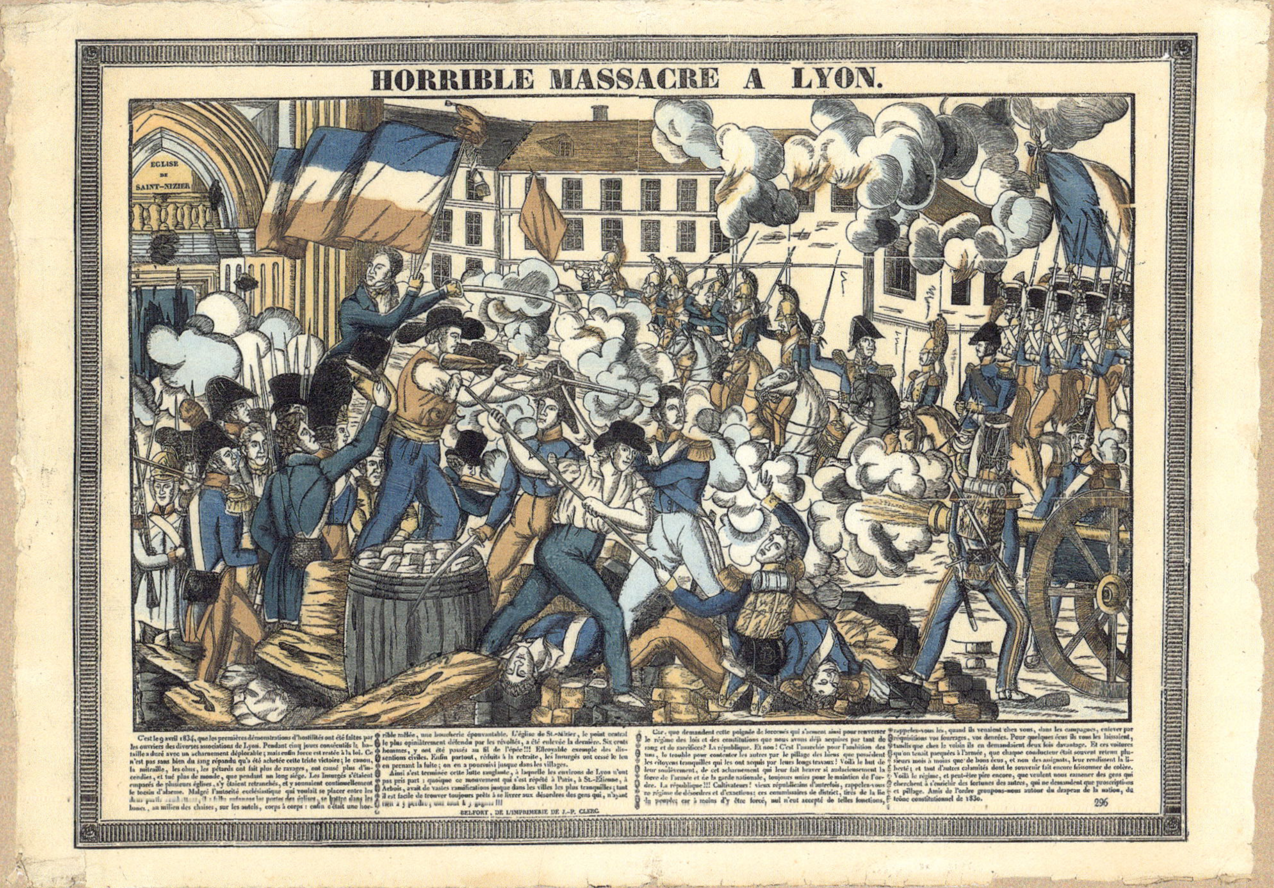

J. P. Clerc, *Horrific Massacre in Lyon, 9 April 1834*, 1834, engraving, donated by Justin Godart, inv. 54.458. © Musée d'Histoire de Lyon - Gadagne.

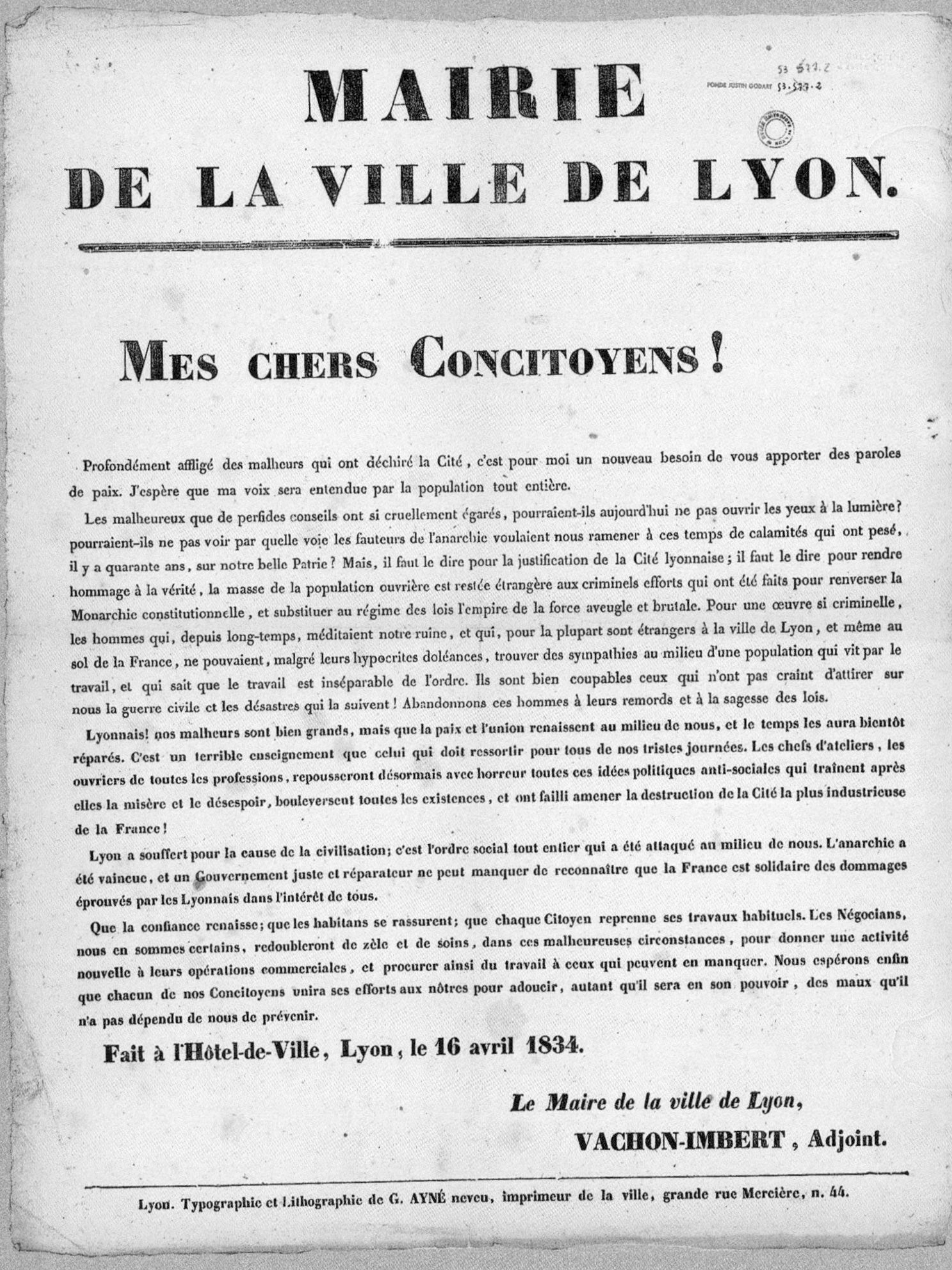

MAIRIE
DE LA VILLE DE LYON.

Mes chers Concitoyens !

Profondément affligé des malheurs qui ont déchiré la Cité, c'est pour moi un nouveau besoin de vous apporter des paroles de paix. J'espère que ma voix sera entendue par la population tout entière.

Les malheureux que de perfides conseils ont si cruellement égarés, pourraient-ils aujourd'hui ne pas ouvrir les yeux à la lumière? pourraient-ils ne pas voir par quelle voie les fauteurs de l'anarchie voulaient nous ramener à ces temps de calamités qui ont pesé, il y a quarante ans, sur notre belle Patrie? Mais, il faut le dire pour la justification de la Cité lyonnaise; il faut le dire pour rendre hommage à la vérité, la masse de la population ouvrière est restée étrangère aux criminels efforts qui ont été faits pour renverser la Monarchie constitutionnelle, et substituer au régime des lois l'empire de la force aveugle et brutale. Pour une œuvre si criminelle, les hommes qui, depuis long-temps, méditaient notre ruine, et qui, pour la plupart sont étrangers à la ville de Lyon, et même au sol de la France, ne pouvaient, malgré leurs hypocrites doléances, trouver des sympathies au milieu d'une population qui vit par le travail, et qui sait que le travail est inséparable de l'ordre. Ils sont bien coupables ceux qui n'ont pas craint d'attirer sur nous la guerre civile et les désastres qui la suivent! Abandonnons ces hommes à leurs remords et à la sagesse des lois.

Lyonnais! nos malheurs sont bien grands, mais que la paix et l'union renaissent au milieu de nous, et le temps les aura bientôt réparés. C'est un terrible enseignement que celui qui doit ressortir pour tous de nos tristes journées. Les chefs d'ateliers, les ouvriers de toutes les professions, repousseront désormais avec horreur toutes ces idées politiques anti-sociales qui traînent après elles la misère et le désespoir, bouleversent toutes les existences, et ont failli amener la destruction de la Cité la plus industrieuse de la France!

Lyon a souffert pour la cause de la civilisation; c'est l'ordre social tout entier qui a été attaqué au milieu de nous. L'anarchie a été vaincue, et un Gouvernement juste et réparateur ne peut manquer de reconnaître que la France est solidaire des dommages éprouvés par les Lyonnais dans l'intérêt de tous.

Que la confiance renaisse; que les habitans se rassurent; que chaque Citoyen reprenne ses travaux habituels. Les Négocians, nous en sommes certains, redoubleront de zèle et de soins, dans ces malheureuses circonstances, pour donner une activité nouvelle à leurs opérations commerciales, et procurer ainsi du travail à ceux qui peuvent en manquer. Nous espérons enfin que chacun de nos Concitoyens unira ses efforts aux nôtres pour adoucir, autant qu'il sera en son pouvoir, des maux qu'il n'a pas dépendu de nous de prévenir.

Fait à l'Hôtel-de-Ville, Lyon, le 16 avril 1834.

Le Maire de la ville de Lyon,

VACHON-IMBERT, Adjoint.

Lyon. Typographie et Lithographie de G. AYNÉ neveu, imprimeur de la ville, grande rue Mercière, n. 44.

Call for peace by Thélis Vachon-Imbert (Deputy Mayor of Lyon), 16 April 1834, poster, donated by Justin Godart, inv. 53.677.2. © Musée d'Histoire de Lyon - Gadagne.

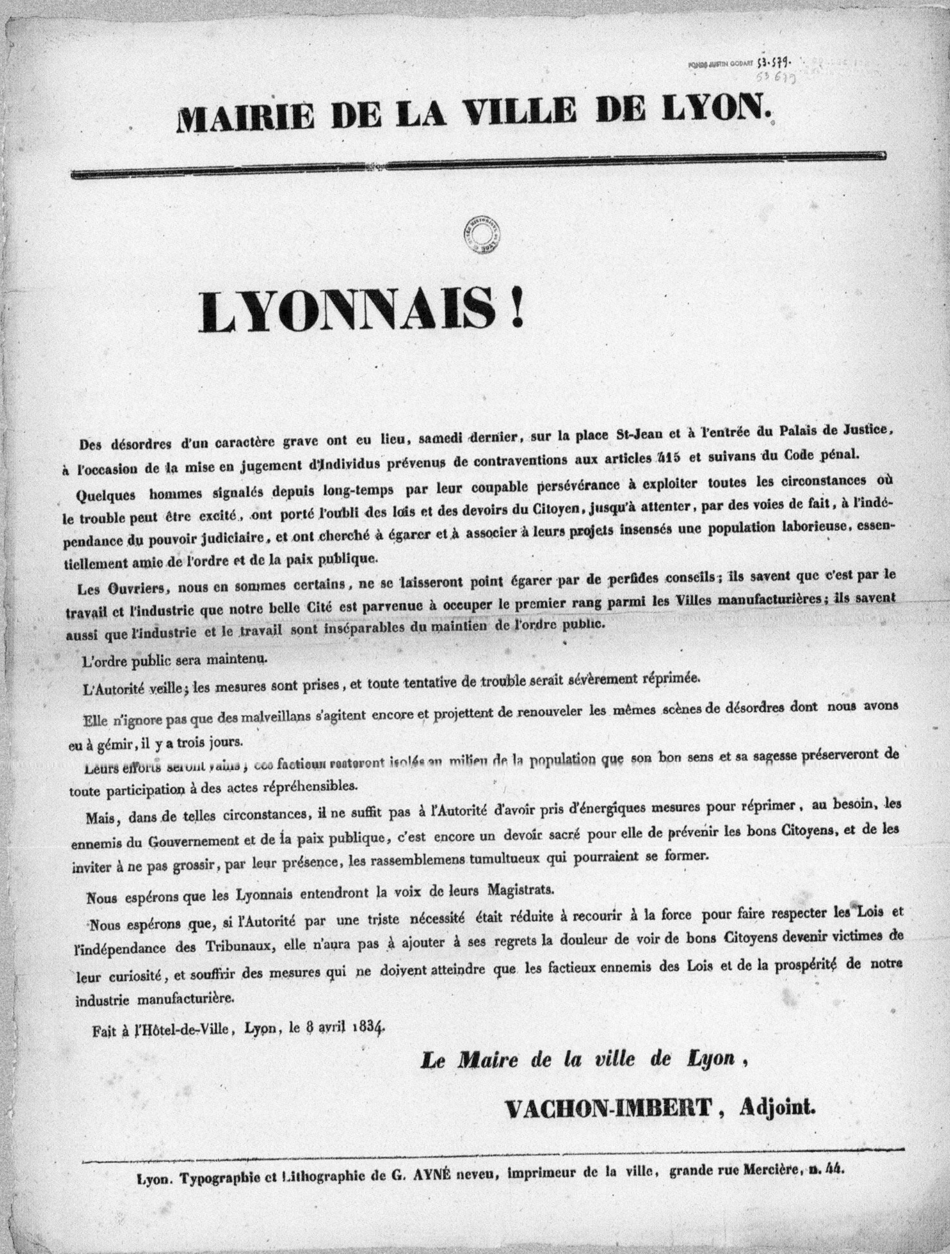

MAIRIE DE LA VILLE DE LYON.

LYONNAIS !

Des désordres d'un caractère grave ont eu lieu, samedi dernier, sur la place St-Jean et à l'entrée du Palais de Justice, à l'occasion de la mise en jugement d'individus prévenus de contraventions aux articles 415 et suivans du Code pénal.

Quelques hommes signalés depuis long-temps par leur coupable persévérance à exploiter toutes les circonstances où le trouble peut être excité, ont porté l'oubli des lois et des devoirs du Citoyen, jusqu'à attenter, par des voies de fait, à l'indépendance du pouvoir judiciaire, et ont cherché à égarer et à associer à leurs projets insensés une population laborieuse, essentiellement amie de l'ordre et de la paix publique.

Les Ouvriers, nous en sommes certains, ne se laisseront point égarer par de perfides conseils; ils savent que c'est par le travail et l'industrie que notre belle Cité est parvenue à occuper le premier rang parmi les Villes manufacturières; ils savent aussi que l'industrie et le travail sont inséparables du maintien de l'ordre public.

L'ordre public sera maintenu.

L'Autorité veille; les mesures sont prises, et toute tentative de trouble serait sévèrement réprimée.

Elle n'ignore pas que des malveillans s'agitent encore et projettent de renouveler les mêmes scènes de désordres dont nous avons eu à gémir, il y a trois jours.

Leurs efforts seront vains; ces factieux resteront isolés au milieu de la population que son bon sens et sa sagesse préserveront de toute participation à des actes répréhensibles.

Mais, dans de telles circonstances, il ne suffit pas à l'Autorité d'avoir pris d'énergiques mesures pour réprimer, au besoin, les ennemis du Gouvernement et de la paix publique, c'est encore un devoir sacré pour elle de prévenir les bons Citoyens, et de les inviter à ne pas grossir, par leur présence, les rassemblemens tumultueux qui pourraient se former.

Nous espérons que les Lyonnais entendront la voix de leurs Magistrats.

Nous espérons que, si l'Autorité par une triste nécessité était réduite à recourir à la force pour faire respecter les Lois et l'indépendance des Tribunaux, elle n'aura pas à ajouter à ses regrets la douleur de voir de bons Citoyens devenir victimes de leur curiosité, et souffrir des mesures qui ne doivent atteindre que les factieux ennemis des Lois et de la prospérité de notre industrie manufacturière.

Fait à l'Hôtel-de-Ville, Lyon, le 8 avril 1834.

Le Maire de la ville de Lyon,

VACHON-IMBERT, Adjoint.

Lyon. Typographie et Lithographie de G. AYNÉ neveu, imprimeur de la ville, grande rue Mercière, n. 44.

Message from Thélis Vachon-Imbert (Deputy Mayor of Lyon), 8 April 1834, poster, donated by Justin Godart, inv. 53.679. © Musée d'Histoire de Lyon - Gadagne.

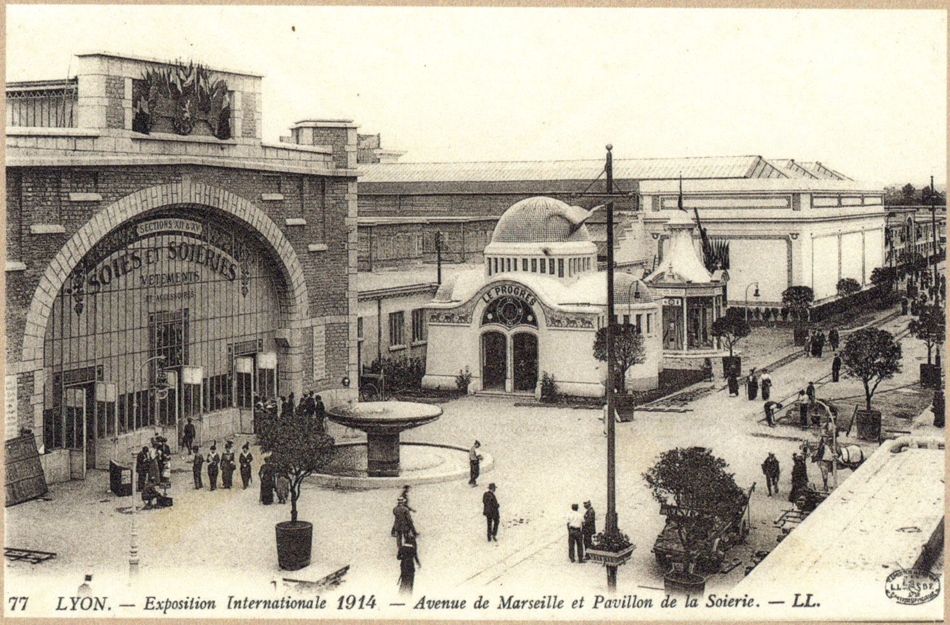

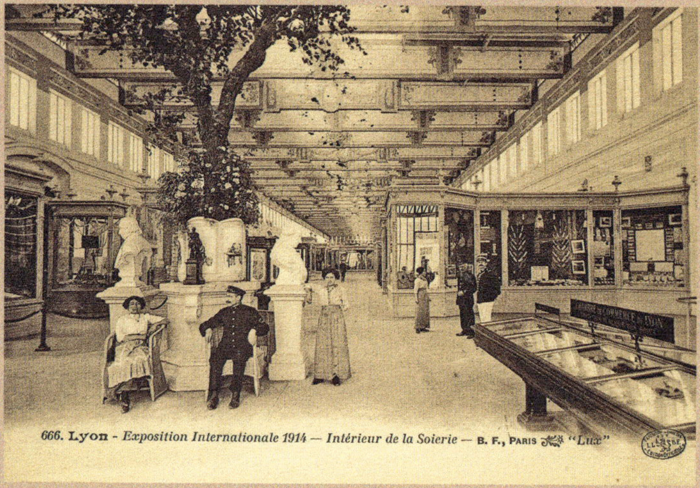

Top *Lyon – 1914 International Exhibition, Marseille Avenue and silk industry pavilion*, postcard, inv. 0131.60. © Musée d'Histoire de Lyon - Gadagne.

Bottom *The silk pavilion in the large hall of Lyon's World Fair*, 1914, postcard. Private collection.

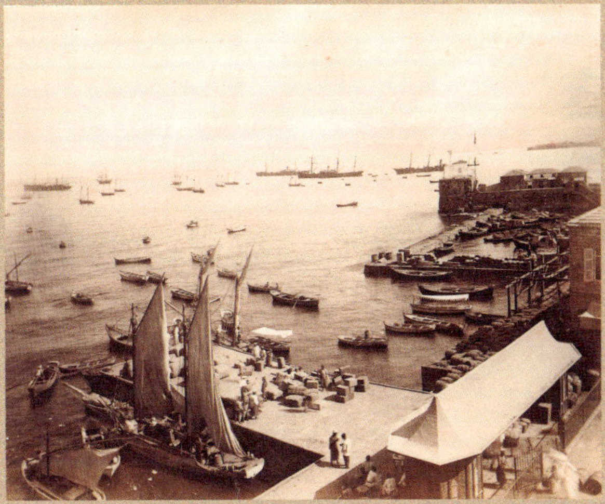

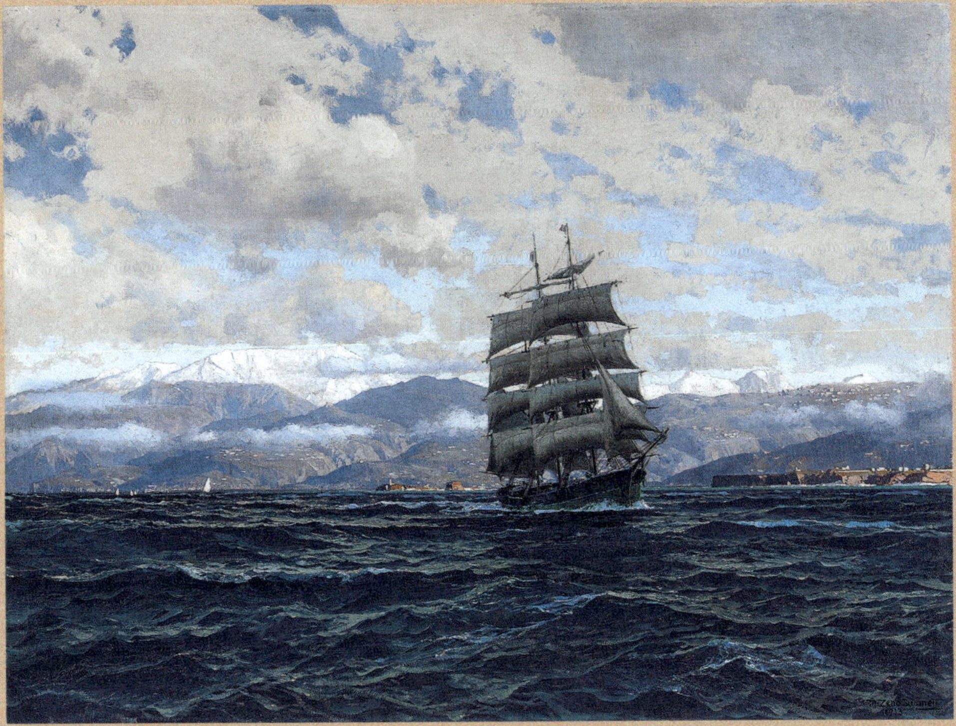

Michael Zeno Diemer, *Three-masted ship in front of Quarantine area in Beirut; in the background, a snow-covered Mount Sannine*, 1933, oil on canvas, 70 x 94 cm. Courtesy Philippe Jabre Art Collection.

Jean-Baptiste Charlier, *View of Beirut port*, late 19th century, albumin print, 22 x 28 cm. Courtesy Philippe Jabre Art Collection.

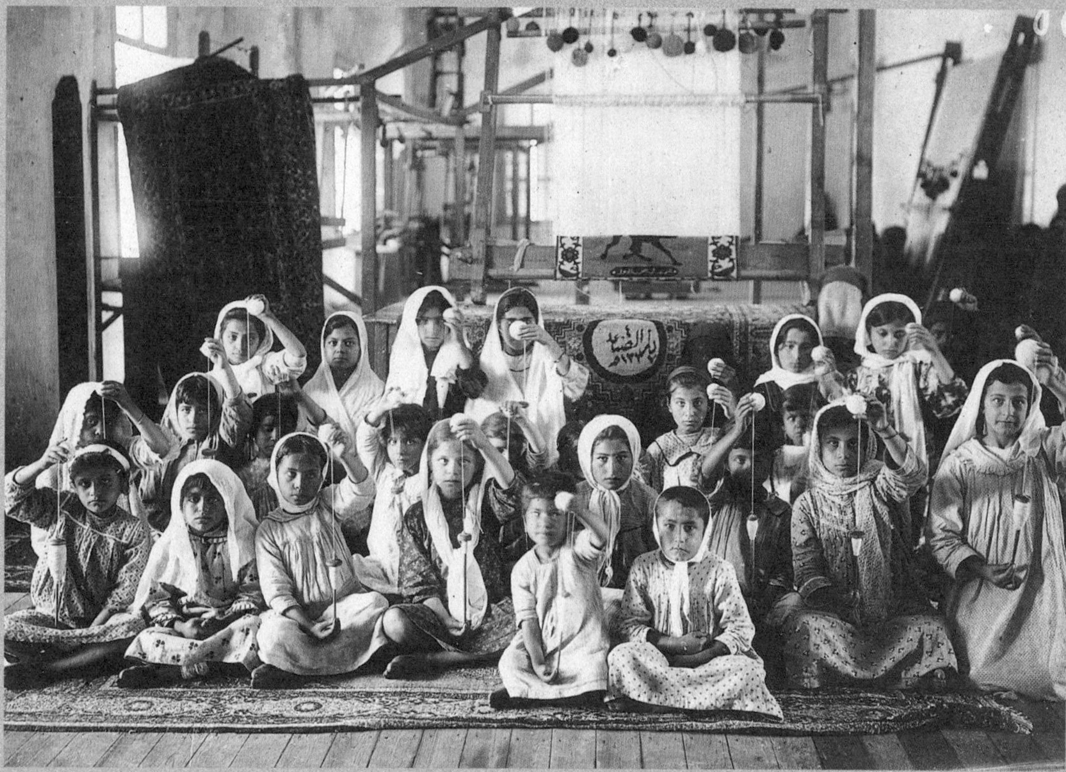

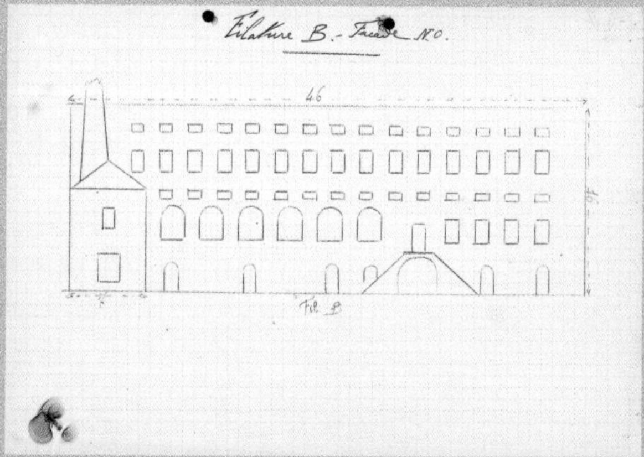

The work of the French Public Welfare – children are taught to spin wool, Mount Lebanon, late 19th century – early 20th century, photograph, inv. A003563. Courtesy Archives du Ministère de l'Europe et des Affaires Etrangères.

Veuve Guérin et Fils, Floor plan of the northwestern façade of factory B at al-Qrayye, ca. 1909. Arch. dép. Rhône, 145J169 .

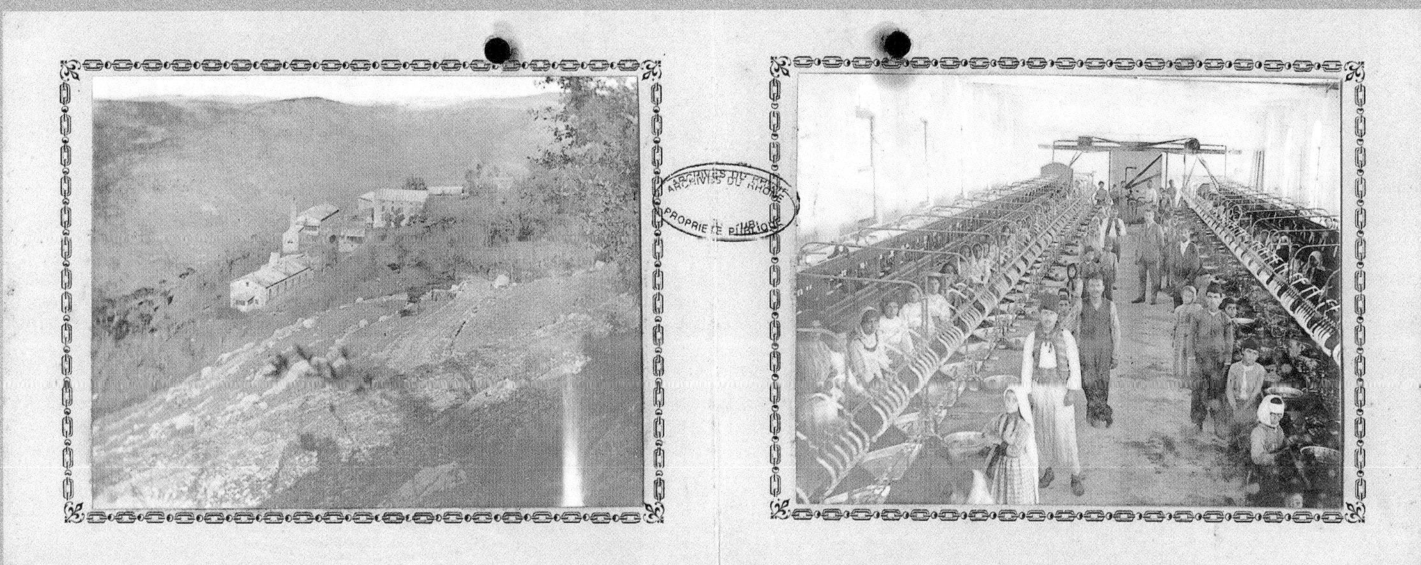

Veuve Guérin et Fils, Photos of the exterior and interior of the silk factory at al-Qrayye on the obverse side of a reception menu, undated. Arch. dép. Rhône, 145J169.

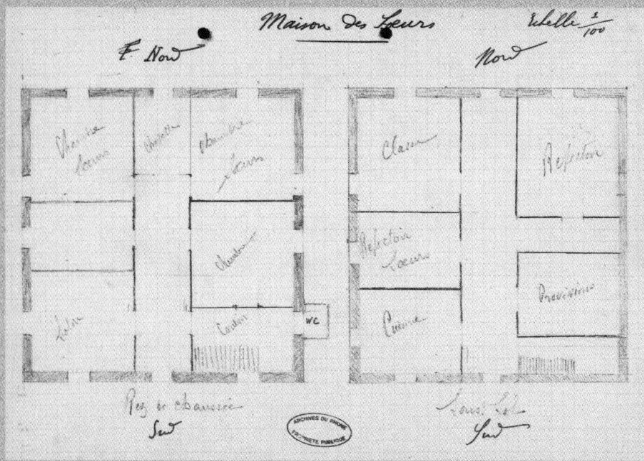

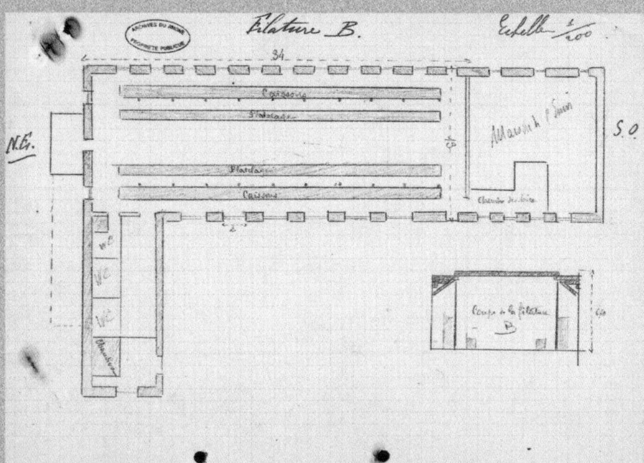

Top Veuve Guérin et Fils, Floor plan of the sisters' residence in the factory of al-Qrayye, ca. 1909. Arch. dép. Rhône, 145J169.

Bottom Veuve Guérin et Fils, Floor plan and cross-section of factory B in al-Qrayye, ca. 1909, Arch. dép. Rhône, 145J169.

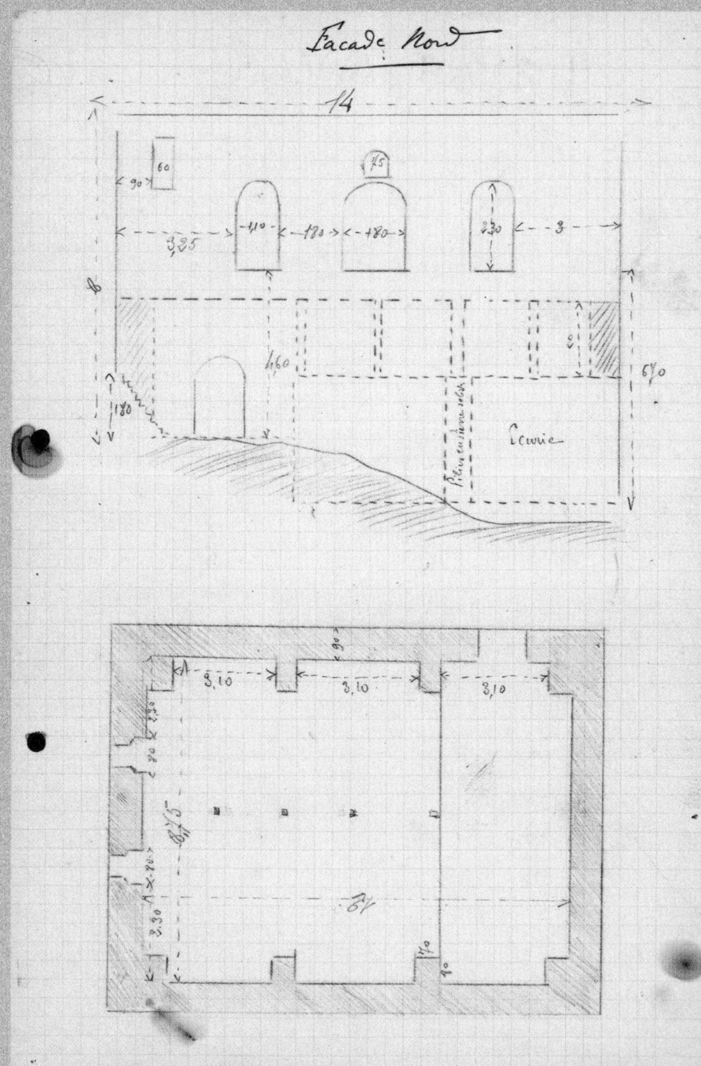

Veuve Guérin et Fils, Floor plan and elevation of the northern façade of one of the factory buildings of al-Qrayye, ca. 1909. Arch. dép. Rhône, 145J169.

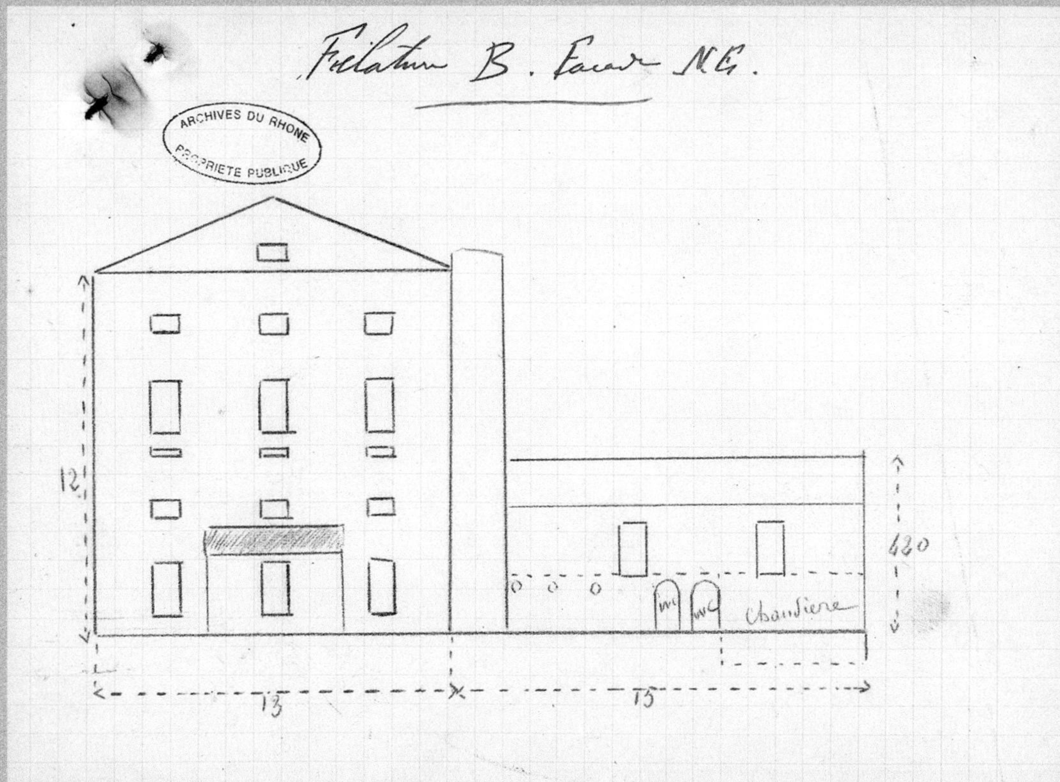

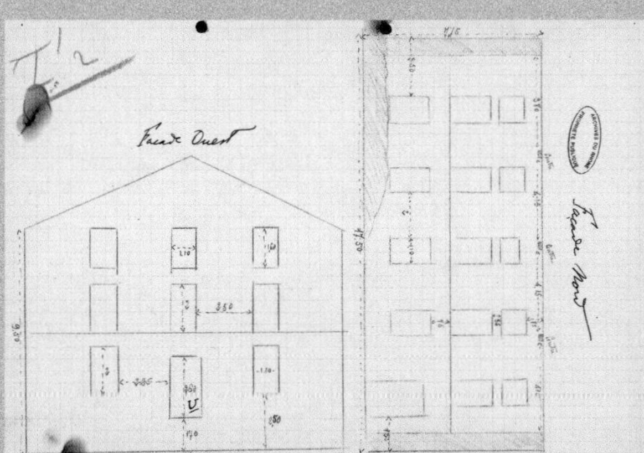

Top Veuve Guérin et Fils, Elevation of the northeastern façade of factory B in al-Qrayye, ca. 1909, 145J169. Arch. dép. Rhône.

Bottom Veuve Guérin et Fils, Elevation of the northern and western façades of one of the factory buildings at al-Qrayye, ca. 1909, 145J169. Arch. dép. Rhône.

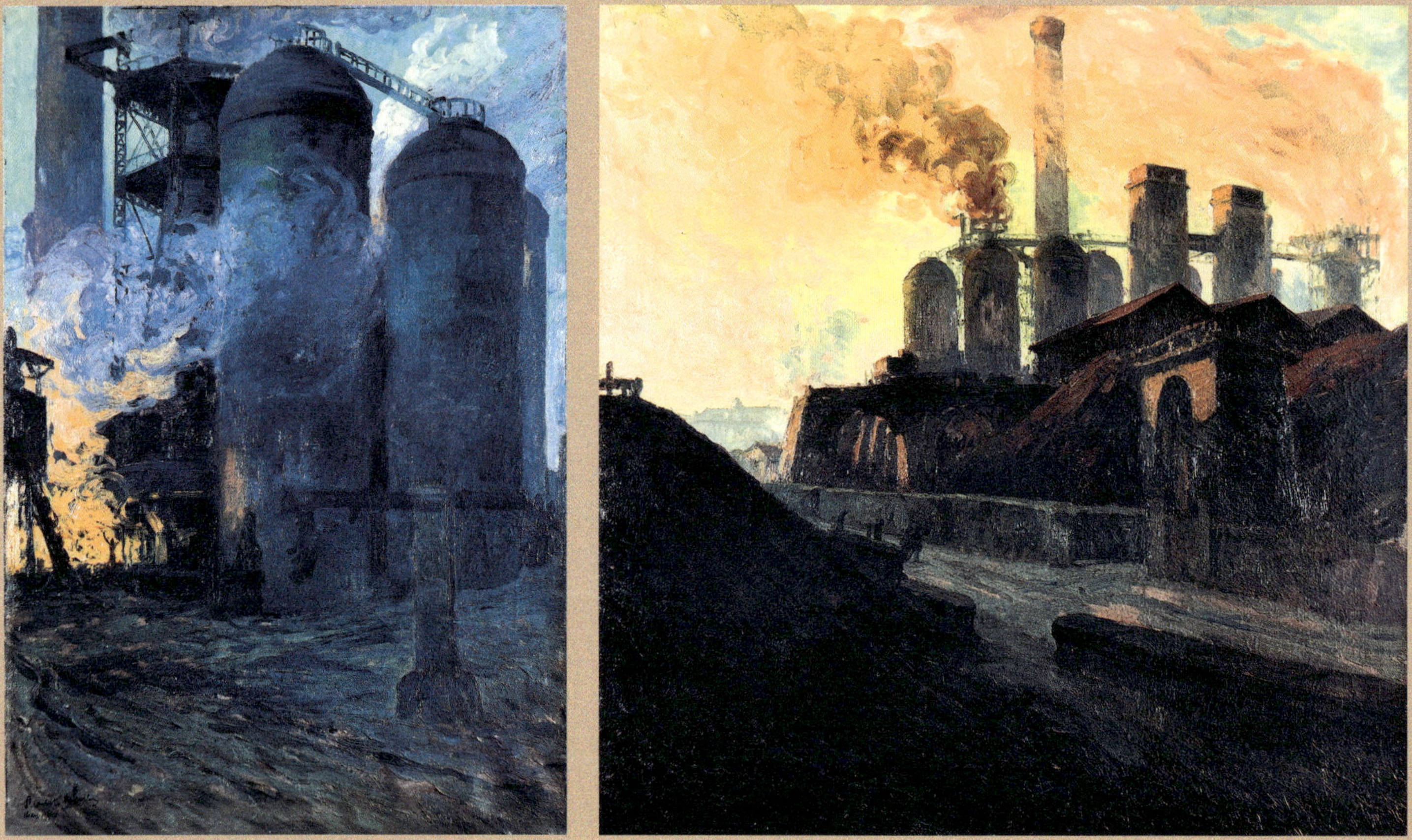

Pierre Combet-Descombes, *The Blast Furnaces for Hunting* (triptych), 1911, oil on canvas, inv. 1999.1.96.1, Inv. 1999.1.96.2, Inv. 1999.1.96.3. Courtesy of the Musée municipal Paul Dini, Villefranche-sur-Saône, donated by Muguette and Paul Dini.

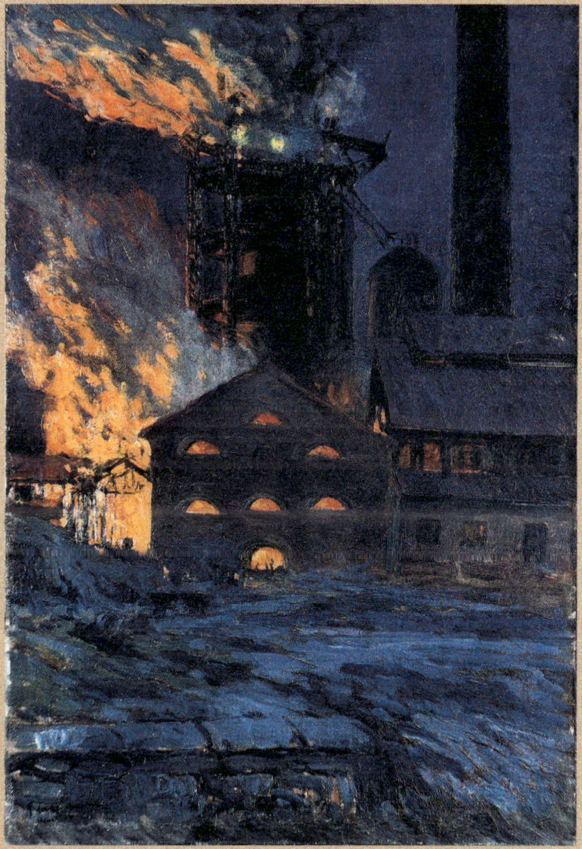

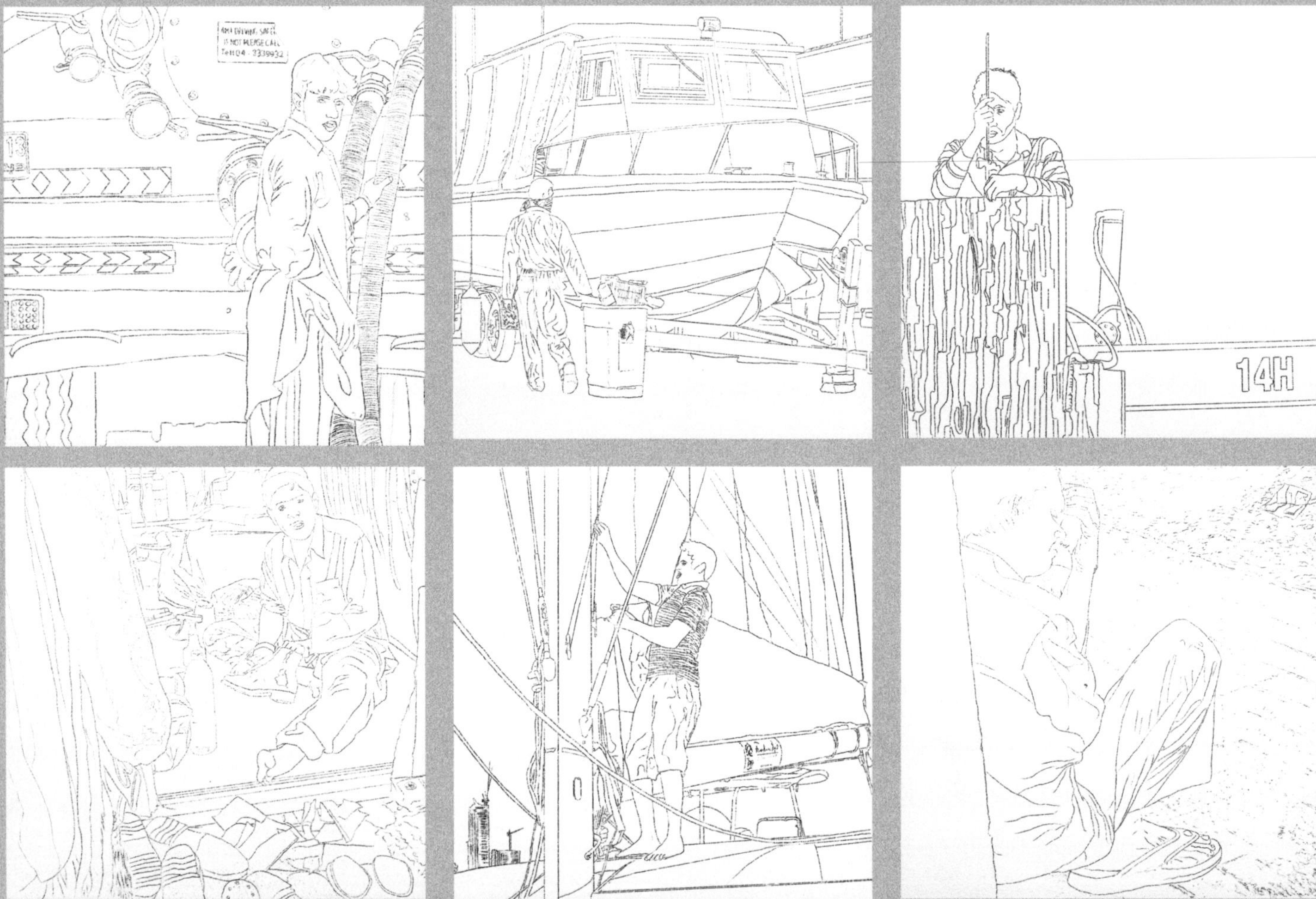

Mohammed Kazem, from the series *Windows*, 2011–2012, graphite on paper, 25 x 25 cm (each), inv. MK/PA 257.11. Courtesy of the artist and Gallery Isabelle van den Eynde.

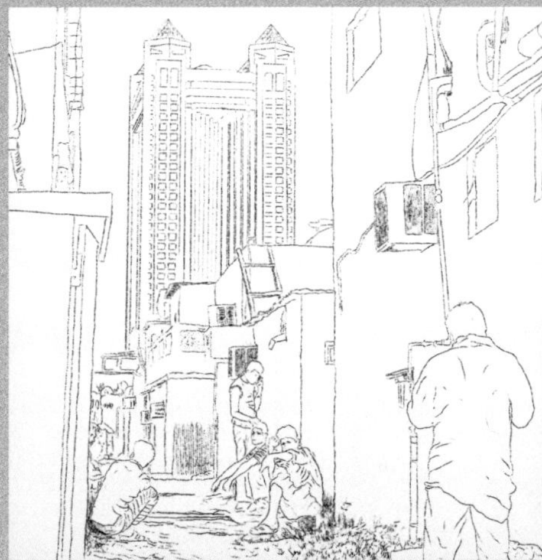

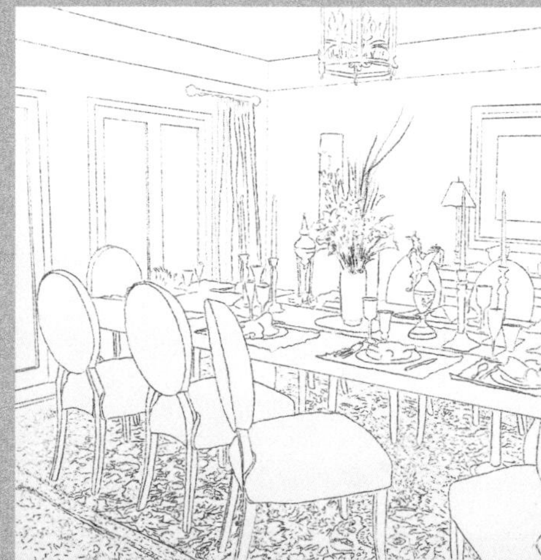

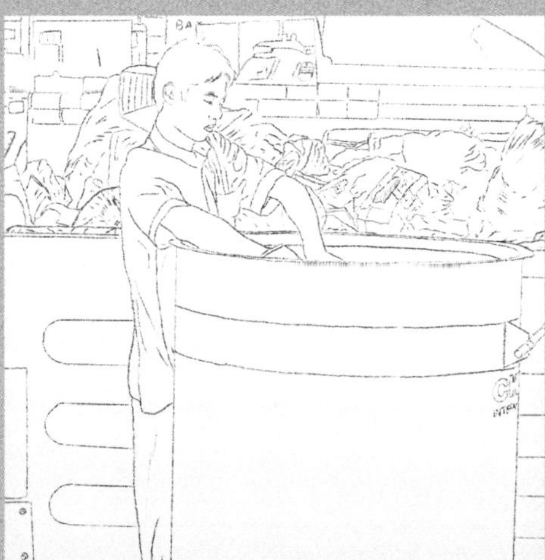

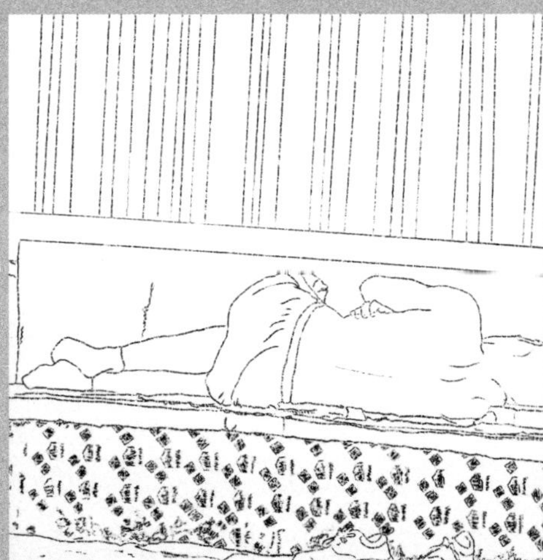

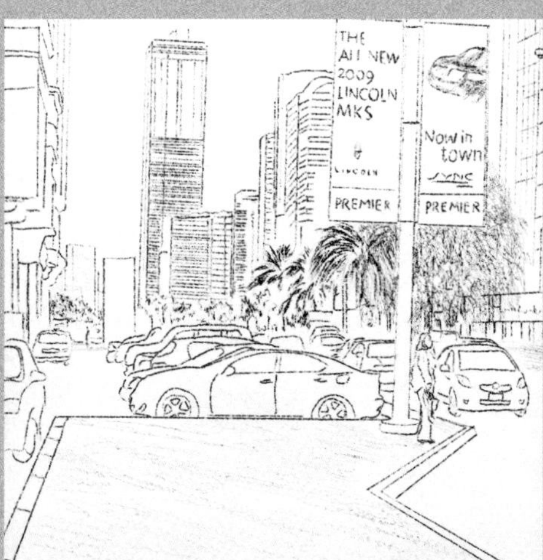
THE
ALL NEW
2009
LINCOLN
MKS
PREMIER
Now in
town
PREMIER

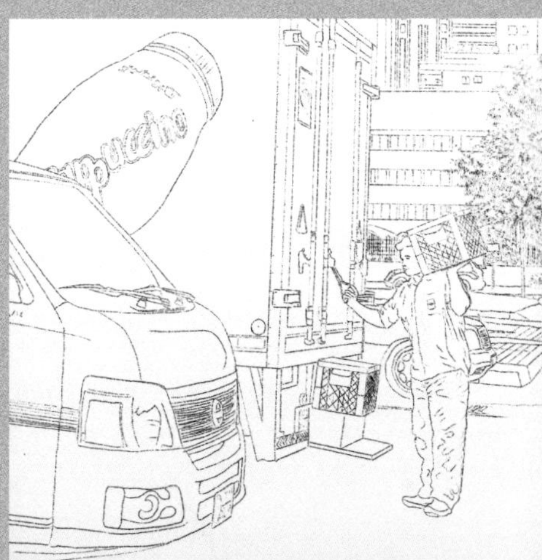

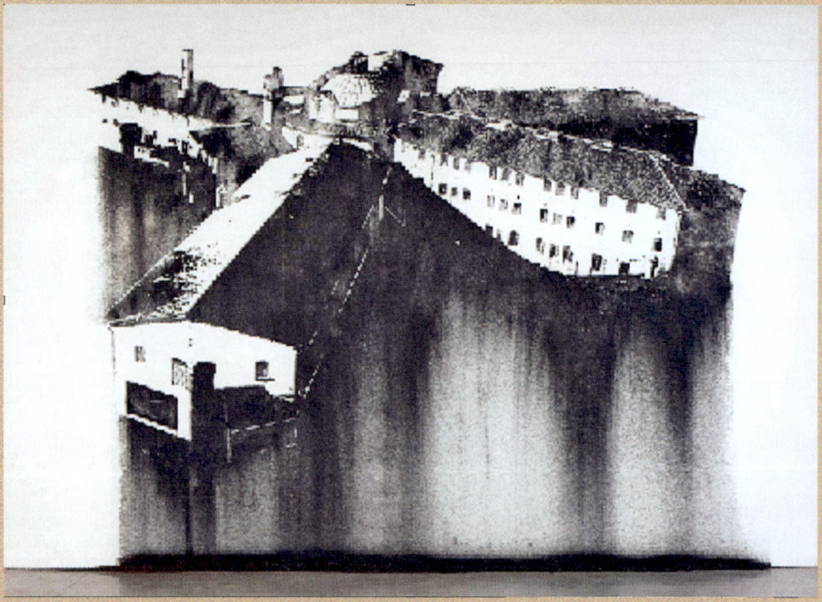

Nicolas Daubanes, *Saint Michel – prison de Toulouse*, 2017, magnetized iron powder, 280 x 300 cm. Courtesy of the artist and Galerie Maubert. © Adagp, Paris, 2022. Photo: Damien Aspe.

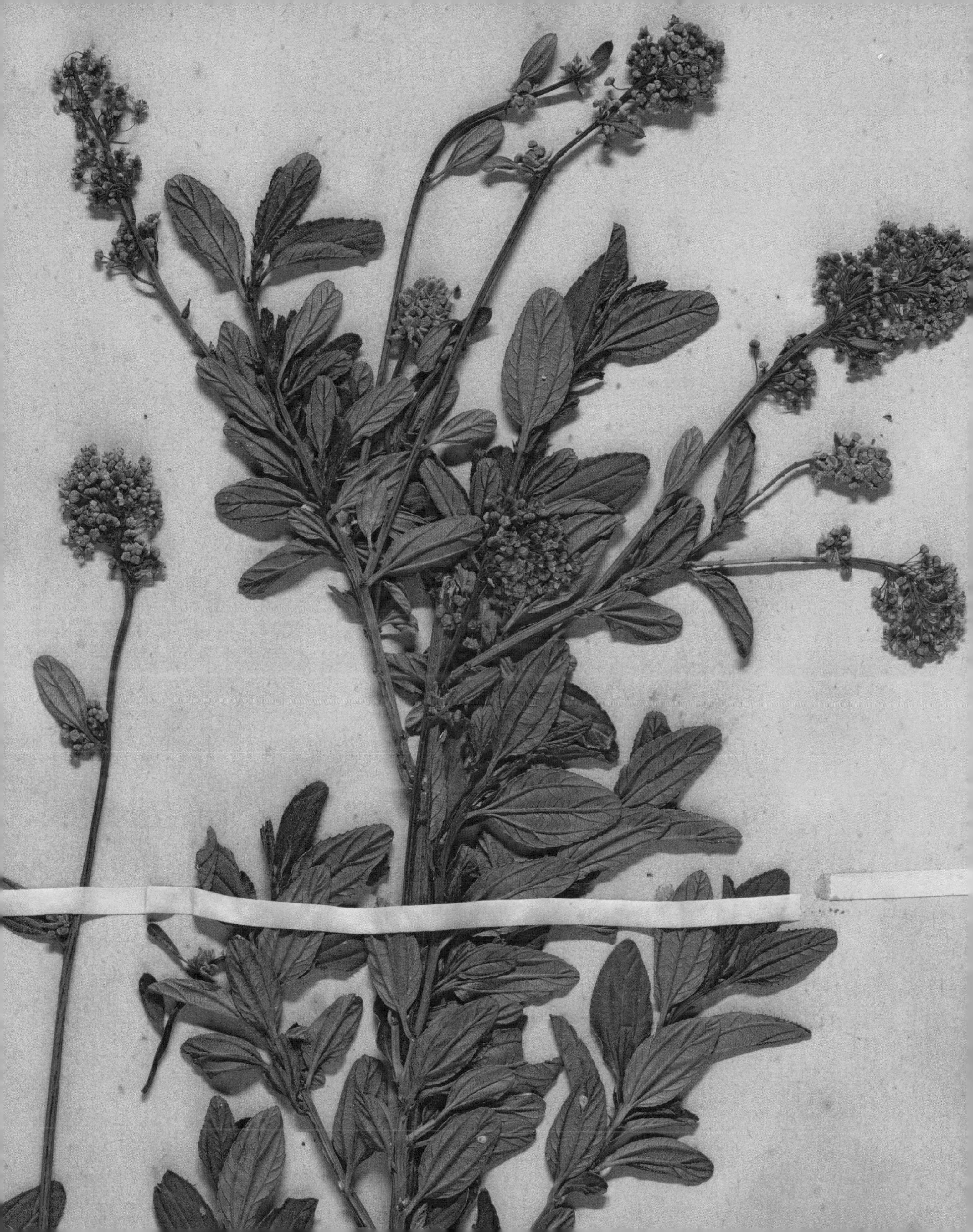

Fragile Heroes

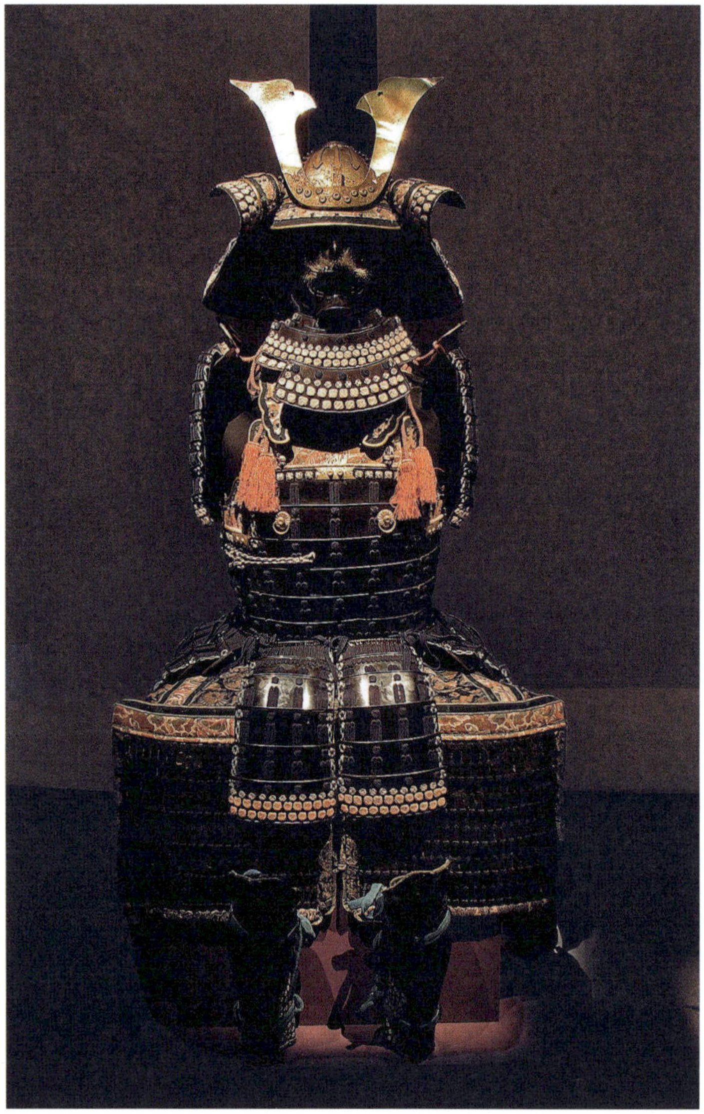

Louise Brunet 03

It is nine in the morning on 15 May 1942. Louise Brunet waits on the pavement in front of the house where he has lived for the last 20 years. Standing with Louise are his wife Mami and their five children. At the age of 55, Louise is a proud, self-made man who owns and operates five greenhouses on a three-acre plot of land in Alameda County in San Francisco's East Bay area. Kiyoshi Yukimura, or Mr. Yuki as Louise's friends and neighbours call him, was born in 1887 at 1344 Kearny Street on the eastern outskirts of San Francisco's Chinatown. Like many first-generation Japanese immigrants, Louise's parents had settled there. After the 1906 earthquake, the family relocated to Japantown in the city's Western Addition neighbourhood.

The hardworking Louise opened his first plant shop on Post Street, the main thoroughfare of Japantown, 25 years earlier. Five years later, newly married with a baby on the way, Louise purchased the house one block to the west on Fillmore Street where he has been living with his family ever since.

Although Louise is standing at the same spot where he usually catches his daily ride to work, the destination of today's journey is unfathomably different, even surreal. Louise's children are huddled together, nestled between him and his wife. Three suitcases lie between their fidgeting feet. They are marked with the family name Yukimura written in bold white paint. Large, vertical identification tags hang around each family member's neck with the same family name and an identifying number: "Yukimura 1/6", "Yukimura 2/6", "Yukimura 3/6", and so on. Louise and his family are among tens of thousands of Japanese Americans being forcibly relocated and incarcerated in what the US Department of Justice euphemistically calls "relocation centers". Following the surprise attack on the US naval base at Pearl Harbor by the Imperial Japanese Navy Air Service on 7 December 1941, President Franklin Roosevelt issued Executive Order 9066 on 19 February 1942. The order authorised the forced "evacuation" of any persons considered to be a security threat and cleared the way for the incarceration of almost every Japanese American for the duration of the war in militarised internment camps. Two-thirds of the detainees are US citizens who were born in the United States and lived in the country their whole lives. Louise, and his family, are among them.

Japan, Mogami-dō Gusoku black samurai armour, 19th century, lacquered steel and leather, silk, metal, inv. 2009.0.436. Musée des Confluences, Lyon.

Louise hears the familiar roar of a bus engine approaching the corner. One of his hands rests gently on his youngest daughter's shoulder. She looks up towards him and whispers, "The bus is coming," as she holds onto his waist. "It is. It is," Louise replies as he gently pats her head. He clasps his other hand firmly around the strap of the large bag that he is carrying on his right shoulder.

Louise had woken up early this morning. He wanted to make sure that some things were not left behind; in particular, heirlooms that his parents had brought back from their hometown of Yokohama. One thing held a special place in Louise's heart: a samurai armour that belonged to his great, great grandfather. Louise had worn parts of it on his wedding day. "This is the gusoku that I wore", Louise's father used to tell him as a child, "on 8 July 1853, the day Japan changed forever." He was referring to the day that US Commodore Matthew Perry commanded four black navy vessels into Japan's Edo Bay, beginning a compelled opening of the Japanese empire to foreign trade. "Our land, our time, our way" was something his father used to declare at almost every family gathering. Louise had never fully grasped the meaning of these words until this morning while standing on the pavement, waiting with his family to begin their forced relocation.

The family climbs into the bus. Ten hours later, they find themselves almost 600 kilometres away in Manzanar – one of ten mainland internment camps – located at the foot of the Sierra Nevada mountains in California's Owens Valley. While exiting the bus, Louise's eldest son refuses to get off. His act of disobedience is the first of many that will ultimately lead to the Manzanar uprising on 5 and 6 December 1942. To quell the insurrection, the US military police will fire into the crowd, killing Louise and his 17-year-old son instantly. Some will say they heard them shouting, "Our land, our time, our way." Others will say they found Louise's samurai armour bloodied on the ground. But this does not occur until seven months later. Today, the armour is packed neatly in Louise's bag.

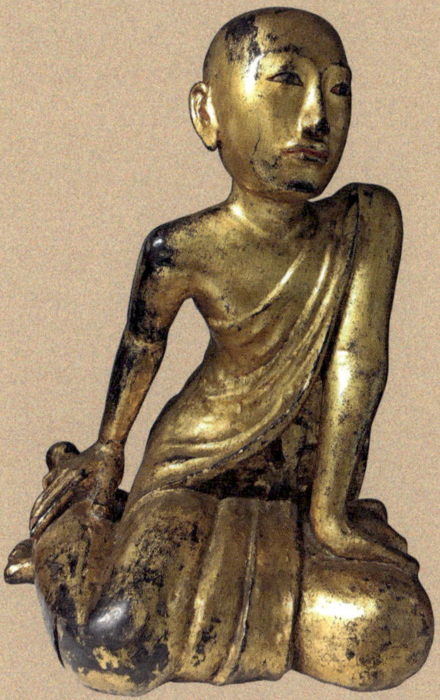

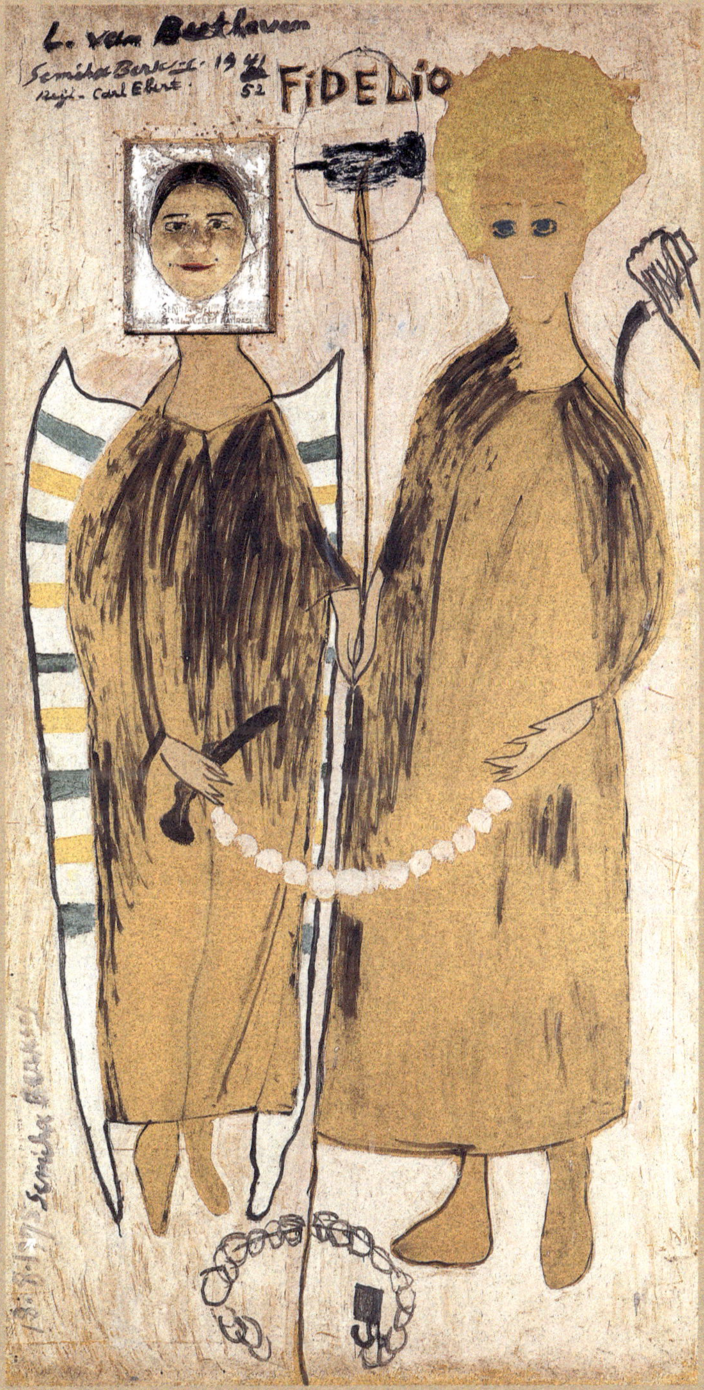

Monk Sāriputta, disciple of Buddha, Myanmar, 19th century, gilded wood, inv. 60005983. Musée des confluences, Lyon.

Semiha Berksoy, *Fidelio*, 1975, oil on Masonite, 244 x 122 cm. Courtesy of the Estate of Semiha Berksoy and Galerist.

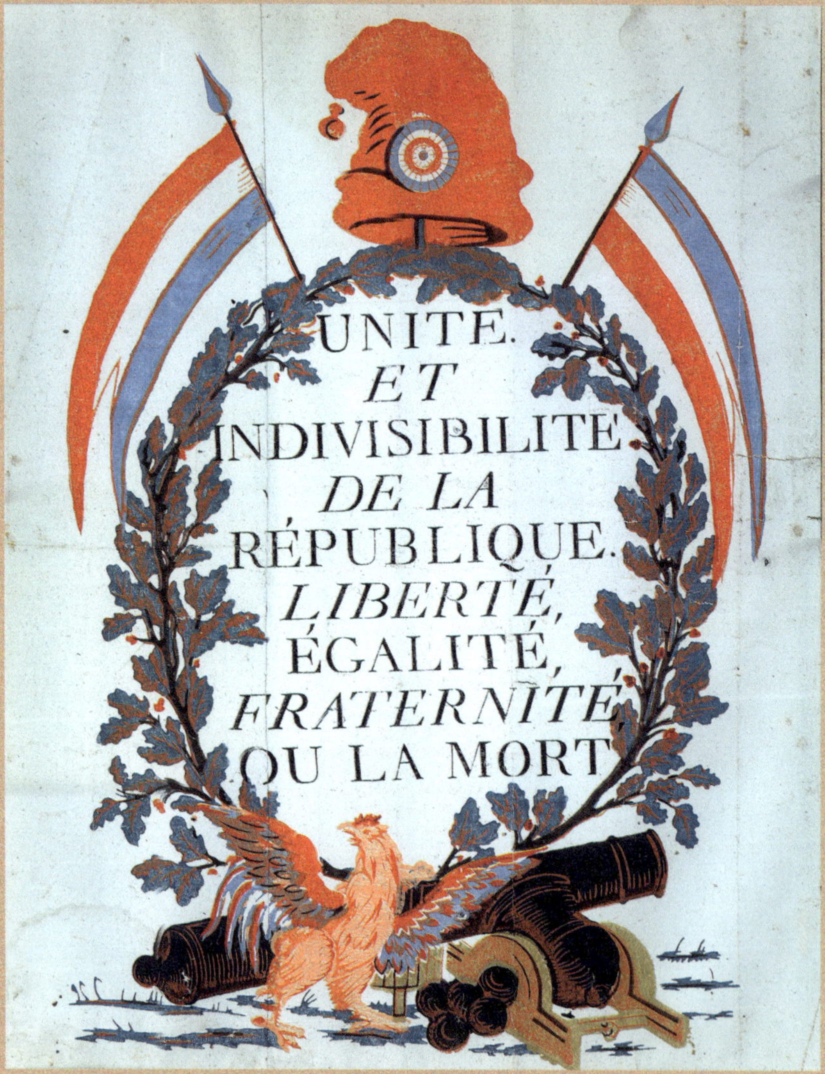

French revolution coloured wallpaper, inv. 386. © Musée d'Histoire de Lyon - Gadagne.

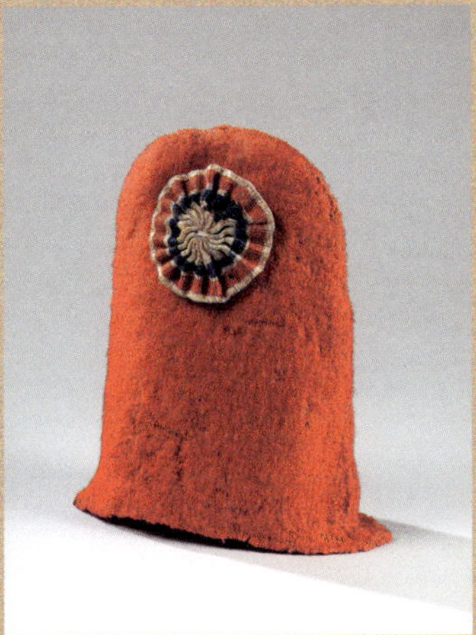

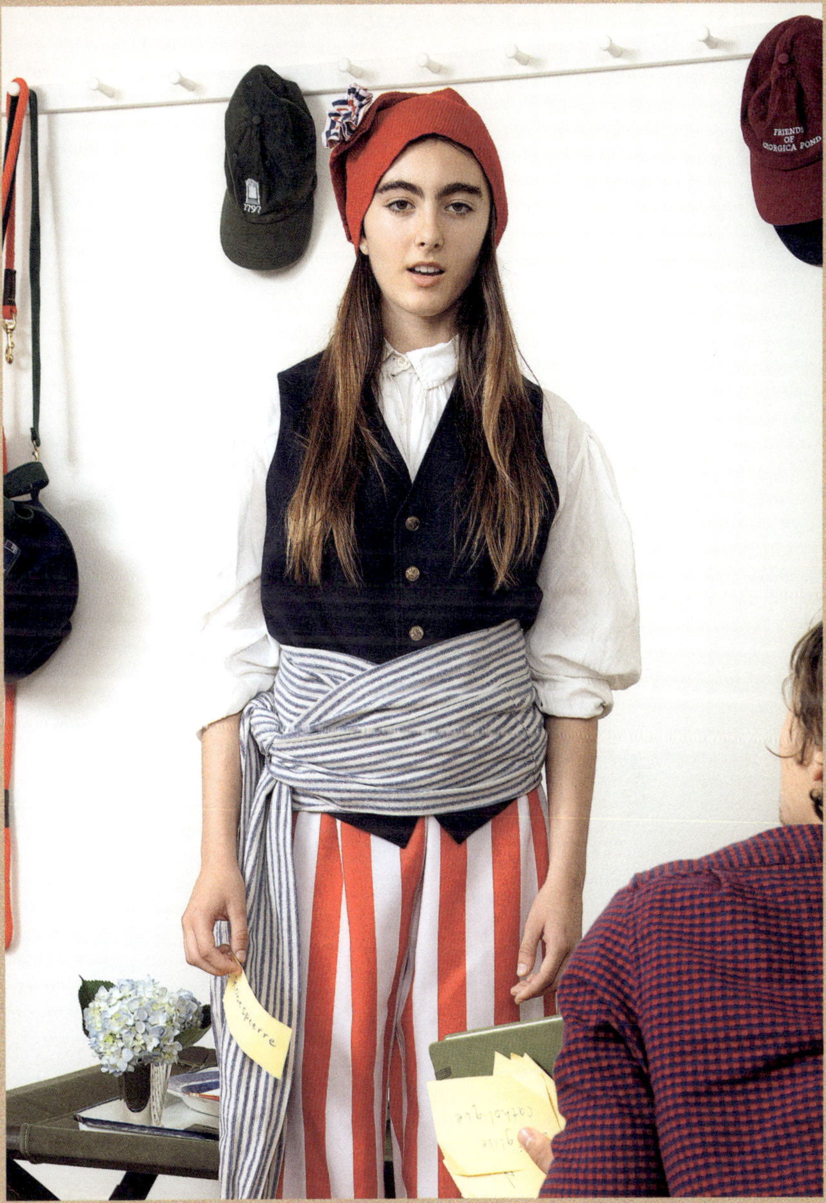

Freedom bonnet, ca. 1791, knitted wool, inv. 391 b. © Pierre Aubert / Musée d'Histoire de Lyon - Gadagne.

Buck Ellison, *French-American*, 2022, archival pigment print, 125.7 x 88.9 cm. Courtesy of the artist.

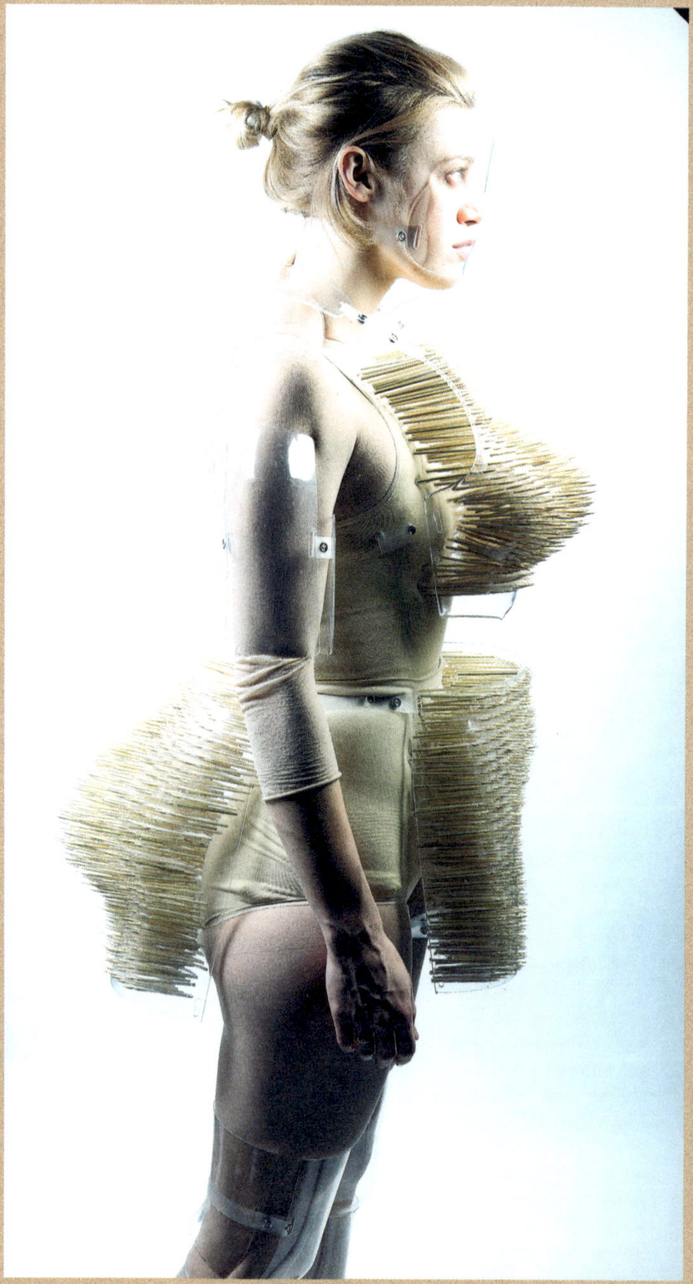

Lucy McRae, *Skin Pours* (Costume for Lady Gaga), 2011, bamboo skewers, plexiglass, panty hose. Courtesy of the artist.

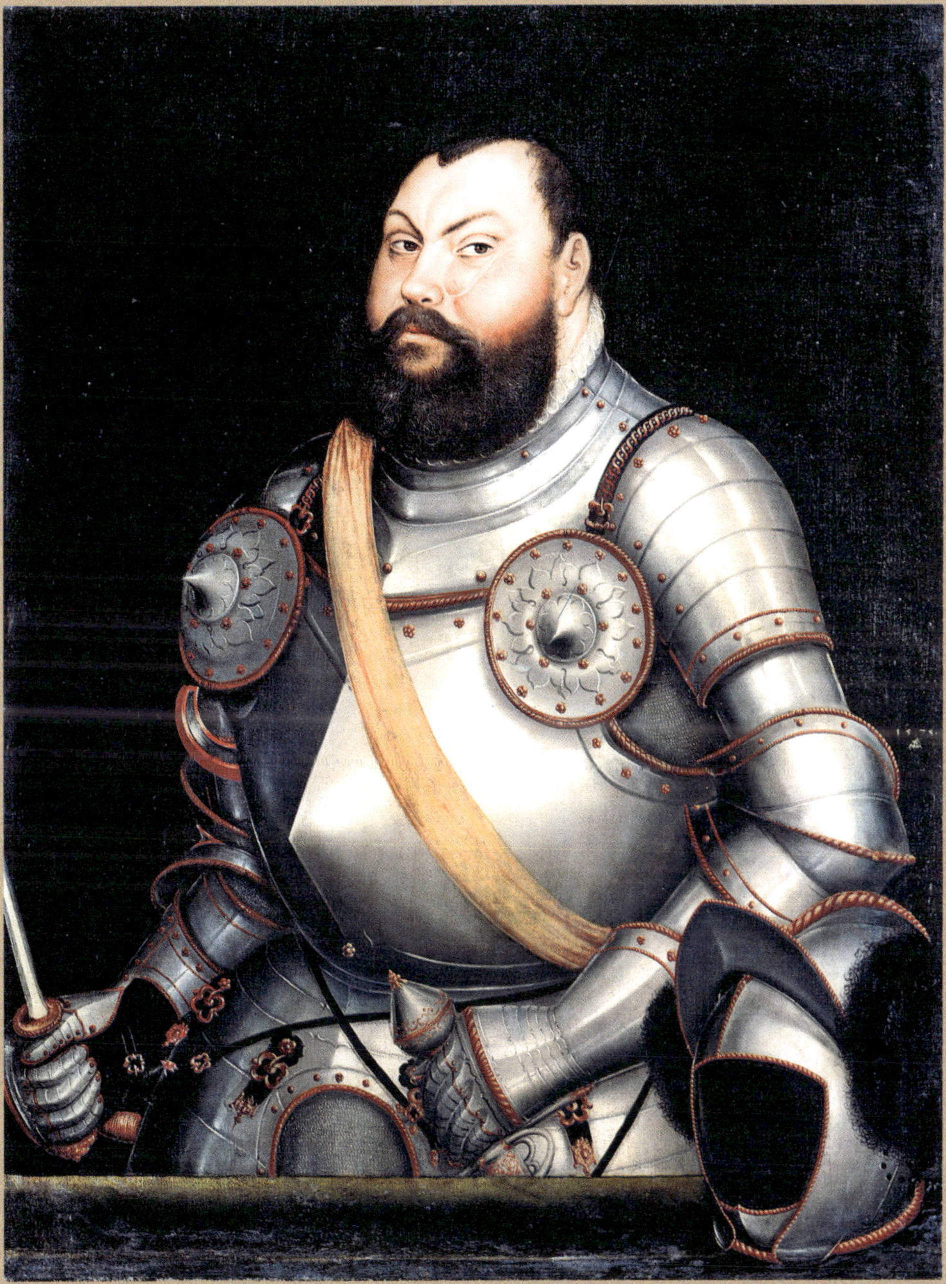

Lucas Cranach the Younger, *Johann Friedrich of Saxony*, 1578, oil on canvas, 138.8 x 111.1 cm, inv. H0073.01. © Albertinum / GNM, Staatliche Kunstsammlungen Dresden.

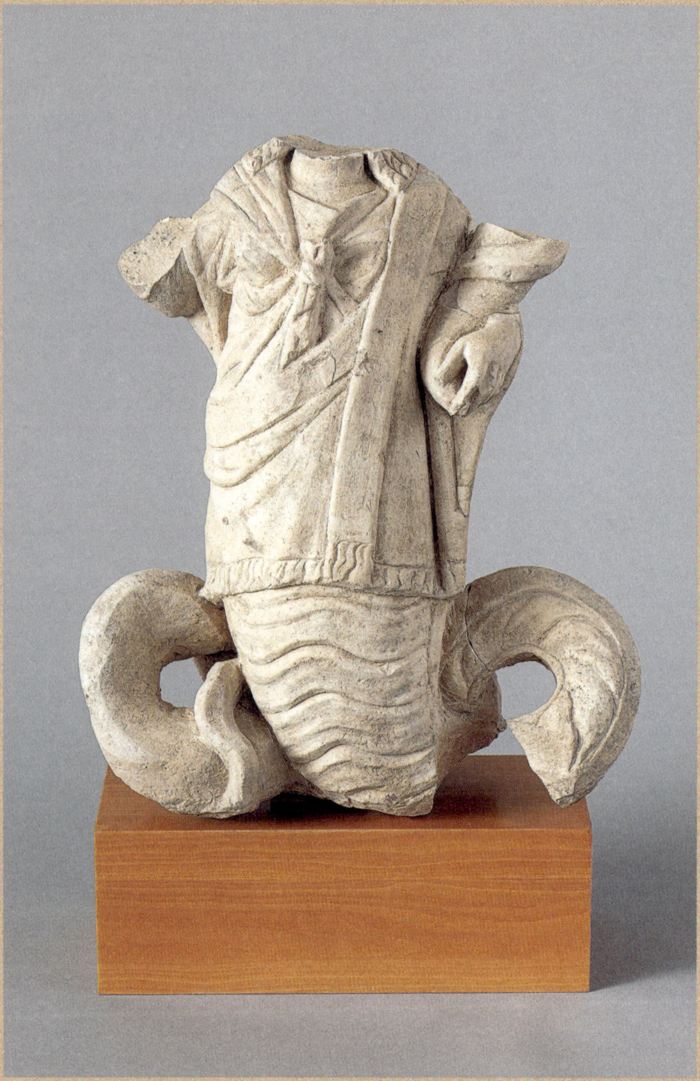

Isis-Thermuthis

Isis-Thermuthis combines the figures of the mythical queen Isis and the goddess Renenutet-Thermuthis (respectively "the nourishing snake" in ancient Egyptian and "the grandmother" in Greek). Mentioned as having the form of a cobra in the Pyramid Texts, she watches over the grain stored in the granaries. This hybrid figure is represented here in her anguiped form, that is, endowed with a snake's tail. Dressed in a tunic and a fringed cloak, she holds an ear of wheat in her left hand – a reminder of her agrarian role. Worship of this goddess, who protected both agricultural and female fertility, peaked during the reign of the Greco-Egyptian pharaohs and the Roman domination of Egypt.

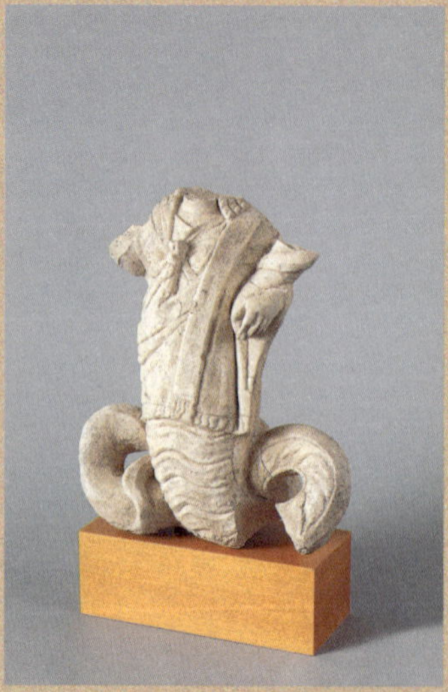

Egpyt (Hellenistic or Roman period), Isis-Thermuthis, 3rd century BCE, inv. SN 210. Musée des Beaux-Arts, Lyon. Photo: Martial Couderette.

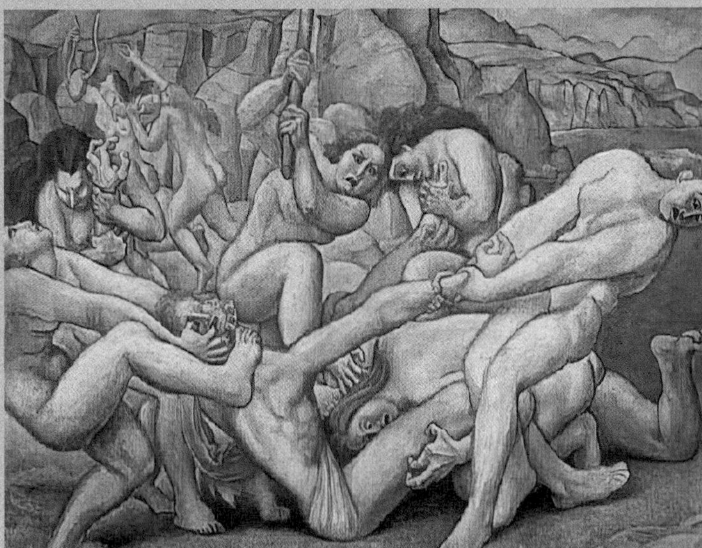

Louis Bouquet, *The Death of Orpheus*,
1919-1929, oil on canvas, 98 x 131 cm. Private collection . © Adagp, Paris, 2022.

The Death of Orpheus

According to the art critic Stanislas Fumet, Louis Bouquet viewed the legendary poet Orpheus as "his hero and the fellow at the centre of his dreams". Although the first preparatory sketches for it date from 1925, The Death of Orpheus *was only completed in 1939, on the eve of World War Two. Since the poet refused to wed any woman other than Eurydice, his dead soulmate, the Maenads accused Orpheus of scorning them. Armed with thyrsi (staffs covered with leaves), these followers of Dionysus decided to rip the poet to pieces. Drunk with fury, they tore off his limbs and thus stopped him from singing.*

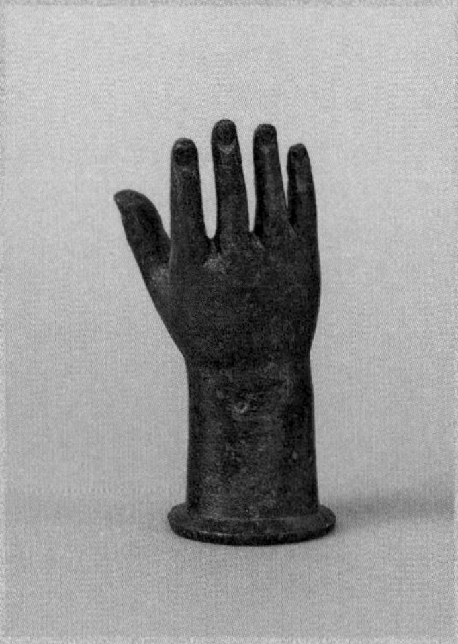

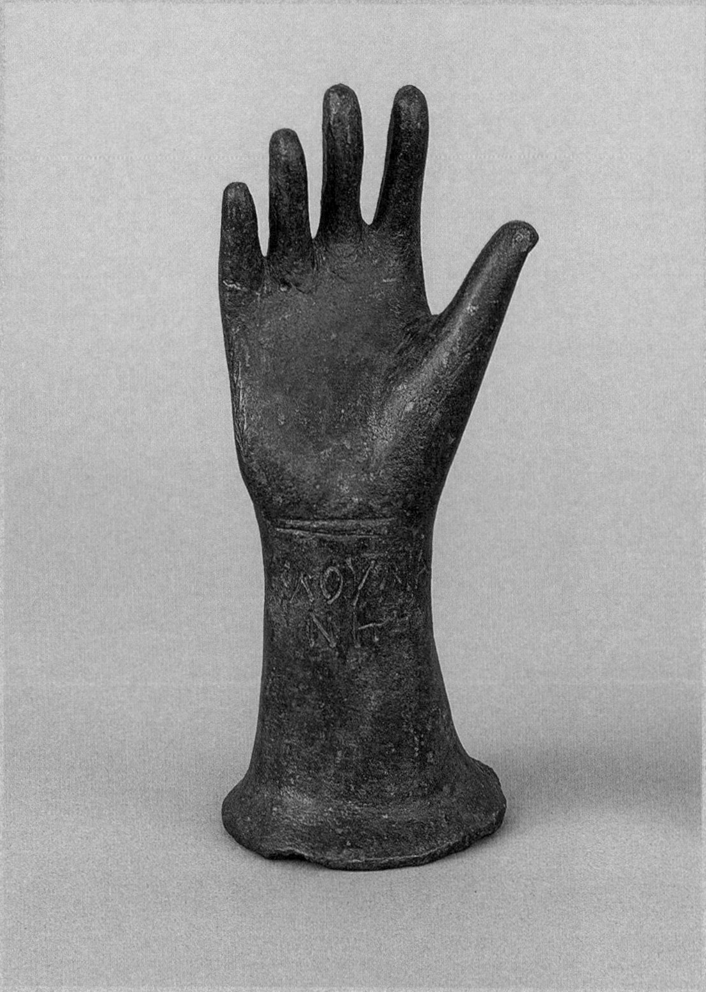

Phoenicia (Roman period), Votive Hands, 2nd–3rd centuries, inv. E 408-11. Musée des Beaux-Arts, Lyon. Photo: Martial Couderette.

Untitled

In her staged photographs, Joanna Piotrowska focuses on human relationships and their bodily expressions. Taking intimate everyday gestures as her starting point, she examine behaviours relating to freedom, power, protection and oppression. Here she represents two pairs of hands, one pressed against the other, in an ambiguous gesture at once evoking confrontation, resistance and support.

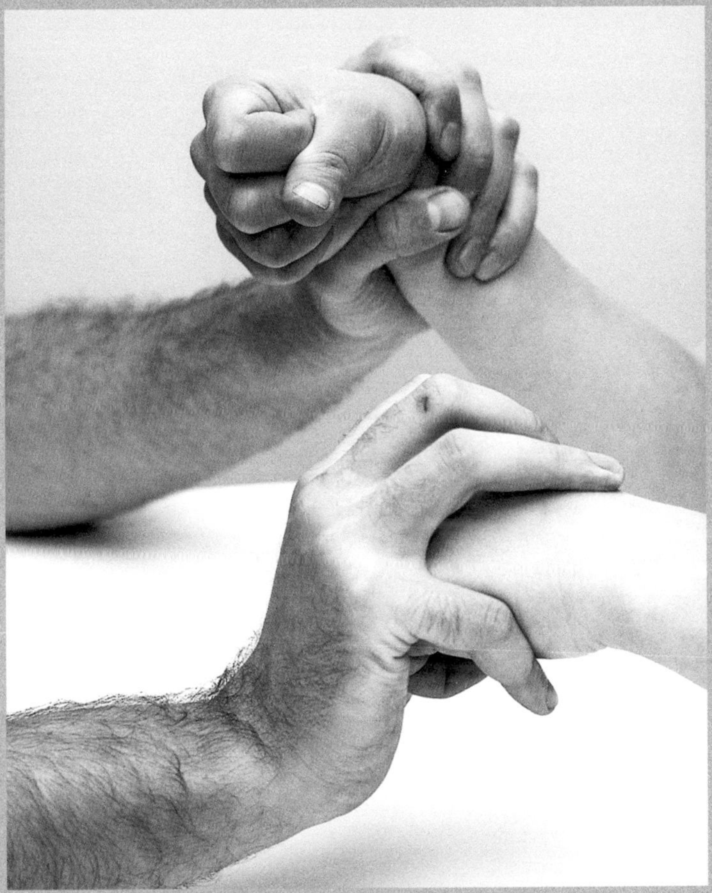

Joanna Piotrowska, *Untitled*, 2015, gelatin silver print, 34.3 x 28.8 cm. © Joanna Piotrowska, Courtesy Galerie Thomas Zander, Cologne and Southard Reid, London.

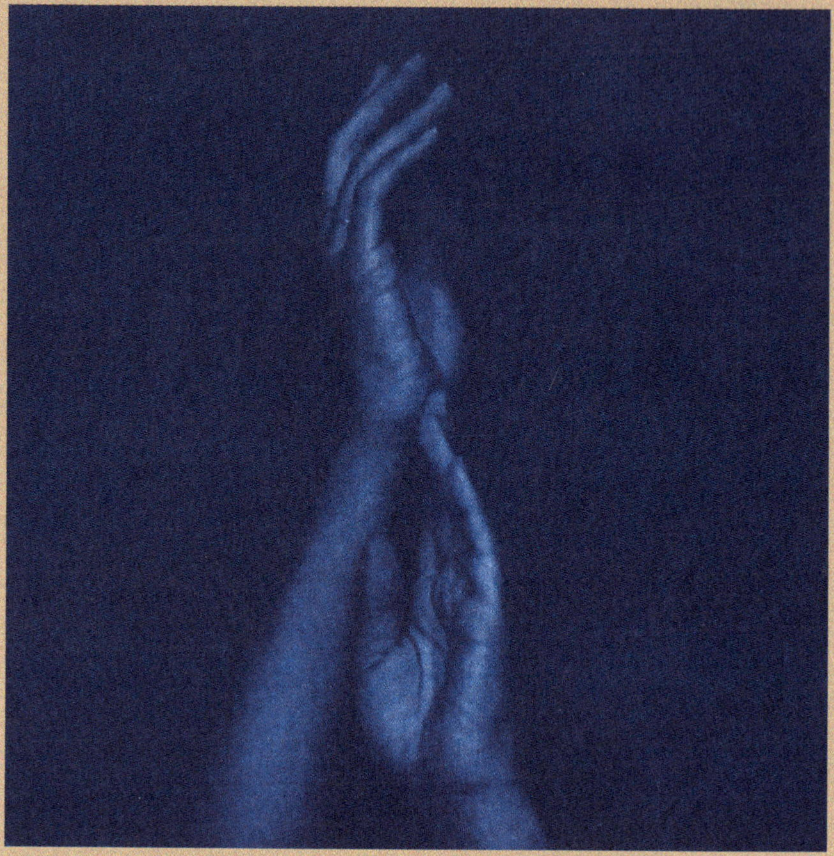

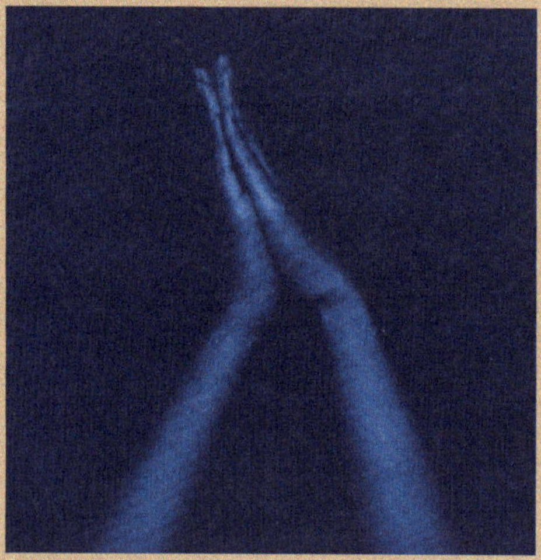

Sarah Brahim, *The Breath*, from the series *Who We Are Out of the Dark*, 2014, cyanotype print on cotton, 20.3 x 27.9 cm. Courtesy of the artist.

Sarah Brahim, *The Gifts*, from the series *Who We Are Out of the Dark*, 2014, cyanotype print on cotton, 20.3 x 27.9 cm. Courtesy of the artist.

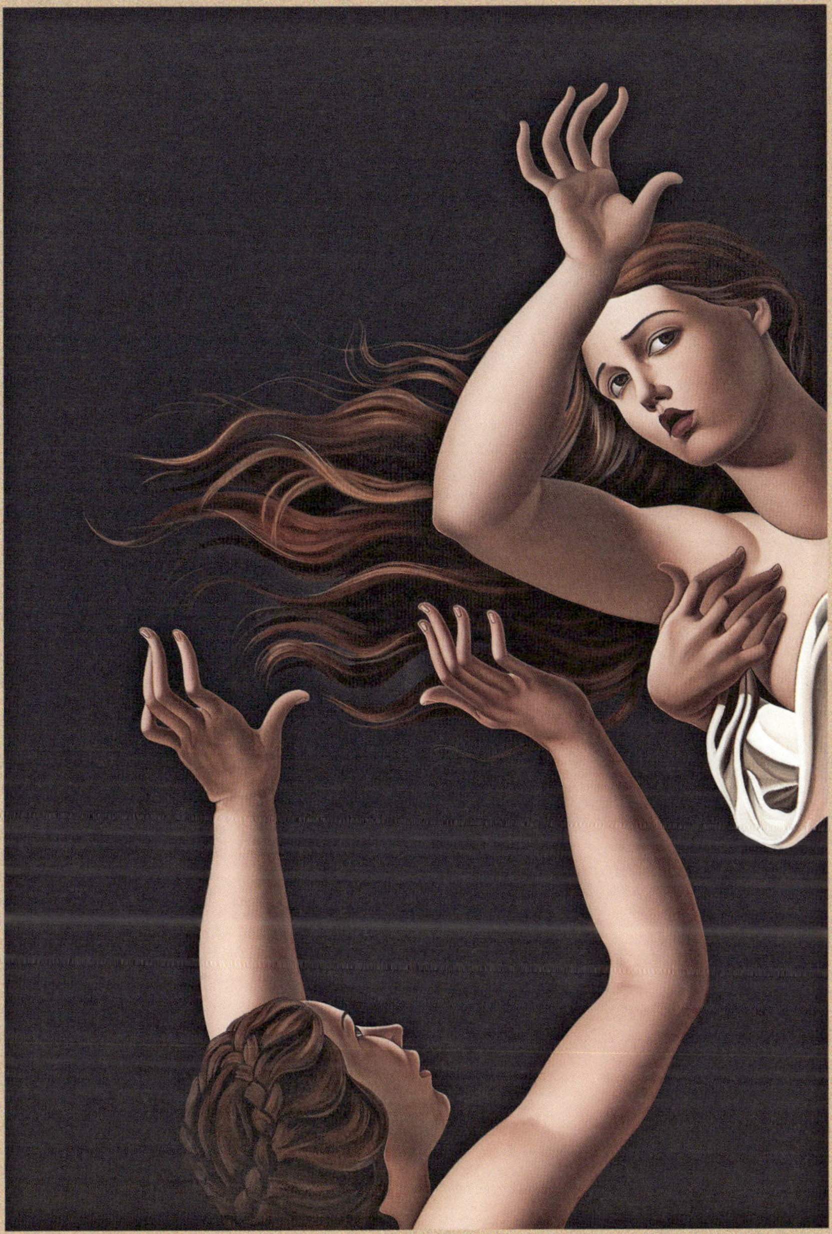

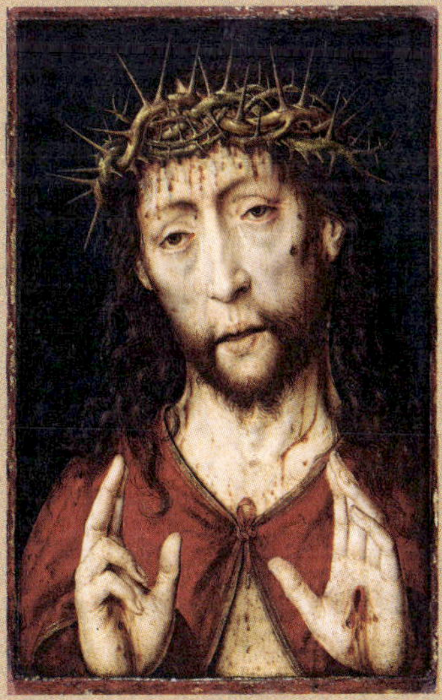

Jesse Mockrin, *Capture*, 2022, oil on linen, 139.7 x 96.5 cm. Courtesy the artist and Night Gallery, Los Angeles. Photo: Nik Massey.

Albrecht Bouts, *Head of Christ Crowned with Thorns*, ca. 1500, oil on wood, inv. B 375. Musée des Beaux-Arts, Lyon.

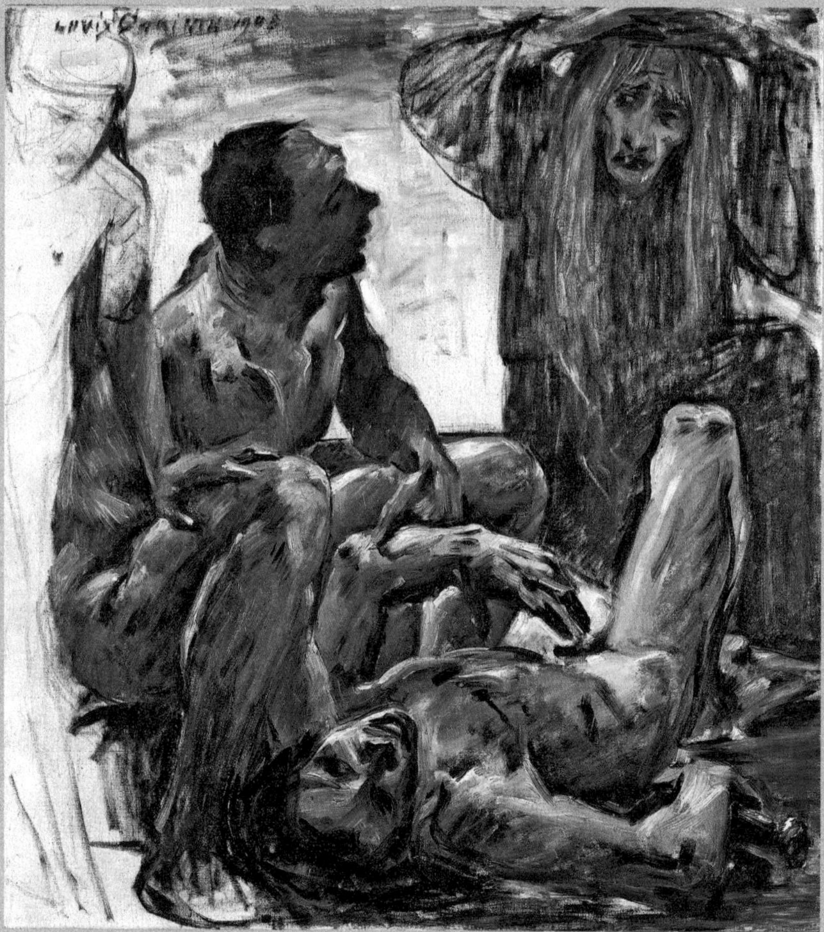

Lovis Corinth, study for the painting *Die Totenklage*, 1908, oil on canvas, 86.5 x 80 cm, Albertinum / Galerie Neue Meister, Inv. no. 95/34. © Albertinum / GNM, Staatliche Kunstsammlungen Dresden. Photo: Ursula Maria-Hoffmann.

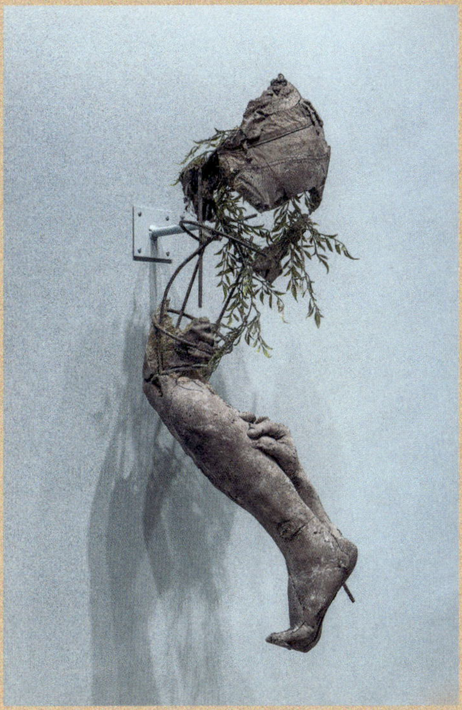

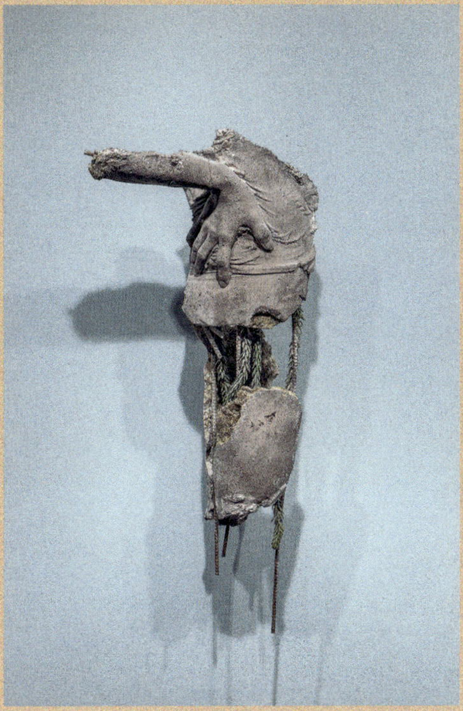

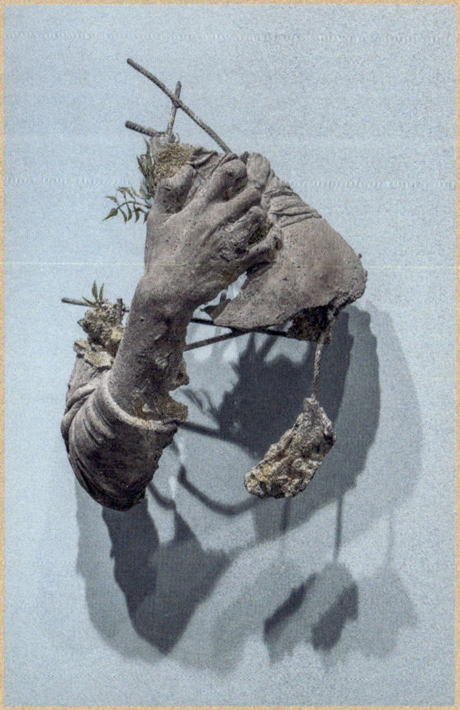

Ugo Schiavi, *Untitled no. 1*, concrete and steel, 130 x 44 x 30 cm, exhibition view, *Le Sang de la Méduse*, Double V Gallery, Paris, France, 2022. Courtesy Double V Gallery, Paris. Photo: Gregory Copitet.

Ugo Schiavi, *Untitled no. 2*, concrete and steel, 80 x 25 x 30 cm, exhibition view, *Le Sang de la Méduse*, Double V Gallery, Paris, France, 2022. Courtesy Double V Gallery, Paris. Photo: Gregory Copitet.

Ugo Schiavi, *Untitled no. 3*, concrete and steel, 55 x 45 x 25 cm, exhibition view, *Le Sang de la Méduse*, Double V Gallery, Paris, France, 2022. Courtesy Double V Gallery, Paris. Photo: Gregory Copitet.

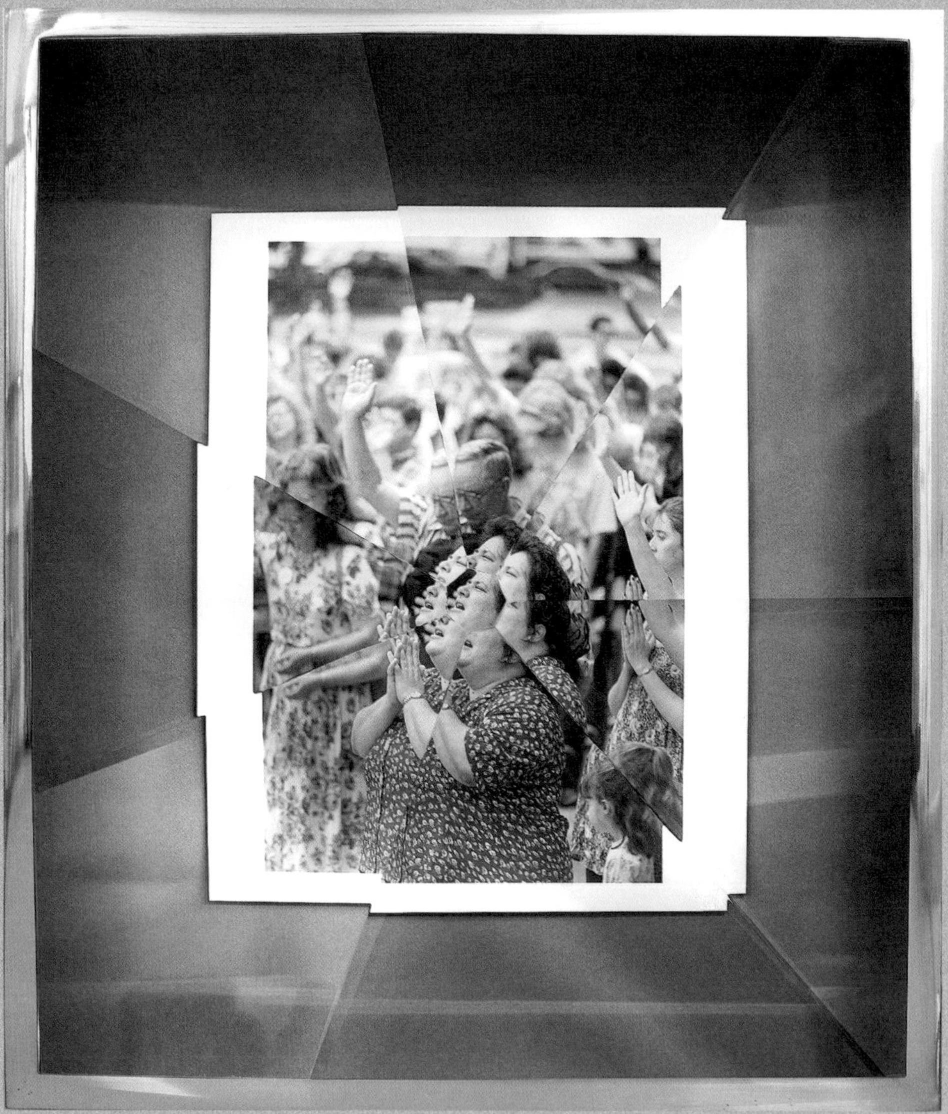

Jeremy Shaw, *Towards Universal Pattern Recognition (National Day of Prayer, Houston, 1993)*, 2022, archival photo, prism and chrome, 42.5 x 37.5 x 16 cm (framed). Courtesy of the artist and KÖNIG GALERIE, Berlin/Seoul/Vienna. Photo: Timo Ohler.

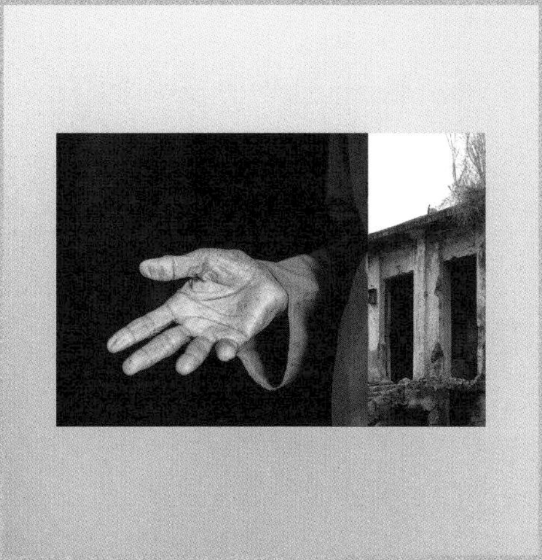

Munem Wasif, from the series *2nd July 2020*, 2022, archival pigment print, 55.9 x 55.9 cm. Courtesy of the artist.

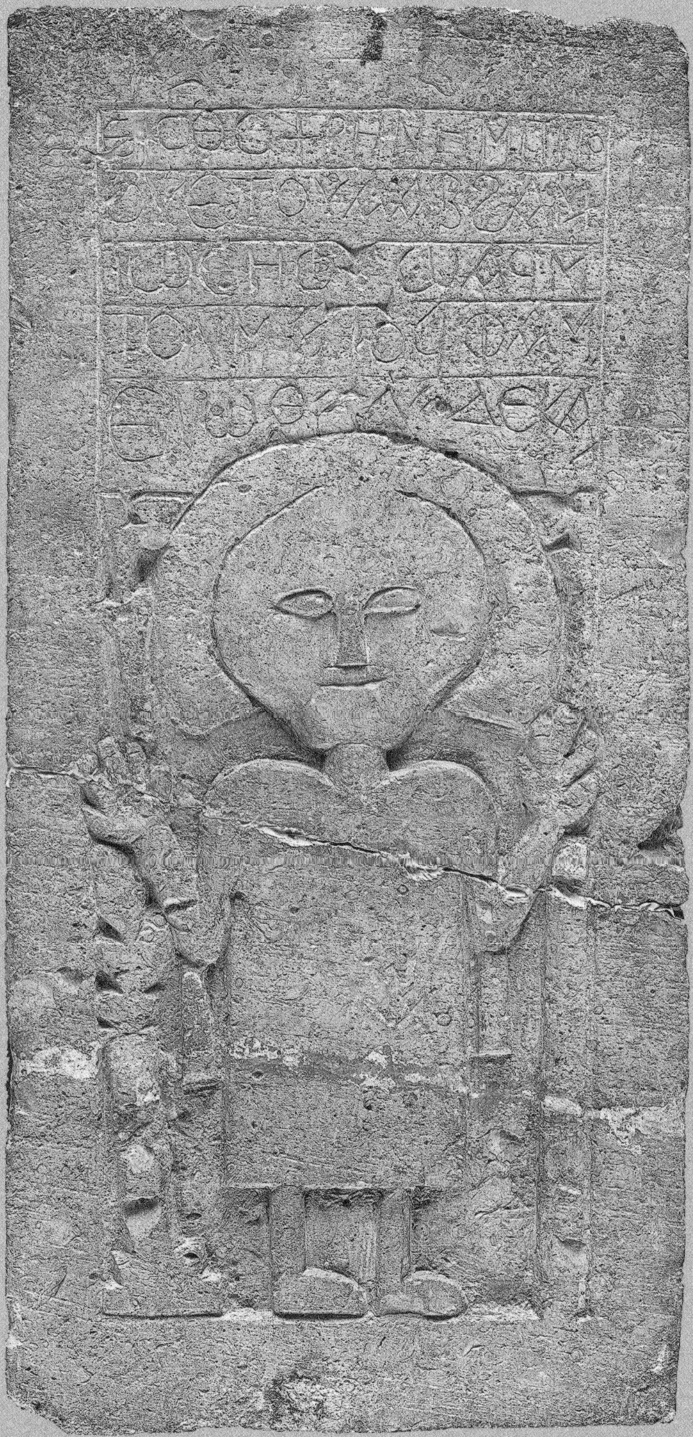

Egypt, Stela of Joseph, 5th-6th centuries, limestone, 53.7 × 26.5 × 3.2 cm, Inv. E 50 I-1720 Musée des Beaux-Arts, Lyon. Photo: Martial Couderette.

Fragile Desires

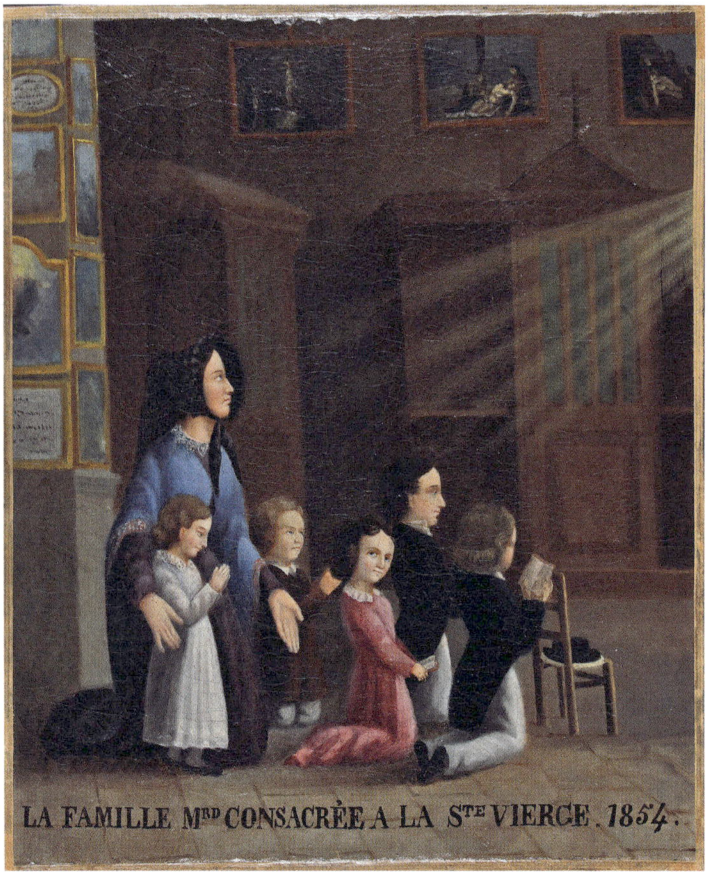

Louise Brunet 04

At eleven years old, Louise Brunet is already at odds with her world. Today's pompous affair is not helping. Her mother woke her and her three siblings up at six in the morning. They were all dressed in their special Sunday clothes and had to be at church at 8:00 a.m. to present themselves to the rector. The whole family is to be consecrated to the Virgin Mary, a tradition in her family for generations. But Louise does not understand why people must blindly carry on doing certain things simply because others have done them for years. Why must she wear this pink dress that her mother chose for her? And more importantly, why can't she be the one kneeling in the front row next to her father instead of her two brothers?

Louise shuffles forward, and her mum tries to pull her back. Louise scoffs at her and refuses to budge. Her father, aware of the kerfuffle that is about to take place, warns her to behave. Louise, compelled by a sense of overwhelming unfairness, starts making small groaning noises, which soon turn into a full-blown tantrum. As it often happens, the day ends in tears: another embarrassment for the family caused by Louise. Things will not get better, at least not for many years.

As a teenager, Louise feels very different. She knows she is attracted to girls but does not know the right words or how to even say them out loud. By the time she turns 20, she has alienated many of the people in her life, but she won't be shamed into denial. She will not conceal her desires. The hurt and anger raging inside her will be the forces that drive Louise to turn her life around. One morning, after a few years working in spinning mills, she simply walks out. In the next four decades, little is known about the places Louise goes, the professions she resorts to or the many lovers she keeps.

Anonymous, *MRD family consecrated to the Virgin Mary*, oil on canvas, 55 x 46 x 2 cm. Fondation Fourvière / Fourvière Museum Lyon. Photo: G. Gambier.

Louise is 51 years old. She resurfaces in Paris, directly across from the Place Blanche and not far from the infamous Moulin Rouge. It is the heyday of Pigalle's red-light years. Lesbian, gay, bisexual and transgendered individuals in Paris are carving out spaces for themselves in the shadows of Montmartre. Only a few women proprietors cater to an almost exclusively female and lesbian clientele, and Louise is one of them. Known as Madame Palmyre, she runs a popular brasserie called La Souris, one of several notable lesbian bars in Pigalle. Every night, she sits enthroned behind her counter with her petit bulldog Bouboule perched right next to her.

Tonight Louise feels particularly carefree. La Souris has been included in the *Guide de Plaisirs à Paris*. She hands a copy of the pamphlet to a fierce brunette, a regular at her bar, and asks her to read it out loud. She begins: "La Souris with its small low rooms and red curtains evokes the appearance of a woman's boudoir. However, this is rather a brasserie for women. At Le Rat Mort or l'Abbaye de Thélème, ladies are looking for men. Here, they are looking for each other. In the evening, you rarely meet a representative of the stronger sex. Instead, masculine women, mistresses of the parlour, dine alone at small tables and offer each other cigarettes, sweets and kisses." "Did you hear that, my Coffee Pot?" Louise shouts across the room to Henri Toulouse-Lautrec, who is busy sketching Louise and her company. He nods in acknowledgement, a pencil between his teeth, his fingers smudging away at his paper.

For the first time in many years Louise is content with a feeling of restfulness only experienced after finally getting to lie down after a long day of hard work. Her mind wanders back to that early morning episode at the church and somehow it doesn't matter anymore. A family does not have to be a mother, father and children. The door swings open and a man and a woman walk in, clearly feeling out of place. Louise turns up. The woman wears a long pink silk dress. "What a lovely outfit," Louise offers, her deep hoarse voice echoing across the hall. "Come in, we might bite, but the drinks are on the house!"

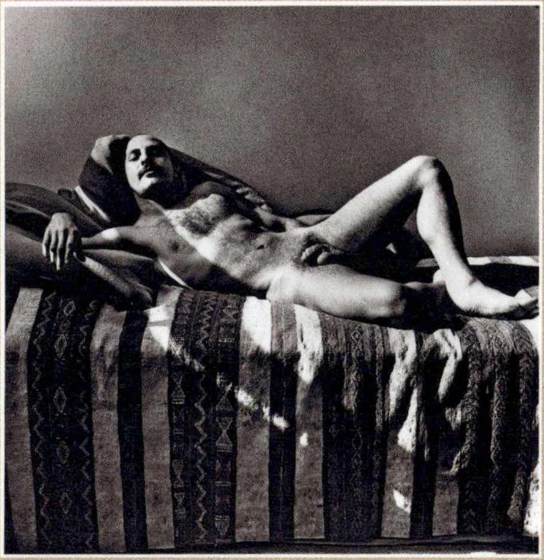

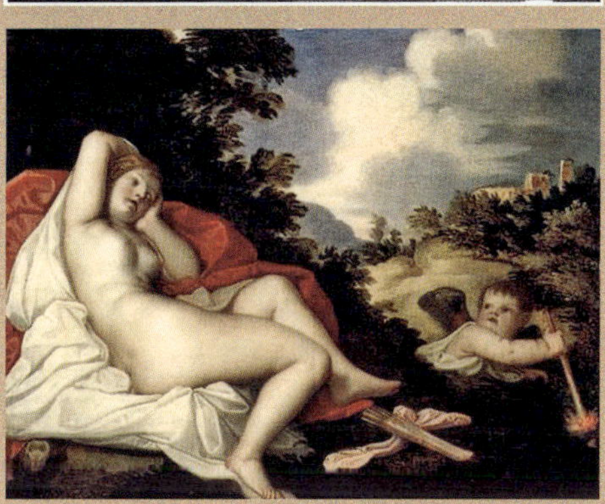

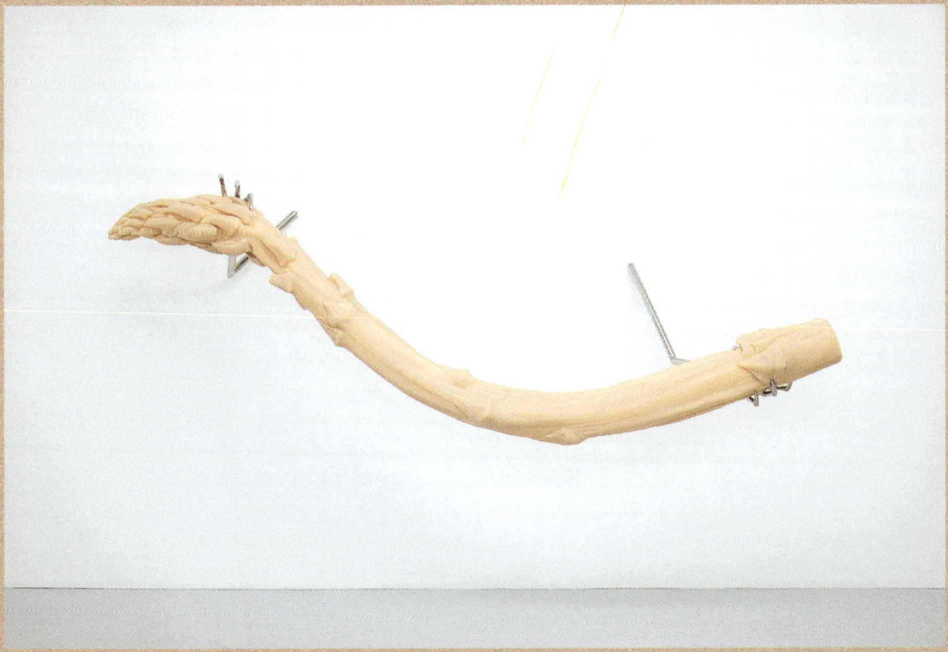

Hannah Levy, *Untitled*, 2022, nickel-plated steel, silicone, polyurethane, 75 x 213 x 60 cm. Courtesy the artist and mother's tankstation Dublin/London.

Top Peter Hujar, *Nicolas Abdallah Moufarrege, Paris*, 1980. © 2022 The Peter Hujar Archive / Artists Rights Society (ARS), New York. Courtesy The Peter Hujar Archive LLC and Pace Gallery, New York. © Adagp, Paris, 2022.

Bottom Alessandro Varotari, also known as Il Padovanino, *Vénus et amour*, undated, oil on canvas, 78 x 101 cm, donated by Monagin of Montrol in 1859, inv. MG 478. © Musée de Grenoble.

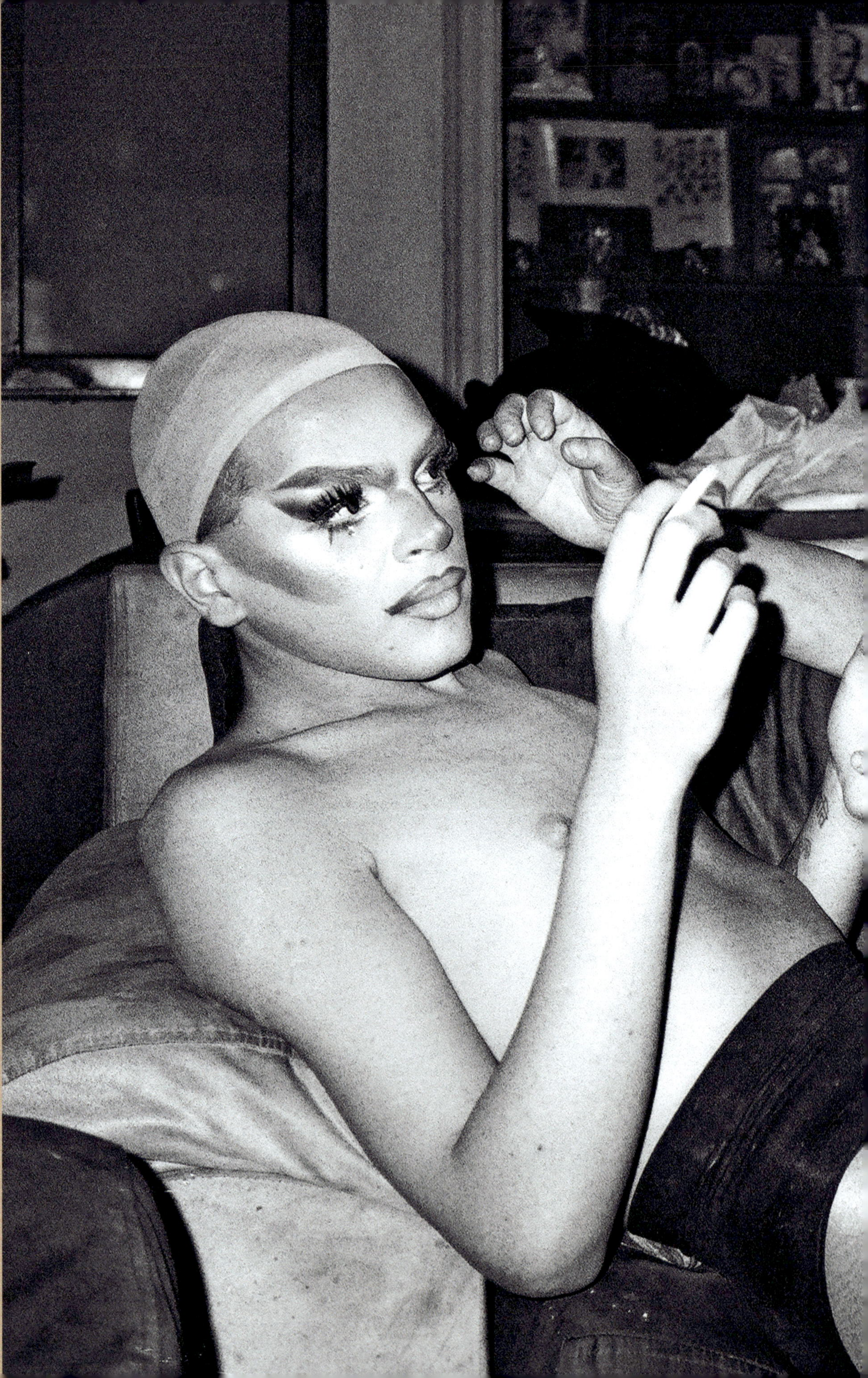

Mohamad Abdouni, *Doris & Andrea – Beirut*, 2019. Courtesy of the artist.

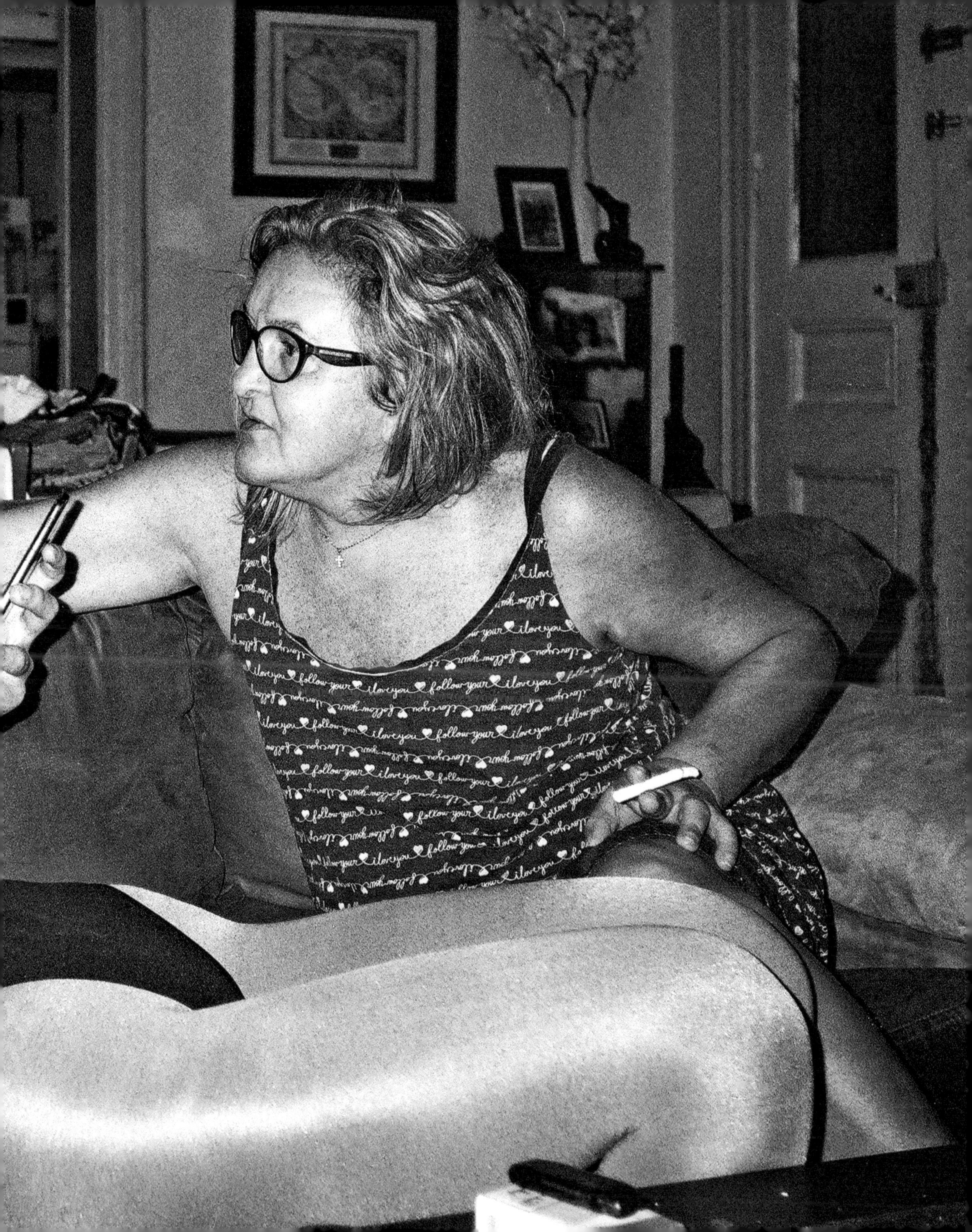
follow your
i love you

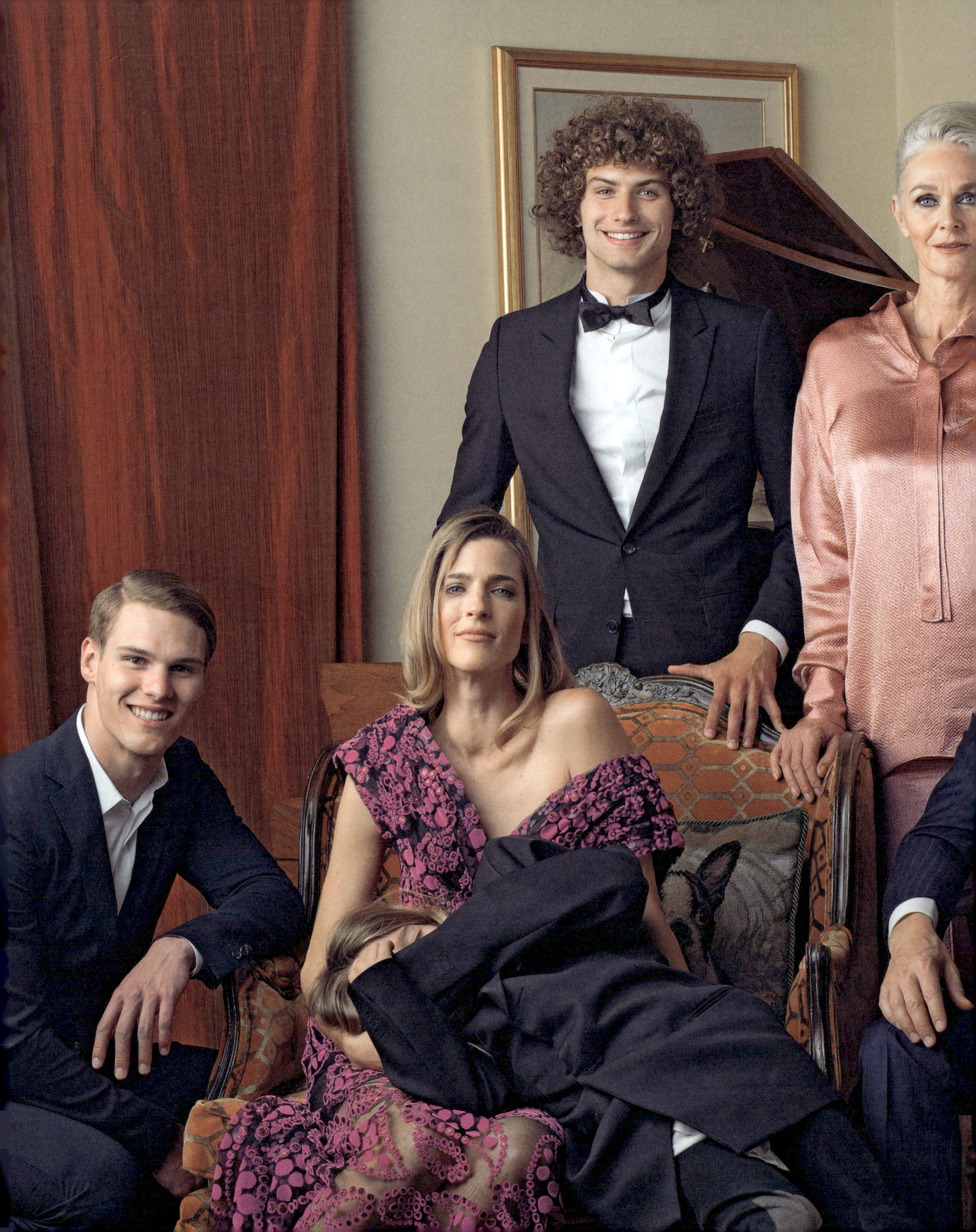

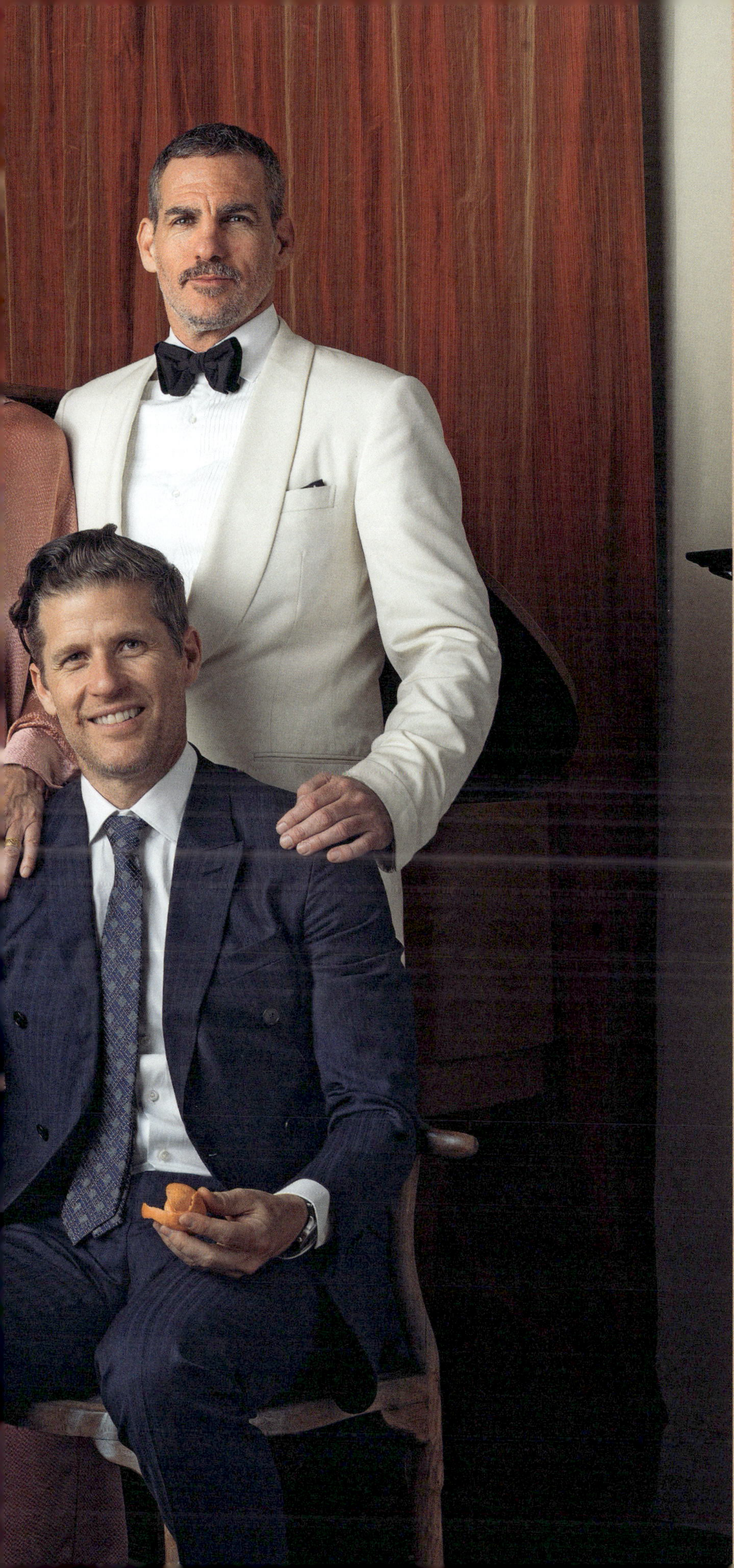

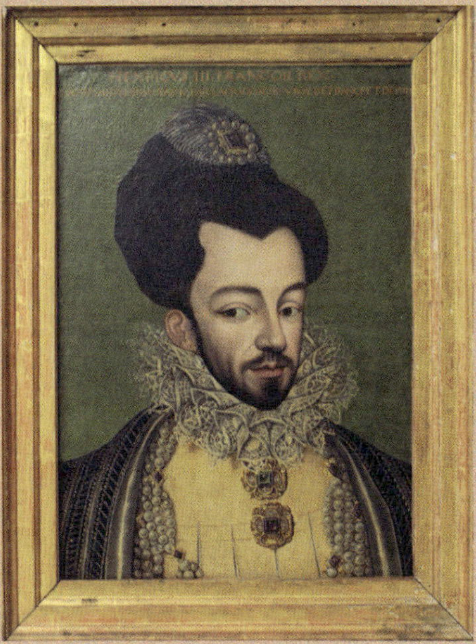

Left Buck Ellison, *Untitled* (*Christmas Card #8*), 2016, 152.4 x 195.6 x 5 cm. Courtesy of the artist.

Right Anonymous, *Portrait of Henri III*, oil on canvas, 56 x 40 cm, inv. 2007.0.853.M_842. Musée des Hospices Civils Lyon.

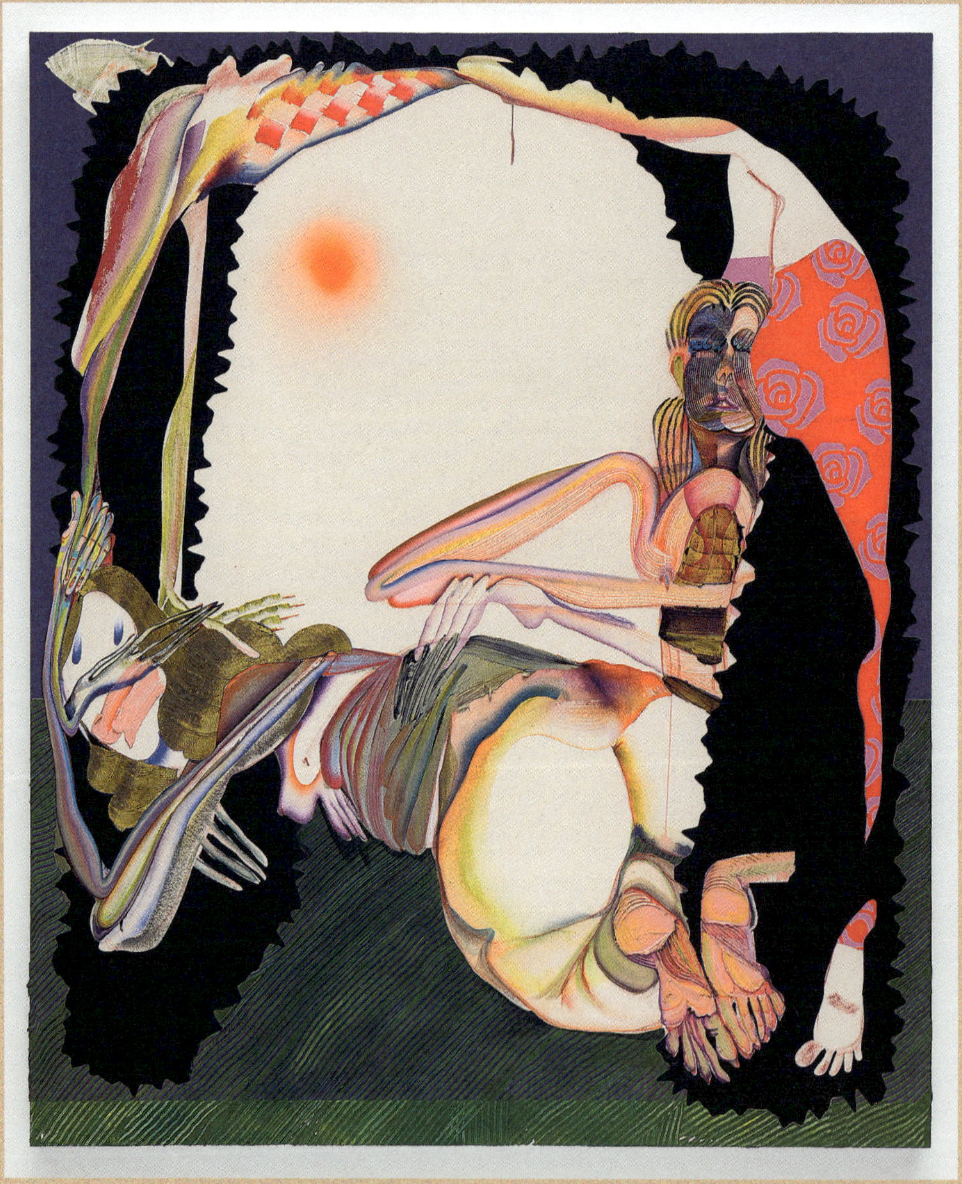

Christina Quarles, *Edge of Tomorrow*, 2020, acrylic on canvas, 182.9 x 152.4 x 5.1 cm. © Christina Quarles. Courtesy the artist, Hauser & Wirth, and Pilar Corrias, London.

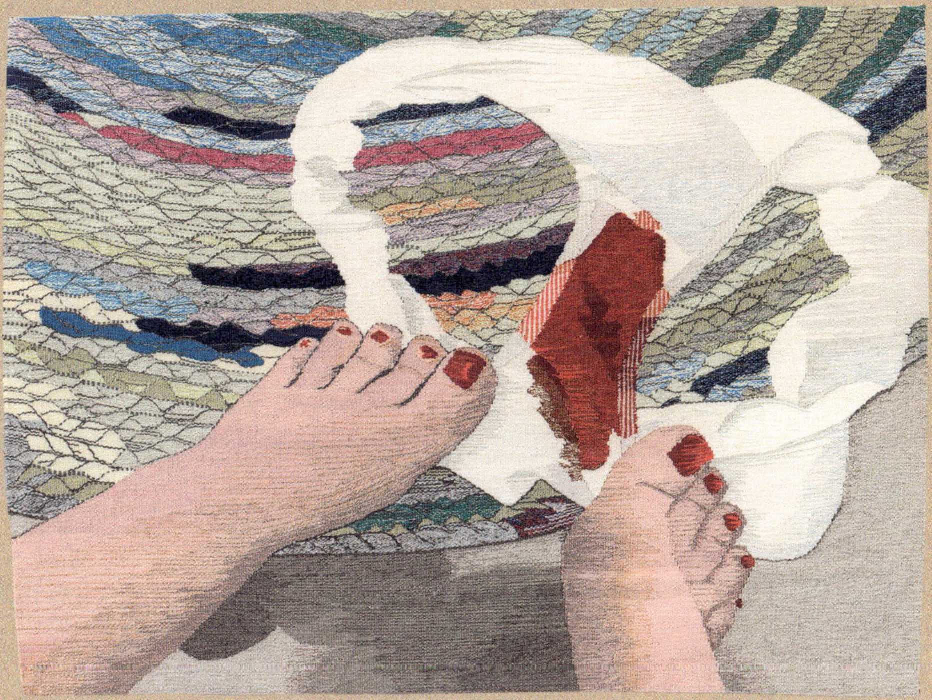

Crimson Landslide

Using traditional tapestry techniques, Erin M. Riley crafts intimate and erotic artworks. Juxtaposing personal photographs, press clippings and images found on the internet, the artist combines memories, fantasies and trauma. She explores experiences of vulnerability to interrogate the fears and anxieties that weigh on the search for personal identity – especially, female identity.

Erin M. Riley, *Crimson Landslide*, 2018, wool and cotton, 88.9 x 121.9 cm. Courtesy of the artist and P·P·O·W Gallery.

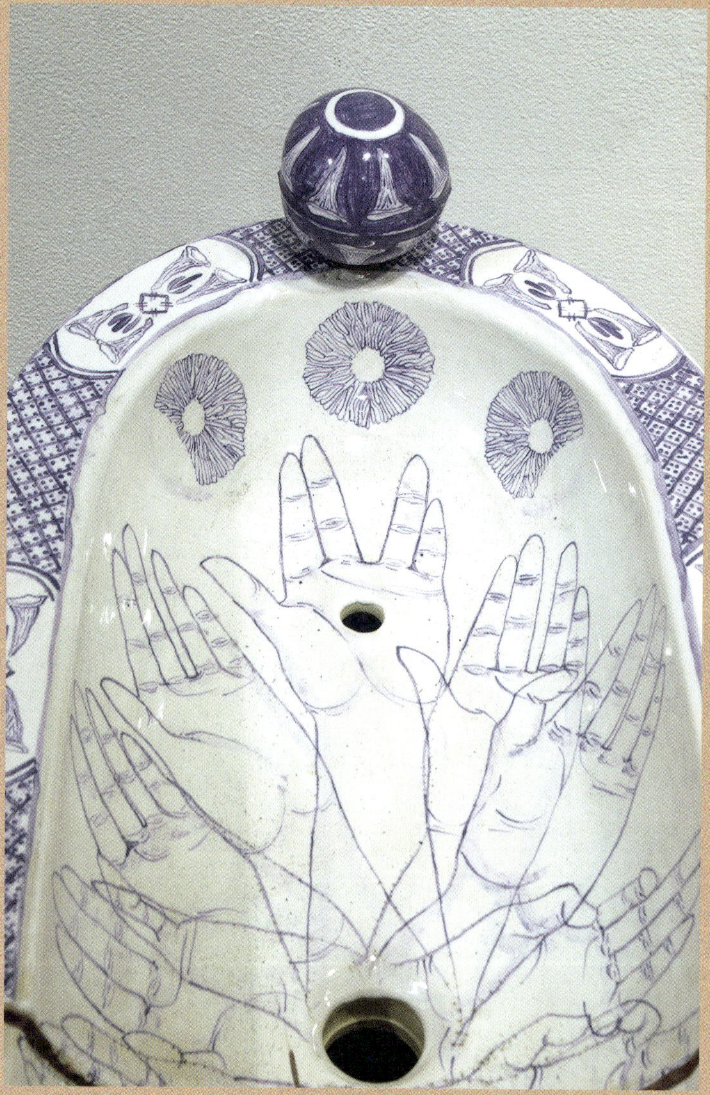

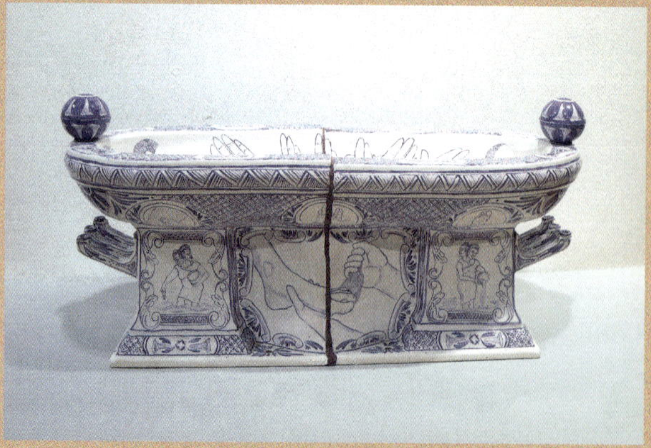

Nicki Green, *Anointed (Double Bidet Basin with Faucets)* (interior detail), 2019, glazed porcelain with epoxy. 48 x 99 x 43 cm. Courtesy of the artist.

Nicki Green, *Anointed (Double Bidet Basin with Faucets)*, 2019, glazed porcelain with epoxy. 48 x 99 x 43 cm. Courtesy of the artist.

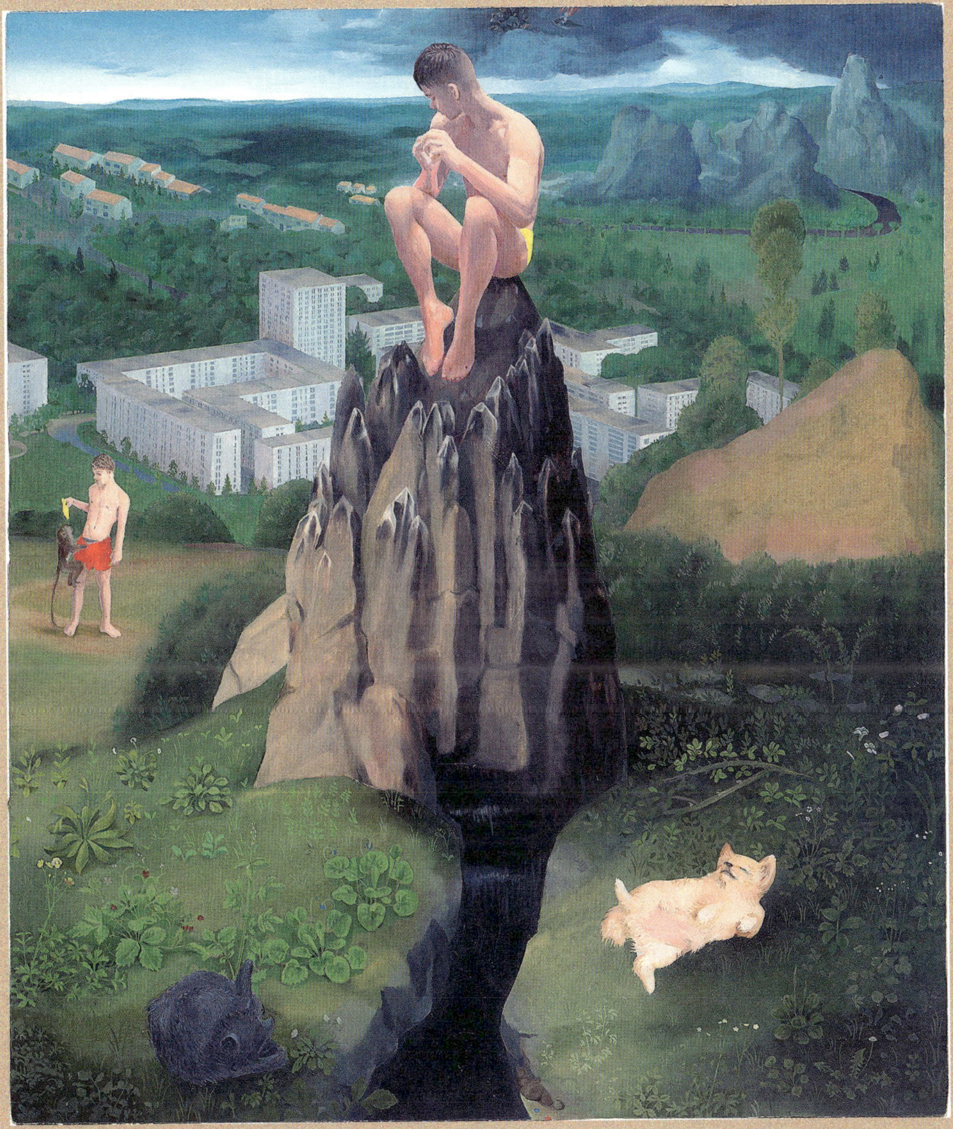

Jean Claracq, *À mon corps défendant*,
2021–2022, oil on wood, 19 x 22 cm.
Courtesy of the artist.

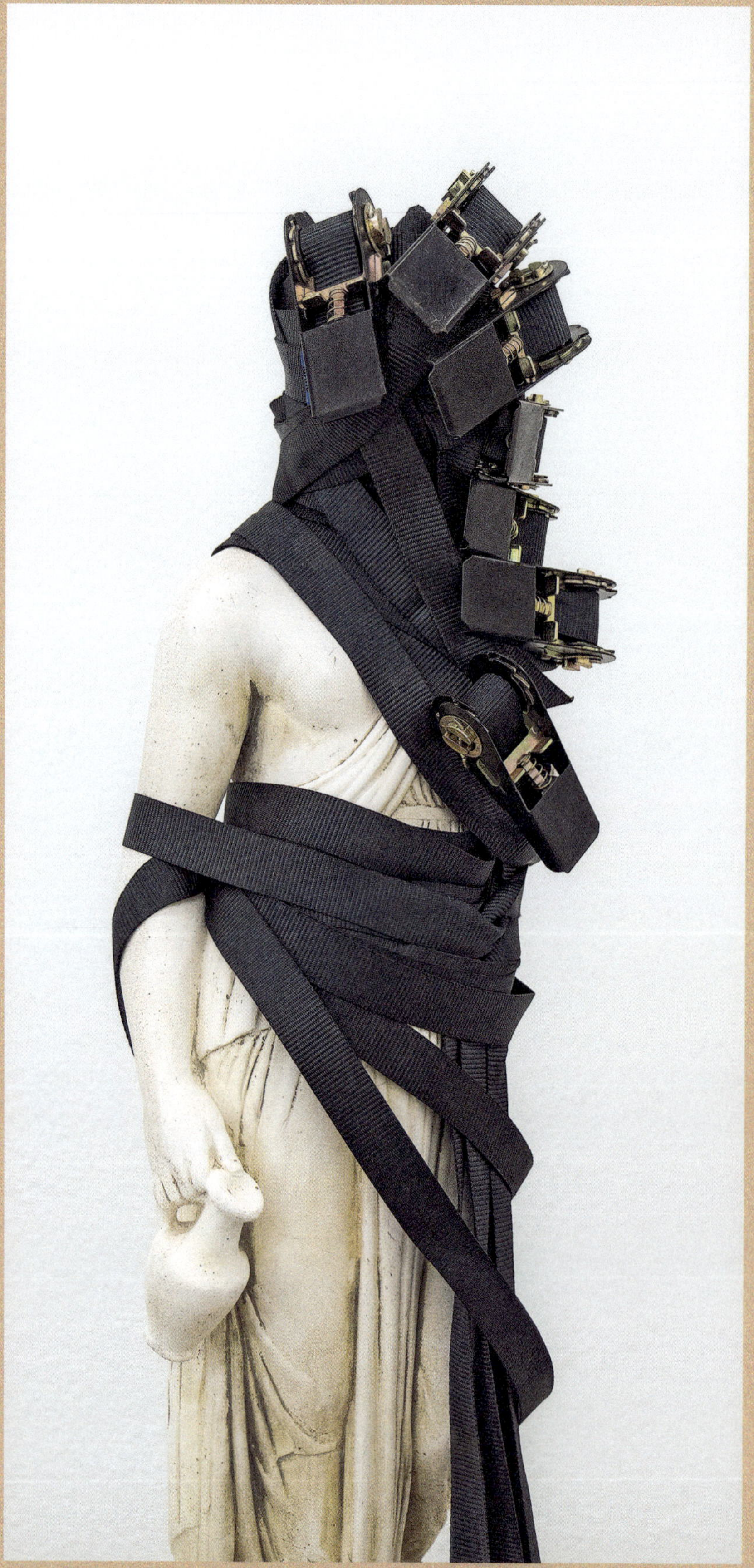

Mater

Referencing the Latin word for the mother figure, Mater *depicts a woman enveloped in straps. In this system of enshrouding restraints, the work suggests both the benefits and drawbacks of protection. Situated on a wooden box used for both displaying and shipping, the statue also hints at heritage conservation methods. The sculpture thus alludes to various forms of caring for others.*

Léo Fourdrinier, *Mater*, 2017, strap, reconstructed stone statue, wood, 190 x 36 x 130 cm. Courtesy of the artist.

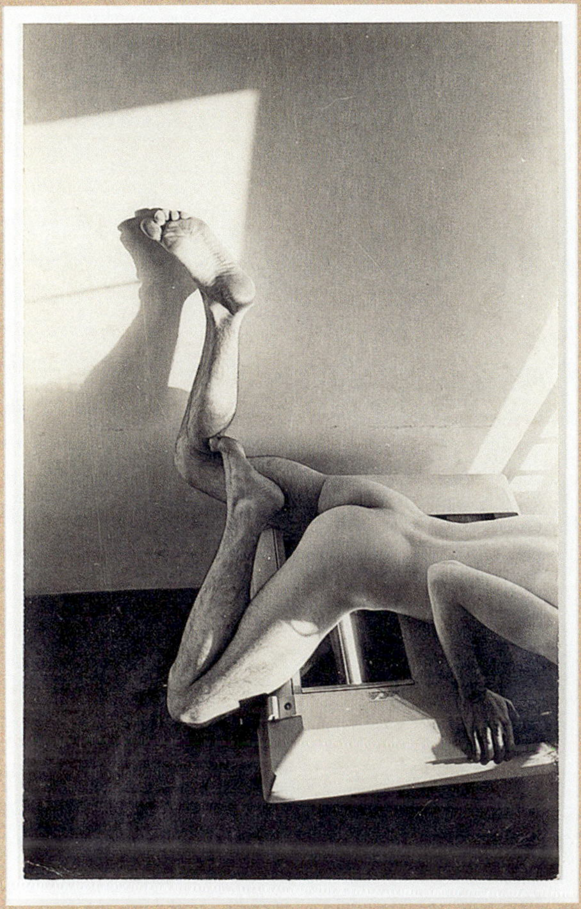

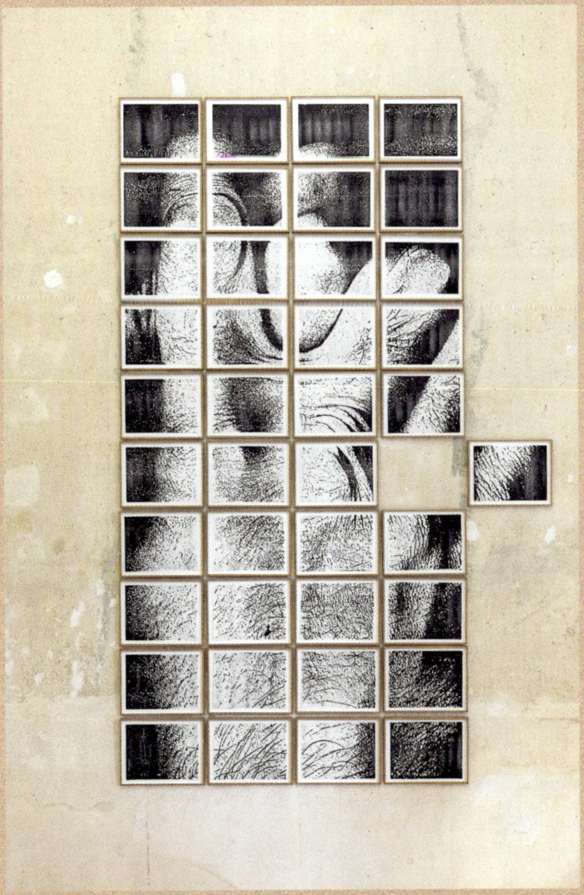

Hudinilson Jr., *Narcisso – Gesto*, 1986, photocopy on paper, 225 x 145 cm. Courtesy Galeria Jaqueline Martins and Clarice O. Tavares. Photo: Regular Studio.

Hudinilson Jr., *Xerox Action*, 1979–1980, photograph, 22 x 14cm. Courtesy Galeria Jaqueline Martins. Photo: Regular Studio.

A Brief History of Princess X

In A Brief History of Princess X*, Gabriel Abrantes retraces the genesis of* Princess X*, a piece by the Romanian sculptor Constantin Brâncuși. While investigating this phallus-shaped portrait of Princess Marie Bonaparte J39*

of psychoanalysis in France – he reflects on the essence of the artmaking process and on the domination-driven nature of relations between the sexes.

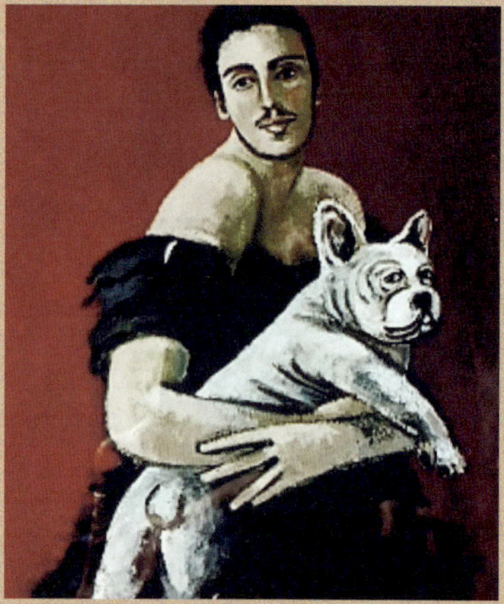

Sylvie Selig, *Tanguy et son chien*, 1992, oil on canvas, 65 x 54 cm. Courtesy of the artist.

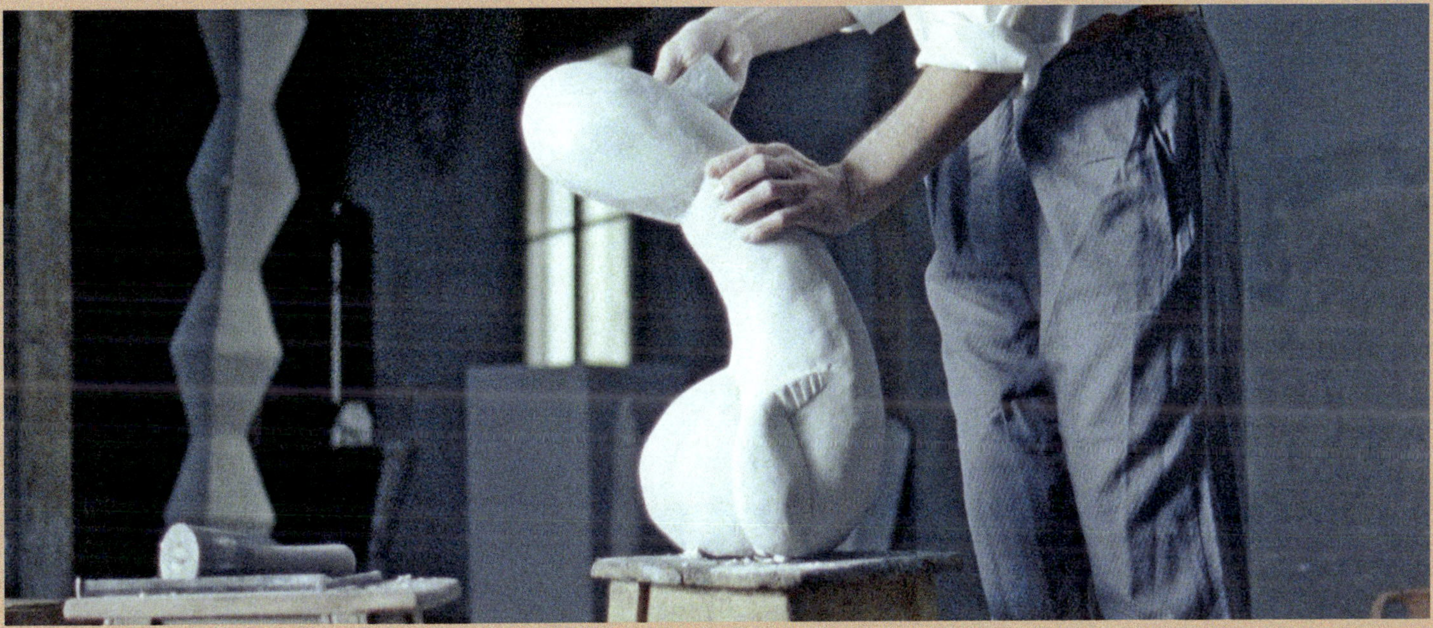

Gabriel Abrantes, still from *A Brief History of Princess X*, 2016, 16mm film. Courtesy of the artist.

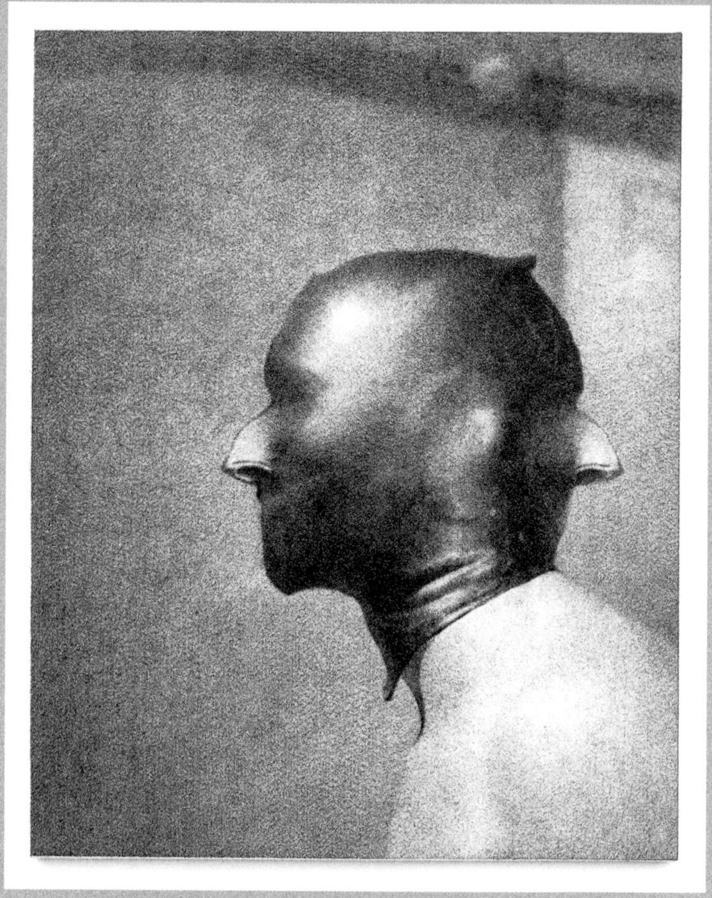

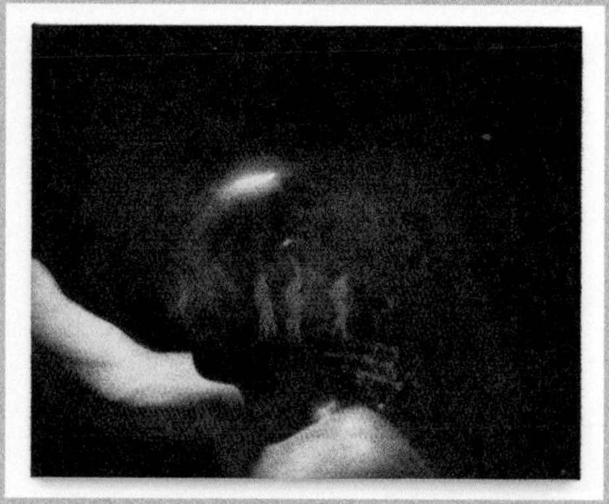

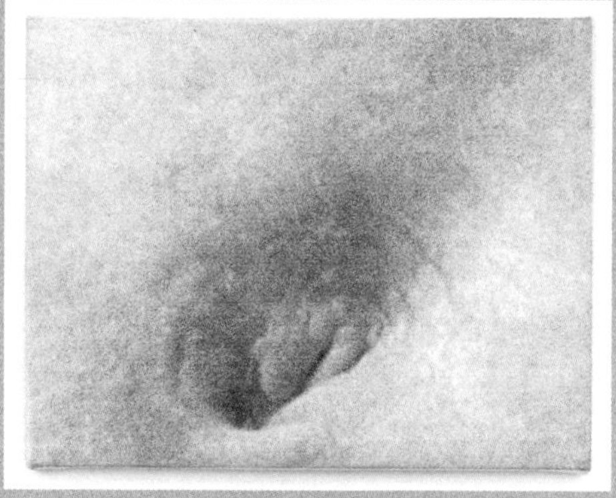

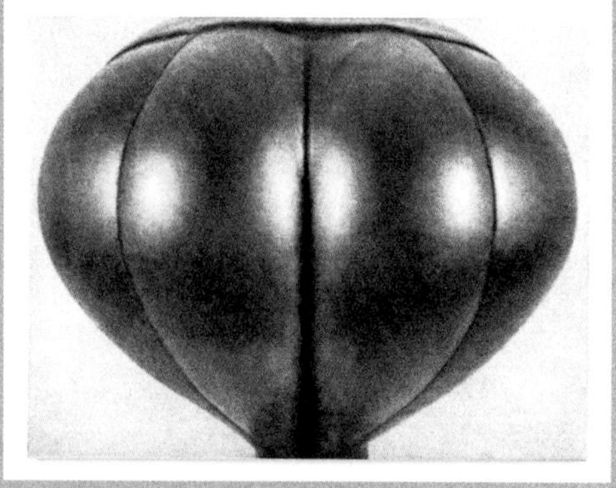

From top to bottom:
Zhang Yunyao, *R (IV)*, 2022, graphite pencil on felt stretched on panel, 45 x 56 cm. Courtesy of the artist and Don Gallery.

Zhang Yunyao, *Sag*, 2022, graphite pencil on felt stretched on panel, 27 x 35 cm. Courtesy of the artist and Don Gallery.

Zhang Yunyao, *OOO*, 2022, graphite pencil on felt stretched on panel, 46 x 45 cm. Courtesy of the artist and Don Gallery.

Zhang Yunyao, *Contour*, 2022, graphite pencil on felt stretched on panel, 65 x 52 cm. Courtesy of the artist and Don Gallery.

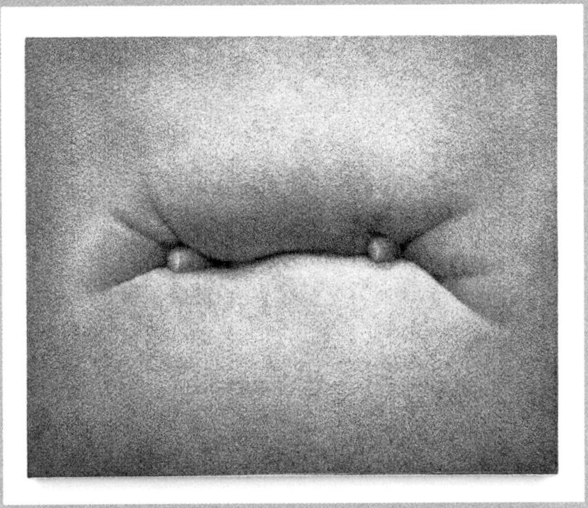

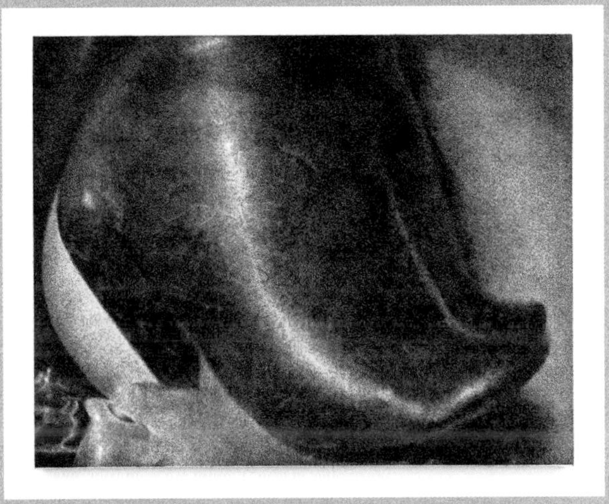

Top Zhang Yunyao, *One Seam & Two Points*, 2022, graphite pencil on felt stretched on panel, 36 x 45 cm. Courtesy of the artist and Don Gallery.

Bottom Zhang Yunyao, *Seal*, 2022, graphite pencil on felt stretched on panel, 37 x 48 cm. Courtesy of the artist and Don Gallery.

Fragile Skins

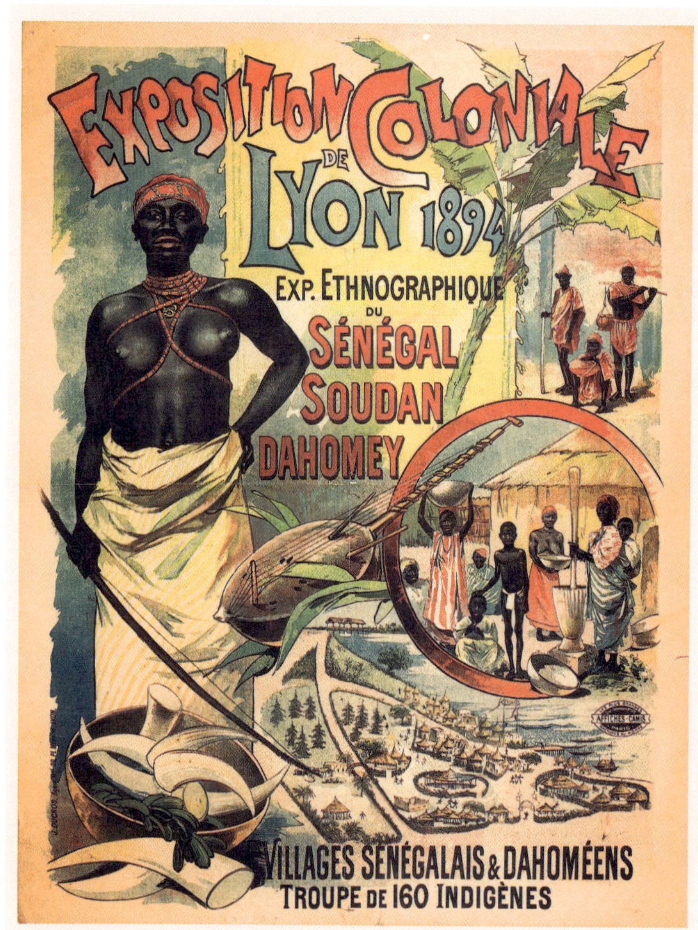

Louise Brunet 05

It is dawn on 1 November 1894. Louise Brunet is making her way up the hill of Fourvière, also known as "the hill that prays". Barefoot and breathless, she can hear the sound of the mob that has gathered in her pursuit. She has been running since noon the day before, after escaping from the tattered sheds in the Parc de la Tête d'Or where she had been forced to live since the previous spring.

Less than a year ago, Louise was still living in Tëngeéj, or Rufisque, near Dakar. A prosperous port town, Tëngeéj as Louise once knew it was quickly disappearing to make way for the administrative compounds of the newly founded French colonial settlements. Her father was a Muslim clergyman or *serini* in Wolof, the language that Louise speaks. He would often tell her stories of the great Lat Joor Ngoone Latiir Joop, the last ruler of the Cayor kingdom before it was defeated by France's colonial army on 6 October 1886.

Memories of home come rushing back. It has only been nine months since Louise disembarked the *Amazone* in Bordeaux. The arduous journey took off from Porto-Novo, a city which had been recently annexed into another French colony, Dahomey. In total, close to 200 individuals were "imported" from various towns and cities across western, central and eastern Africa. Only 160 survived.

The 1894 Colonial Exhibition in Lyon, imprimerie Camis, poster, inv. 2006.51.2. Musée des Confluences.

Louise and the many Sudanese, Dahomian and other Wolof people were brought to Lyon to inhabit the African Village of the Éxposition Coloniale of 1894. Marketed as a scientifically-sound ethnographic display, the exhibition blatantly disregarded the distinct backgrounds, histories, languages and cultures of the so-called natives to present an essentialist, colonial portrait of the Africa continent. Day after day for nine long months, Louise was put on display, bare-chested and clad with props she had never worn before. She was forced to pretend to be the wife, mother and daughter to people from other African cities, some more than 3,000 kilometres away from her hometown of Tëngeéj. They had all been "recruited" by the failed businessman Johannès Barbier, who promoted himself as an ethnographic expert on Africa. He first made a name for himself when *L'illustration* published some of his scandalous photographs of an 1891 massacre in Bakel. In what was clearly a pre-arranged mise en abyme, the images showed decapitated Tukolor fighters who had failed to halt the French colonial seizure of their land.

A few days before the colonial exhibition had ended, rumours began circulating around the camp that Barbier, with help from Clément Ulysse Pila, a notable silk merchant and member of the Lyon Chamber of commerce who had organised the colonial displays, would be moving the exhibition to other cities where plans for future iterations were underway. Louise could not tolerate one more day of humiliation, so she escaped.

Climbing up the steep steps towards the city's famous Basilica, she makes sure to cover her face under a loose, hooded garment that she had taken from the camp. She desperately tries to hide her bare hands – not out of shame but in fear for her life.

Louise flings open the doors of the Virgin's Chapel, which has been standing since the twelfth century and remains the historic and religious heart of this hilltop sanctuary until today. The walls are covered with ex-votos, small lay paintings on canvas; they are often made by worshippers as tokens of gratitude to their saints for saving them from death, sickness or war. One ex-voto makes Louise stop. The depicted scene shows a light-skinned man dressed in European garb surrounded by three dark-skinned figures. An inscription reads: "To Mary, helpful mother. Bishop Collomb and his missionaries saved by her protection from the fury of the savages. Caledonia, 19 July 1847". At this moment, the whole of history and its injustices weigh heavily on Louise's shoulders, and she feels defeated for the first time. She thinks to herself, "Who are the savages?"

Walking out to the edge of the hill, she takes in the view of the entire city below. The mob arrives shortly after, but there is no trace of Louise. They shout, "The witch has made herself disappear."

Louise's Wolof name remains unknown.

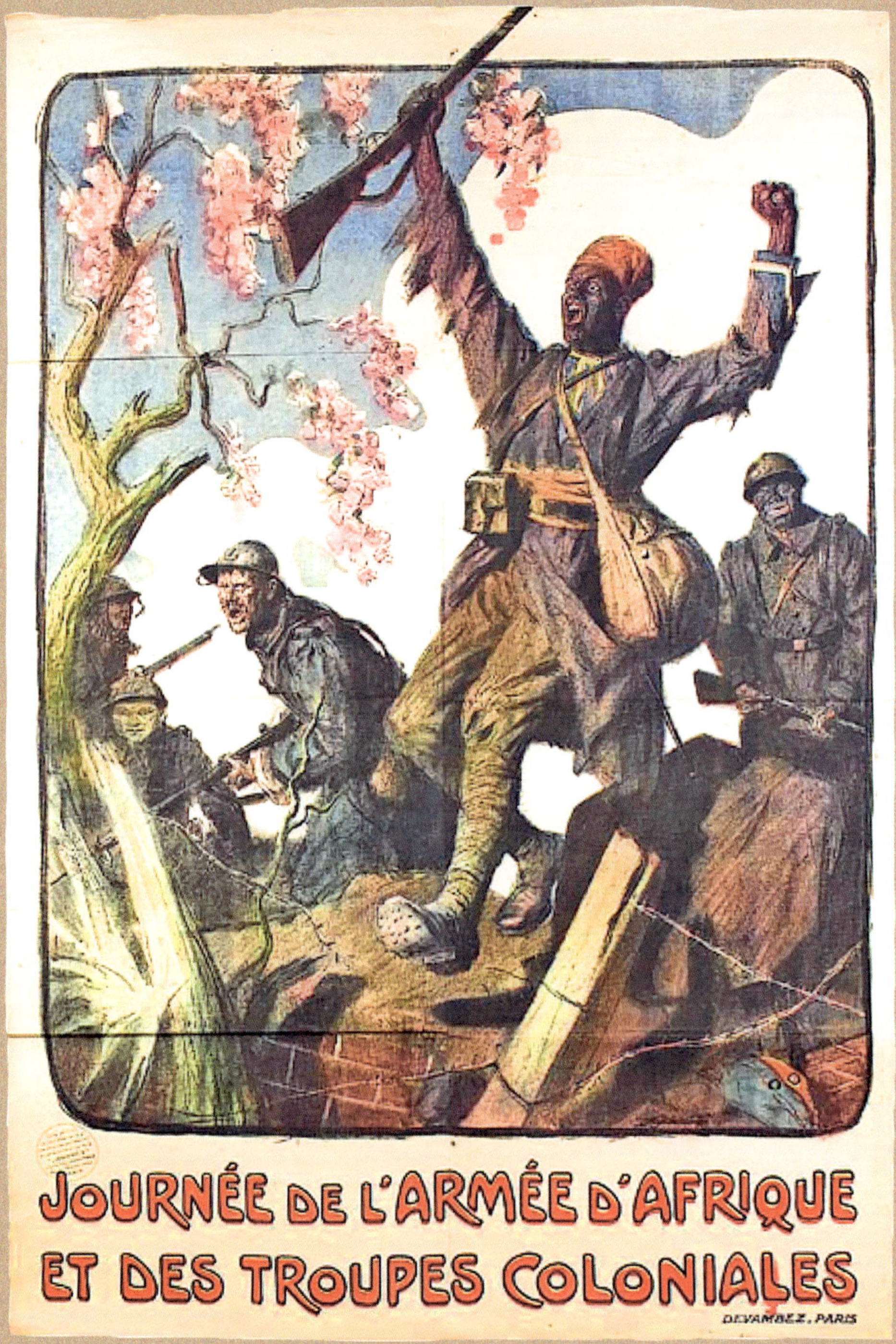

Lucien Jonas, *Day of the African Army and Colonial Troops*, Maison Devambez, Paris, 1917, inv. 2007.0.693. Musée des Confluences.

Gouraud from the porch of the Résidence des Pins Palace

General Gouraud (1867-1946) was the High Commissioner of France in the Levant in 1919-1922. His defence of French interests involved protecting the large Lyon silk manufacturers in Lebanon. For this reason, he was hosted several times in Lyon with great pomp. On 1 September 1920 he declared the foundation of the State of Greater Lebanon, which was immediately placed under French mandate, thus separating Lebanon from what is now Syria.

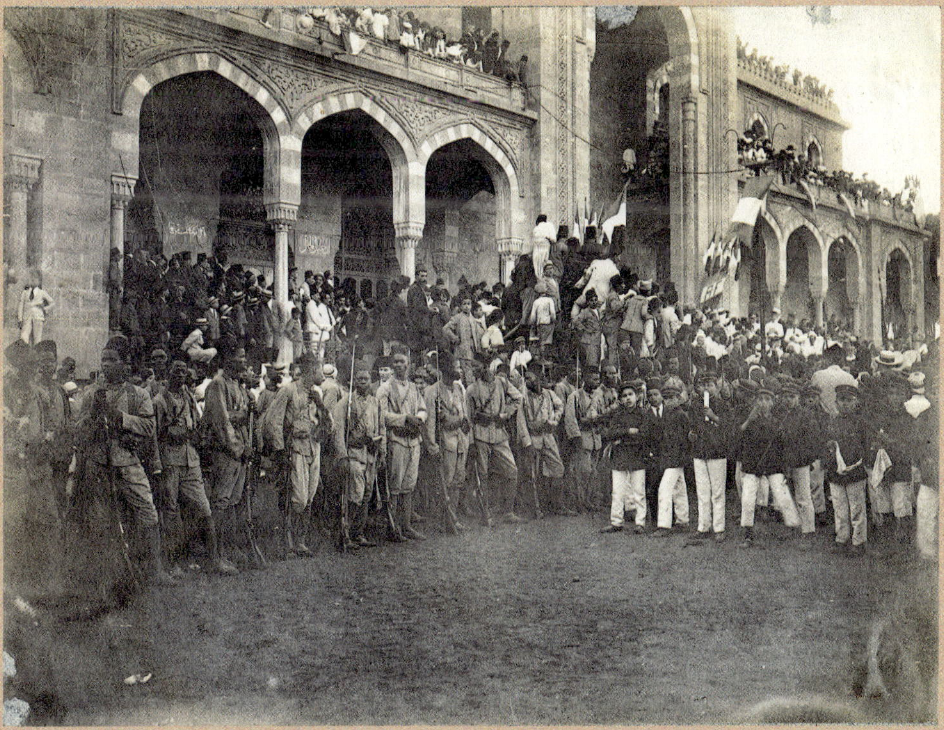

Declaration of Greater Lebanon at the Résidence des Pins, Beirut – The Senegalese Brigade in the foreground, 1 September 1920, photograph, inv. A003574. Archives du Ministère de l'Europe et des Affaires Etrangères – La Courneuve / Collection Gouraud.

International Exhibition of the City of Lyon

When the Lyon city council decided to hold a World's Fair in 1914, it wanted to promote the policies implemented by Mayor Édouard Herriot, elected in 1905. The council sought to "publicise [...] all the progress achieved in the fields of administration and of municipal hygiene". The official poster for the event, designed by architect Tony Garnier, declared that "hygiene should be the 'only source' of every law". Topped by a view of the main entrance to the slaughterhouses, with cars and trams symbolising the modern age, the poster features in its central section the imposing Tony Garnier Hall – the exhibition's venue for machinery and heavy industry.

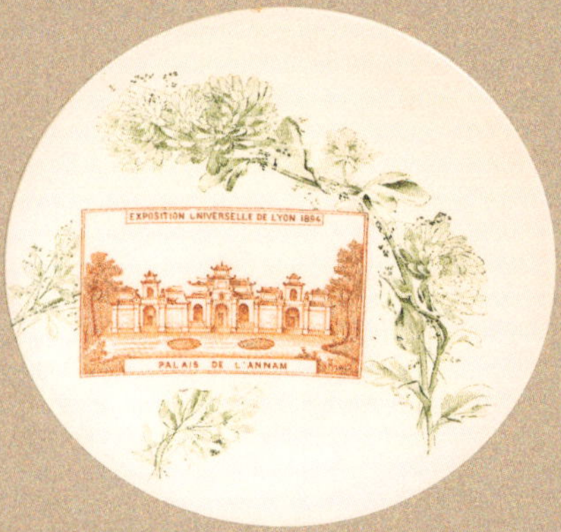

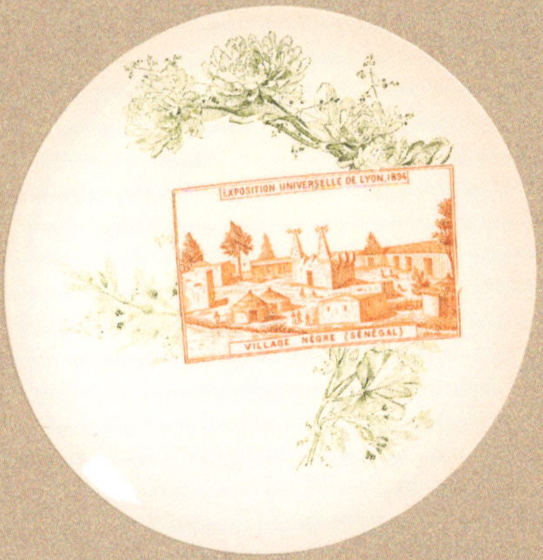

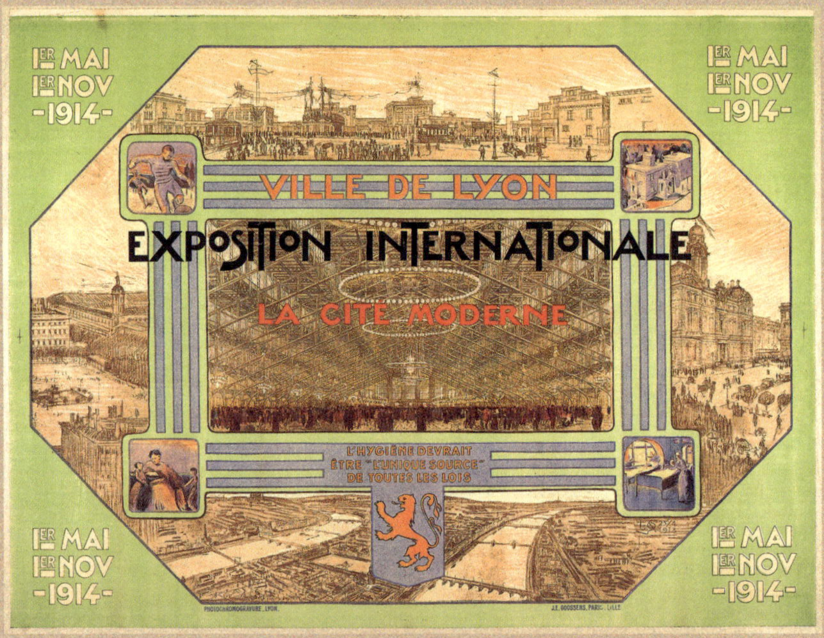

Top Palace at the Annam (present-day Vietnam) pavilion, 1894 World Fair, Lyon, Sarreguemines earthenware, inv. 96.28.2. © Musée d'Histoire de Lyon - Gadagne. Photo: Xavier Schwebel.

Bottom Senegal Pavilion at the 1894 World Fair, Lyon, Sarreguemines earthenware, inv. 96.28.2. © Musée d'Histoire de Lyon - Gadagne. Photo: Xavier Schwebel.

Tony Garnier, *International Exhibition of the City of Lyon*, 1914, The Modern City, 25 April 1913, photochromic print, inv. 938.3. © Musée d'Histoire de Lyon - Gadagne.

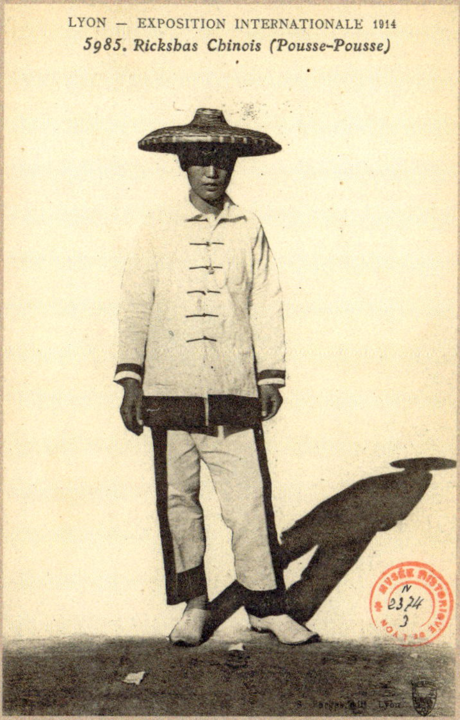

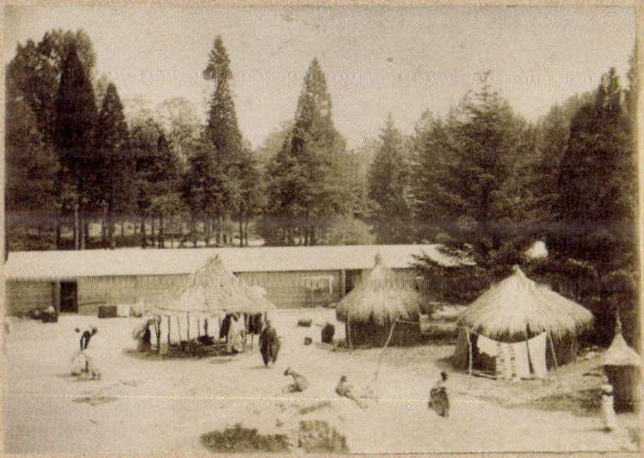

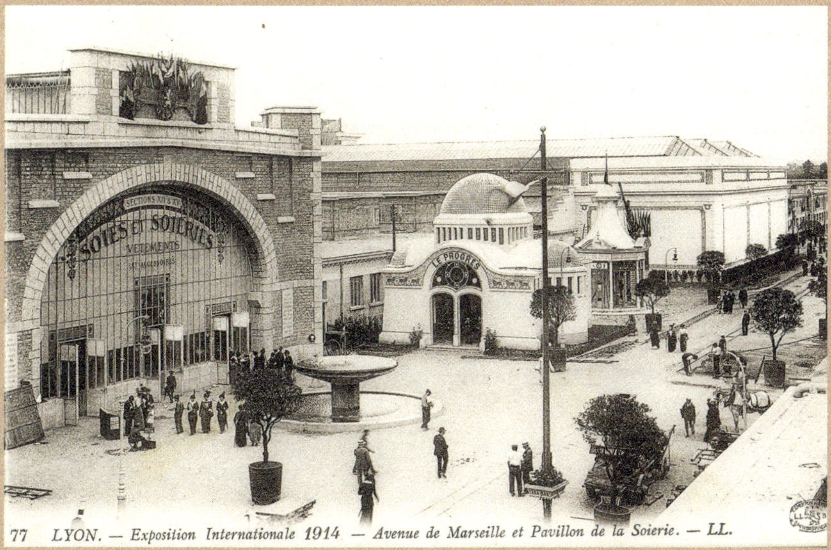

1914 International Exhibition, Silk Pavilion, Marseille Avenue, Lyon, postcard, inv. 013.1.60. © Musée d'Histoire de Lyon - Gadagne.

Top *Chinese Rickshaw*, also known as *pousse-pousse*, postcard, 1914, inv. N 2374.3. © Musée d'Histoire de Lyon - Gadagne.

Bottom *A glimpse of a village at the 1894 World Fair in Lyon*, photographic print, inv. N 3641.14. © Musée d'Histoire de Lyon - Gadagne.

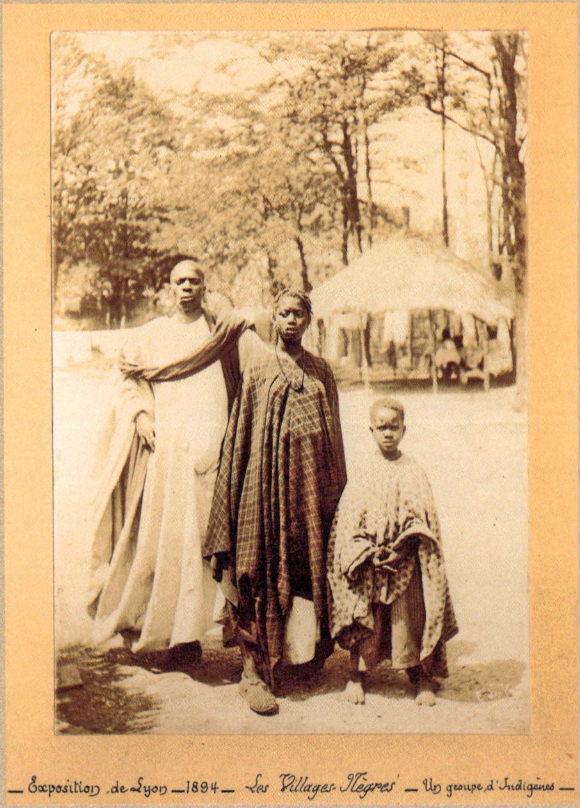

1894 World Fair in Lyon, photographic print, inv. N 3641.20.

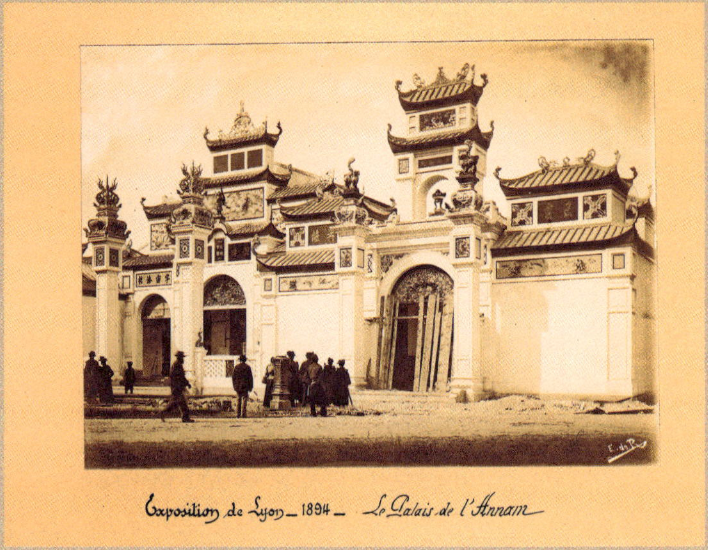

Annam (present-day Vietnam) Palace, Lyon World Fair, 1894, photographic print, inv. N 3641.12.

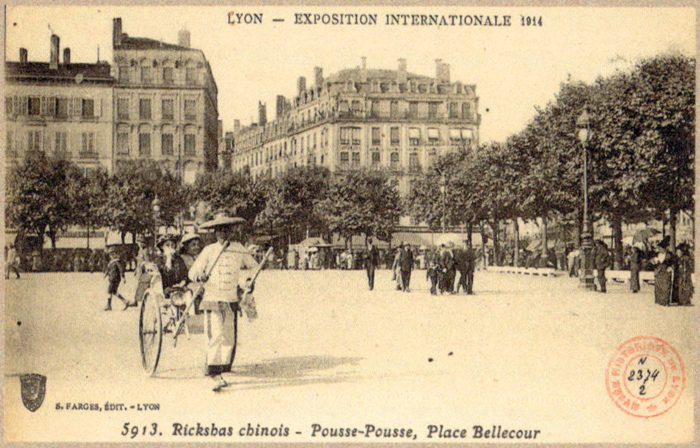

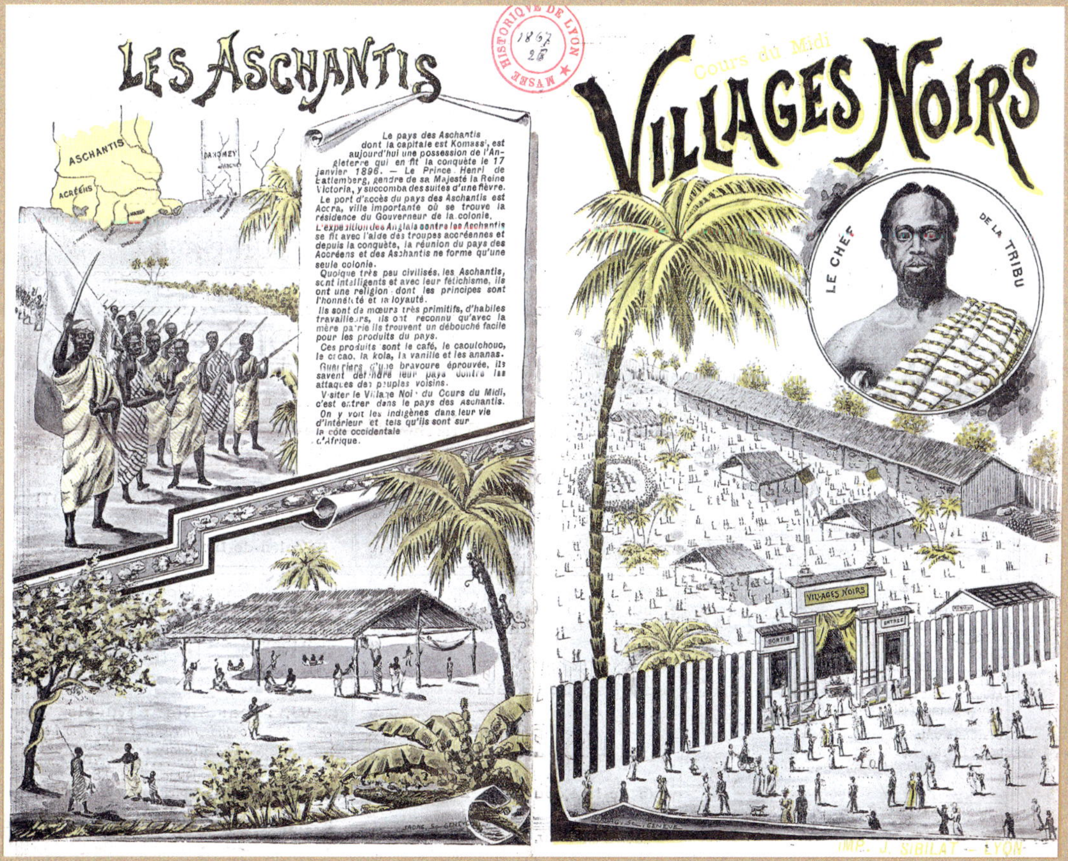

Top *Chinese Rickshaw*, also known as *pousse-pousse*, postcard, 1914, inv. N 2374.3. © Musée d'Histoire de Lyon - Gadagne.

Bottom *The Asante*, Lyon, leaflet, inv. 1867.26. © Musée d'Histoire de Lyon - Gadagne.

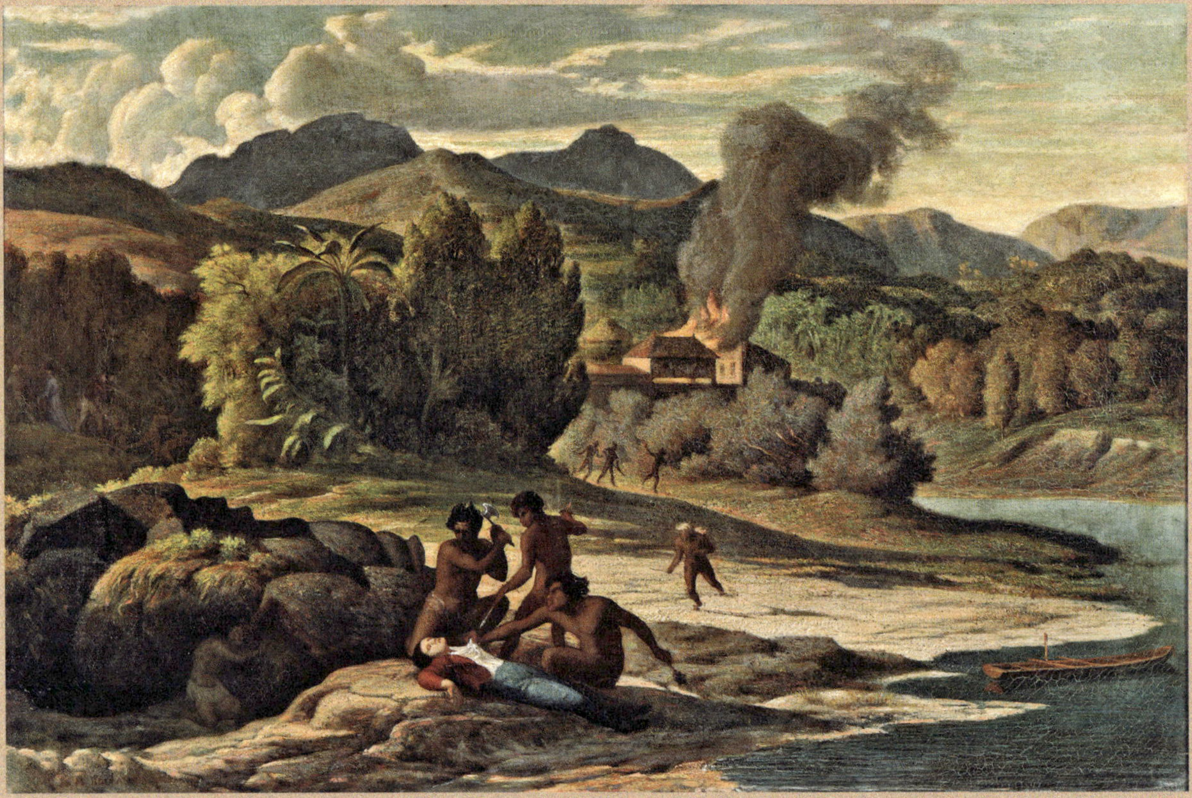

Anonymous, *To Mary, Helping Mother, Bishop Collomb and his missionaries saved by her protection from the fury of the savages, New Caledonia*, 19 July 1847, oil on canvas, 71 x 46 cm, inv. P 104. Fondation Fourvière / Musée de Fourvière. Photo: G. Gambier.

Woman Holding a Mirror

In the 19th century, hundreds of terracotta figurines were found in necropolises lining the roads in the ancient Greek town of Tanagra. Originally a small settlement in the region of Boeotia, it soon became famous for these figurines and was subsequently synonymous with their production during the Hellenistic period (late 4th – 3rd centuries BCE). They reflect the taste for coroplaths *(literally, modellers of young girls) and their graceful, original depictions. The young woman here, wearing a* chiton *(long pleated tunic) beneath her* himation *(wool cloak), tilts her head slightly towards a mirror held in her left hand.*

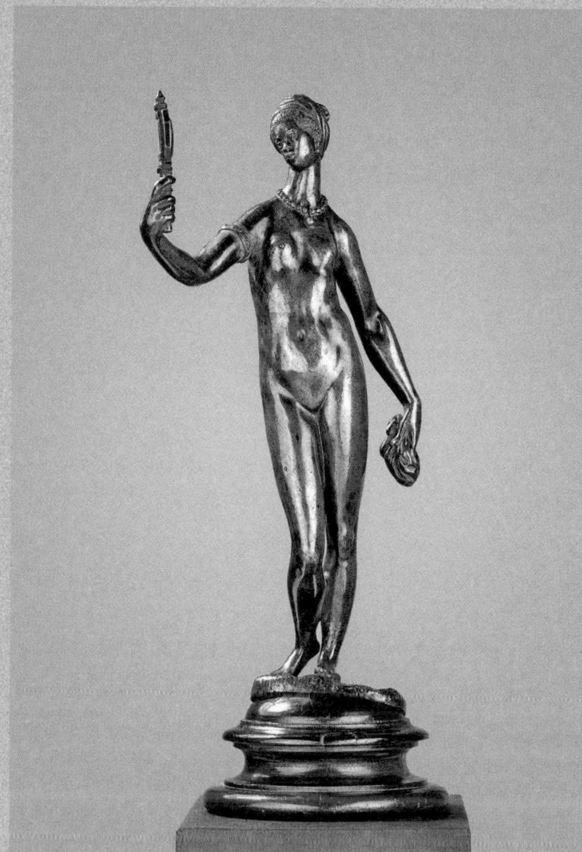

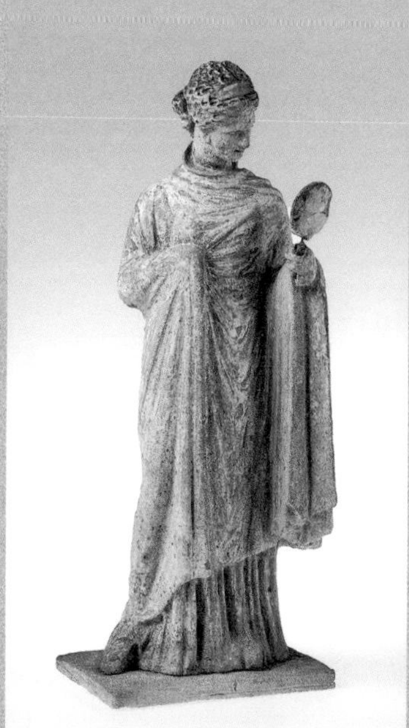

Woman holding a mirror, 3rd century BCE, polychromatic terracotta, 23.8 x 9.2 x 7.6 cm, inv. E 106-2. Musée des Beaux-Arts, Lyon.

Johann Gregor von der Schardt, *African woman with a mirror* (so-called *Black Venus*), France, 1st half of the 17th century, bronze, round wooden base, 35.3 cm, base diameter: 12.6 cm, inv. IX 59. © Grünes Gewölbe, Staatliche Kunstsammlungen Dresden.

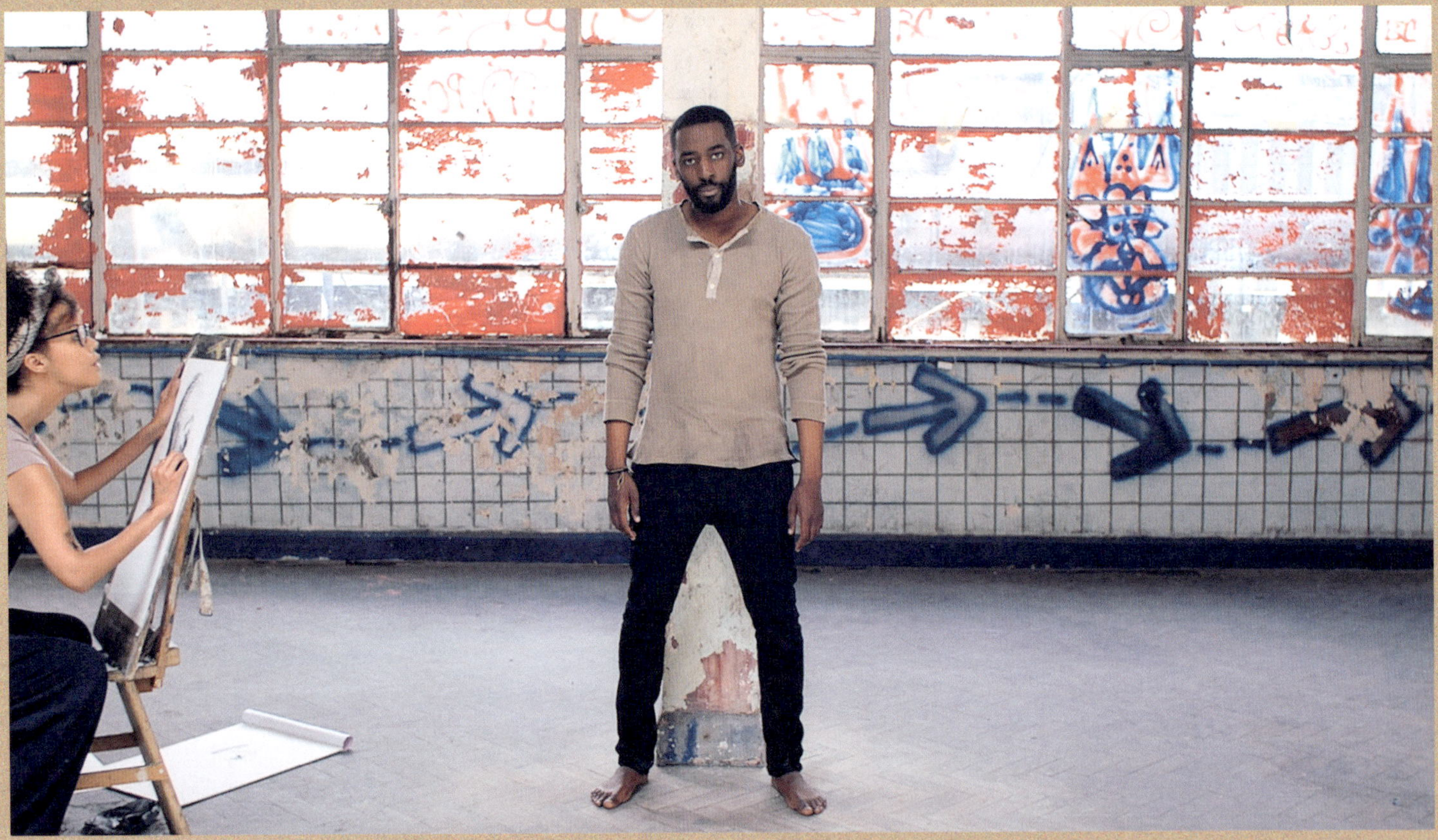

Phoebe Boswell, still from *Dear Mister Shakespeare*, single-screen film, 5 min, 22 sec, 2016. Courtesy of the artist.

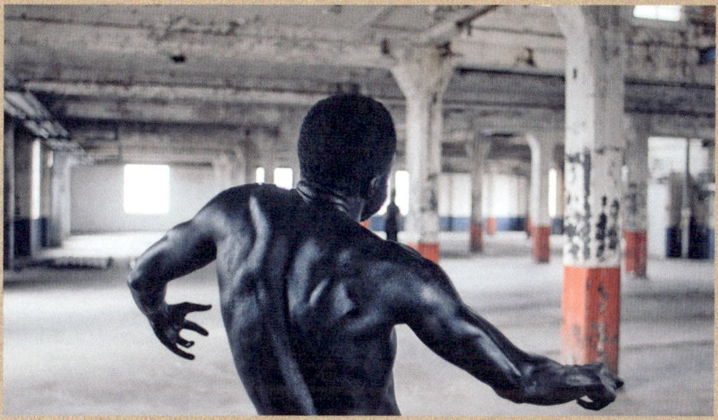

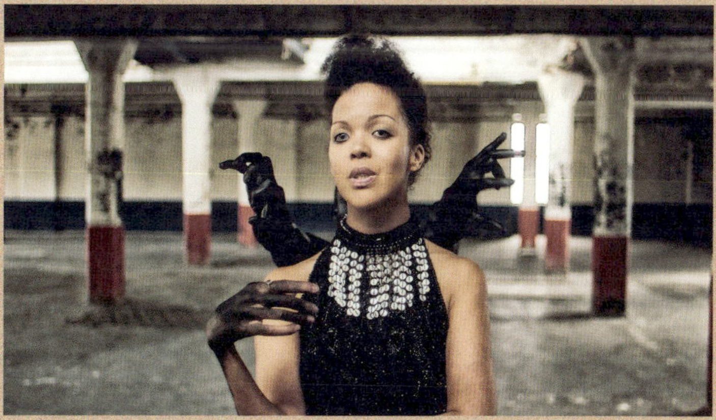

Phoebe Boswell, still from *Dear Mister Shakespeare*, single-screen film, 5 min, 22 sec, 2016. Courtesy of the artist.

Fragile Representations

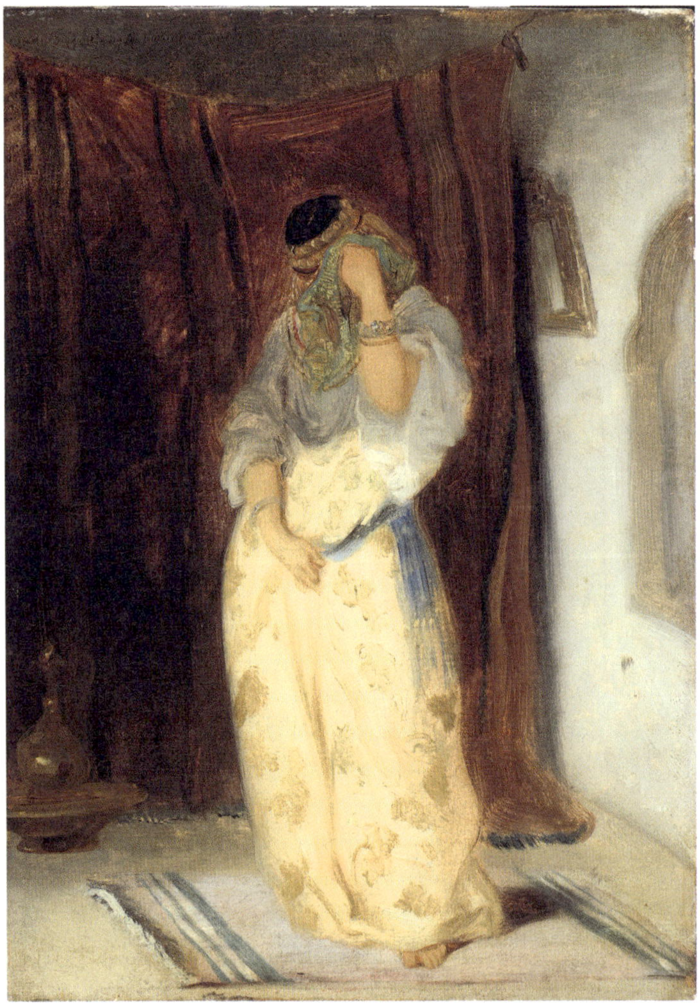

Louise Brunet 06

Louise feels a sudden sharp pain in her right leg. It had started in the ball of her foot, pierced through her knee and rippled up her spine. The pangs have significantly increased over the past four days that she has spent sitting for Mr. Boulanger's new painting. She clenches her fist, as she hopelessly tries to maintain the same pose that the artist has instructed her to keep for the last three hours. She grins while her knees quiver beneath her. But Rose, as she is known by the painters who employ her, is determined not to reveal her physical weakness. How could she, when her body has been her main source of livelihood for more than 30 years?

Louise started sitting at the age of 16, mostly as a live model for painting classes at the École national supérieure des Beaux Arts in Paris. However, it wasn't until 1824 that she would be solicited by established artists for significant paintings requiring many days and sometimes weeks of work. That year Eugène Delacroix first presented his painting of her to the public. He titled it *Mademoiselle Rose* after her. The painting took a whole week to finish, and not once did Louise's body falter. Delacroix did not talk to her other than to instruct her on how to pose. On the last day while making the final touches to the painting, Delacroix turned to her. "What do they call you?" he asked. "Rose," Louise responded. And that was it. Delacroix asked Louise to pose for him on several other occasions in the future, but he was not a man of many words.

Louis Boulanger, *Moorish Woman*, 1849, oil on canvas, 62 x 51.2 cm (framed), donated by l'Association des amis du musée, 1954, inv. 1954-45. Musée des Beaux-Arts, Lyon.

Today, Mr. Boulanger, on the other hand, is happy to talk about all sorts of things. Trying hard to ignore her pain, Louise wanders into her thoughts. Boulanger's voice rambles on about the previous night's dinner with Victor Hugo, which makes it even harder for Louise to switch off. She closes her eyes. She thinks about the details of a painting she has been working on recently. Not many people know, certainly not Mr. Boulanger, that Louise is an accomplished painter herself. Several years ago, with her modelling career at its peak, she put a good chunk of the money she had saved into one of the few classes that allowed women to paint from live models. This provided her with invaluable knowledge about the depiction of bodily proportions and movements. Louise had even succeeded, under a pseudonym of course, to exhibit some of her paintings at the annual Salon de Paris organised by the École nationale supérieure des Beaux Arts. Her *Portrait d'une jeune fille* was even praised by a couple of critics. Boulanger was not included in the Salon. In a fairer world, Louise would be the artist standing behind the easel while Boulanger sat in front, shuddering in pain.

The thought of Boulanger modelling for her brings a smirk to Louise's face. "No, no, no," Boulanger snaps. He grabs a veil from a trunk of accessories that lies next to him, thrusts it towards Louise and asks her to hold it in front of her face. "It is a painting of a woman in a harem", he explains, "and therefore, as tradition has it in all Oriental countries, your face must be covered." Boulanger's ideas of the so-called Orient are in line with the zeitgeist. His paintings, like those of Gérôme and Louise's first patron Delacroix, purport to show an authentic glimpse of a location and its inhabitants. They depict an exotic and, therefore, racialised and often sexualised culture from a distant place where women are subdued yet titillating.

Louise complies at first and holds the veil in front of her face, her head tilted slightly downward. At this point her pain is unbearable. She drops her arms, lifts her head up and tries to calm herself by breathing slowly in and out. "Cover your ugly face, I said," Boulanger yells. Louise feels the blood rushing in her veins. Anger seems to be the only feeling that overrides her pain. "My name is Rose. I also paint," she says with a calmness that comes from nowhere and walks out: away from Boulanger, Delacroix, a world dominated by men, the last 25 years of her life, her ageing body and every false image in which it has appeared. This was 173 years ago. Many images are still misleading, many names are still uncovered. Louise keeps on walking.

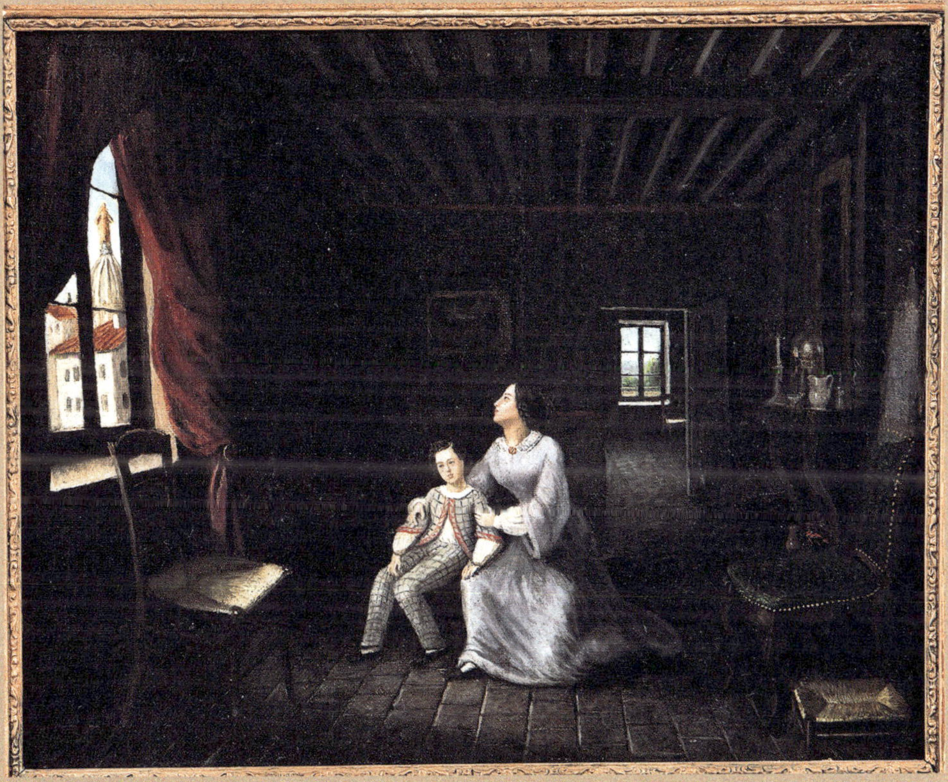

Anonymous, *A Child's Healing*, after 1852, oil on panel, gilt wood frame, 39 x 47.5 cm, inv. P160. Fondation Fourvière / Musée de Fourvière. Photo: G. Gambier.

La promessa sposa

Painting with watercolour and acrylic, and only in Payne's grey, a dark blue-grey hue, Giulia Andreani evokes forgotten histories. As a "memory worker", she composes her pictures from various sources: archival documents, vintage photographs and internet screen grabs. La promessa sposa *is a portrait of Franca Viola, a young Sicilian woman who in 1966 refused a "rehabilitating marriage" with the man who had raped her – an arrangement which, according to Sicilian tradition and Italian law, would have enabled the rapist to escape prosecution.*

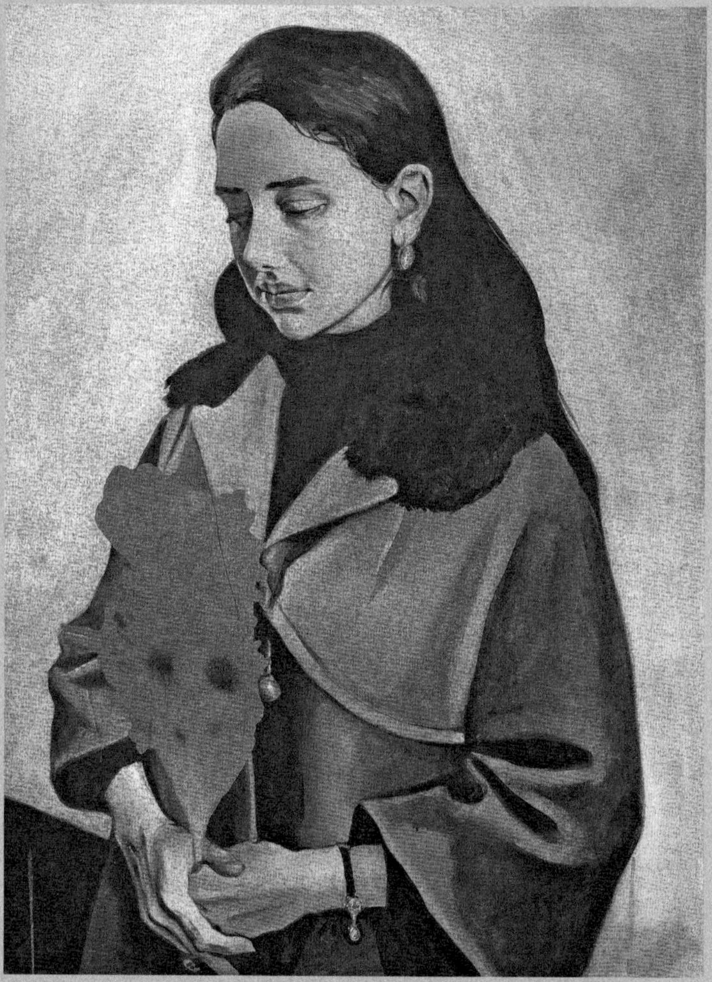

Giulia Andreani, *La Promessa Sposa*, 2021, acrylic on canvas, 81.5 x 60.5 cm. © Giulia Andreani / Private Collection Courtesy Galerie Max Hetzler Berlin/Paris/London. Photo: Charles Duprat.

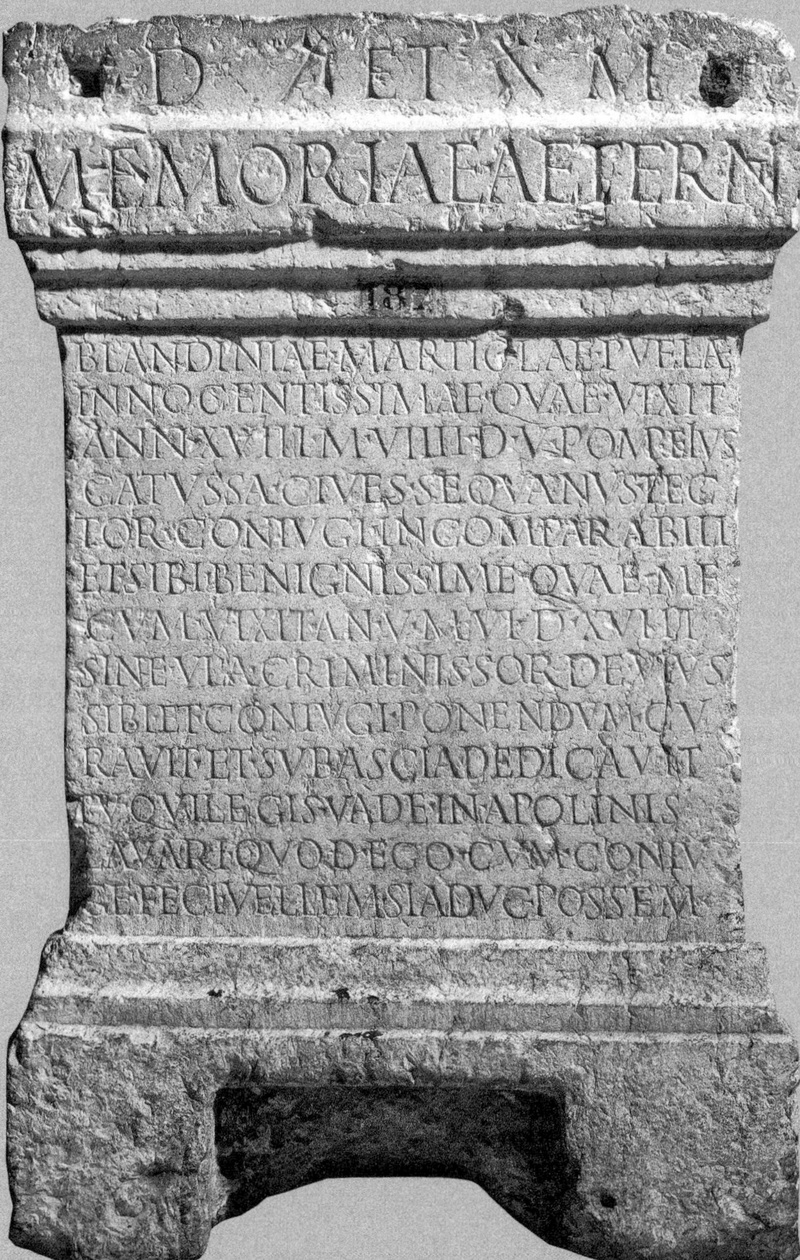

Epitaph of the wife of a stucco craftsman, 2nd–3rd centuries, limestone, 75 x 42 cm, inv. AD187. © Lugdunum – Musée & Théâtres romains, Lyon. Photo: Jean-Michel Degueule.

Epitaph of the wife of a stucco craftsman

On this stela, discovered on the side of an ancient Roman road on the outskirts of Lyon in 1815, a touching epitaph is engraved and dedicated by a husband to his wife, Blandinia Martiola, an enigmatic figure who died at the age of 18. This stela was made between the second and third centuries, during a period of political crisis within the Roman Empire, which saw its borders give way for the first time to invasions from the east. Although the crisis stabilised by the end of the third century, it nevertheless marked the beginnings of the slow decline of the empire, until its complete fall in 476. Like the thousands of Roman antiquities found around the world, this stela, which calls for living in the present moment, is a witness to the pomp and decline of an empire and the lives of its citizens.

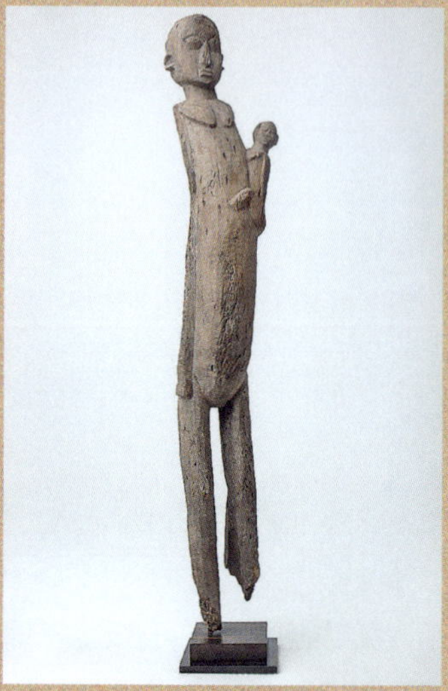

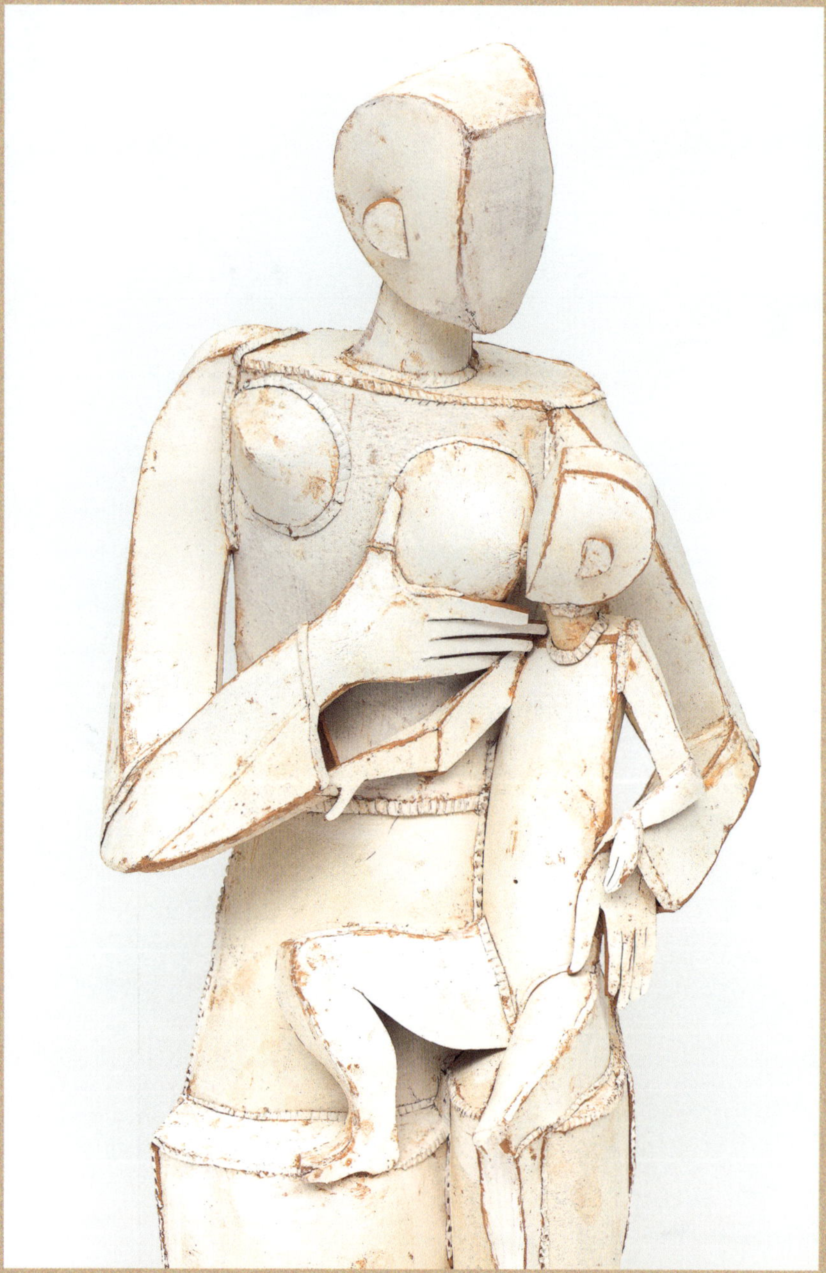

Lobi Mother and Child

*This wooden mother and child (*bùthìba kõtín*) is a particular example of a woman-with-child motif. It was made by the Lobi people and comes from Burkina Faso. It serves to symbolically protect the future mother; such incarnations of ancestors are used by healers to ward off attacks by roaming spirits. The very long, spindly arms are typical of Lobo wood sculpture.*

Ann Agee, *Medieval Madonna* (detail), 2021, earthenware with colored slips, 66 x 27.6 x 21.9 cm. Courtesy of Ann Agee and P·P·O·W, New York.

Lobi-Birifor culture (Burkina Faso), *Lobi Motherhood*, 20th century, inv. 2007.10.2. Musée des Confluences.

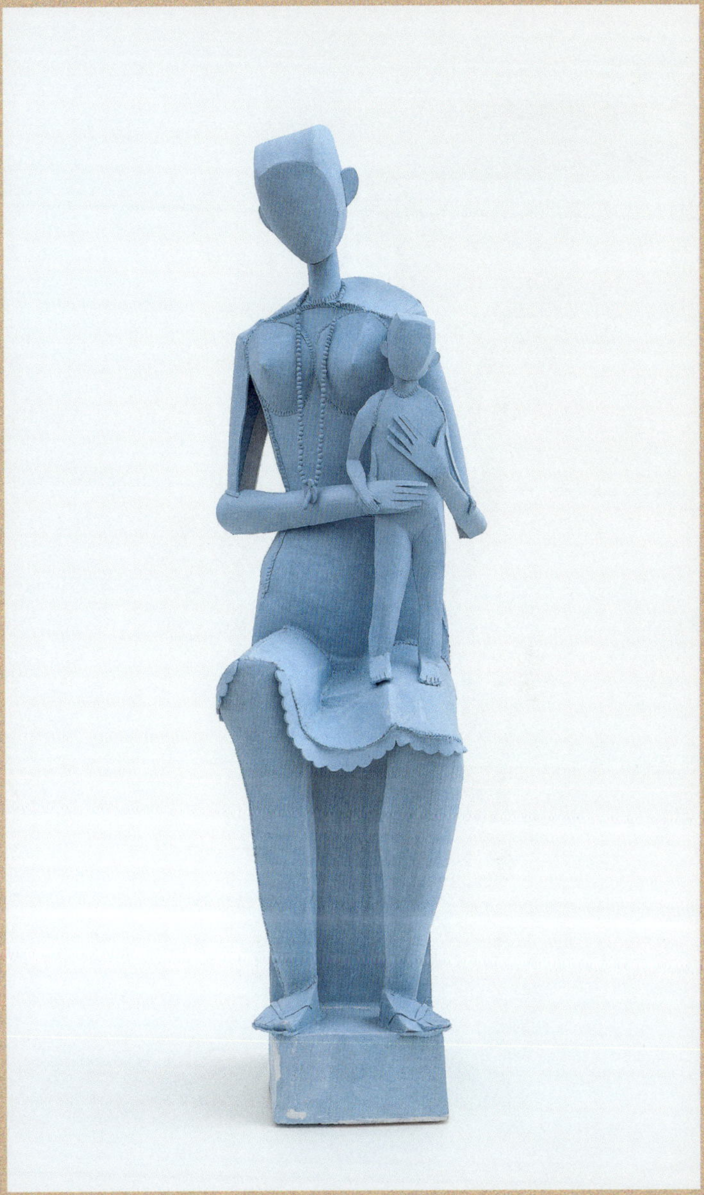

Cult of the Penis Madonna

Inspired by popular Italian saltcellars from the late 17th to early 18th centuries in the collection at the Davanzati palace in Florence, Ann Agee's Madonnas of the Girl Child *series depicts girls being rocked, supported or breastfed by their mothers. These sculptures – moulded from different kinds of clay using various techniques and fired at different temperatures – are suggestive of the divine child motif. By replacing the Christ with a female figure, Agee's ceramic pieces reimagine the gender standards of traditional devotional articles.*

Ann Agee, *Cult of the Penis Madonna*, 2021, pigmented porcelain with cotton thread, cast bronze and epoxy putty, 84.5 x 30.5 x 24.8 cm. Courtesy of Ann Agee and P·P·O·W, New York.

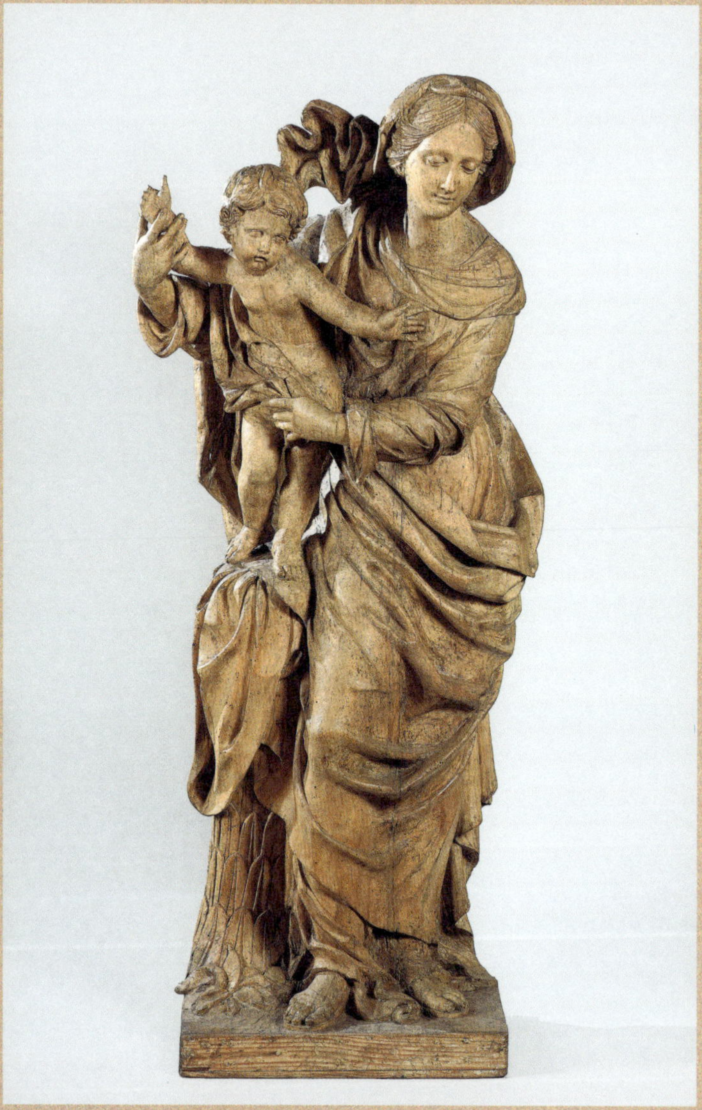

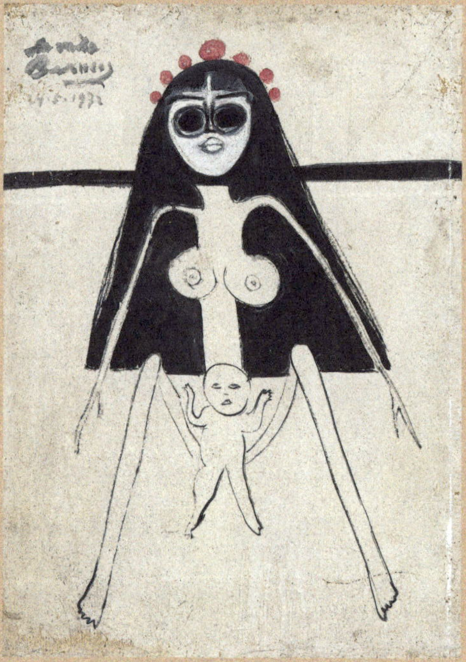

Antoine Coysevox, *Virgin Mary and Child*, 18th century, linden wood, inv. 168. © Musée d'Histoire de Lyon - Gadagne. Photo: Pierre Aubert.

Semiha Berksoy, *'Birth' My Mother*, 1972, oil on hardboard, 100 x 70 cm. Courtesy of Şirin Ediger.

Madonna and Child with the Infant Saint John the Baptist

Intended for private prayer, Madonna and Child with the Infant Saint John the Baptist *is an exemplar of Carlo Portelli's youthful oeuvre. Painted around the time that the artist joined the Brotherhood of Saint Luke, it is in the grand tradition of Florentine painting from the Quattrocento period as taught by his master Ridolfo Ghirlandaio. Yet his acidic palette, cold elegance and brilliant technique are reminiscent of early-16th-century Mannerism, confirming Portelli's affinity for the works of Bronzino and Francesco Salviati.*

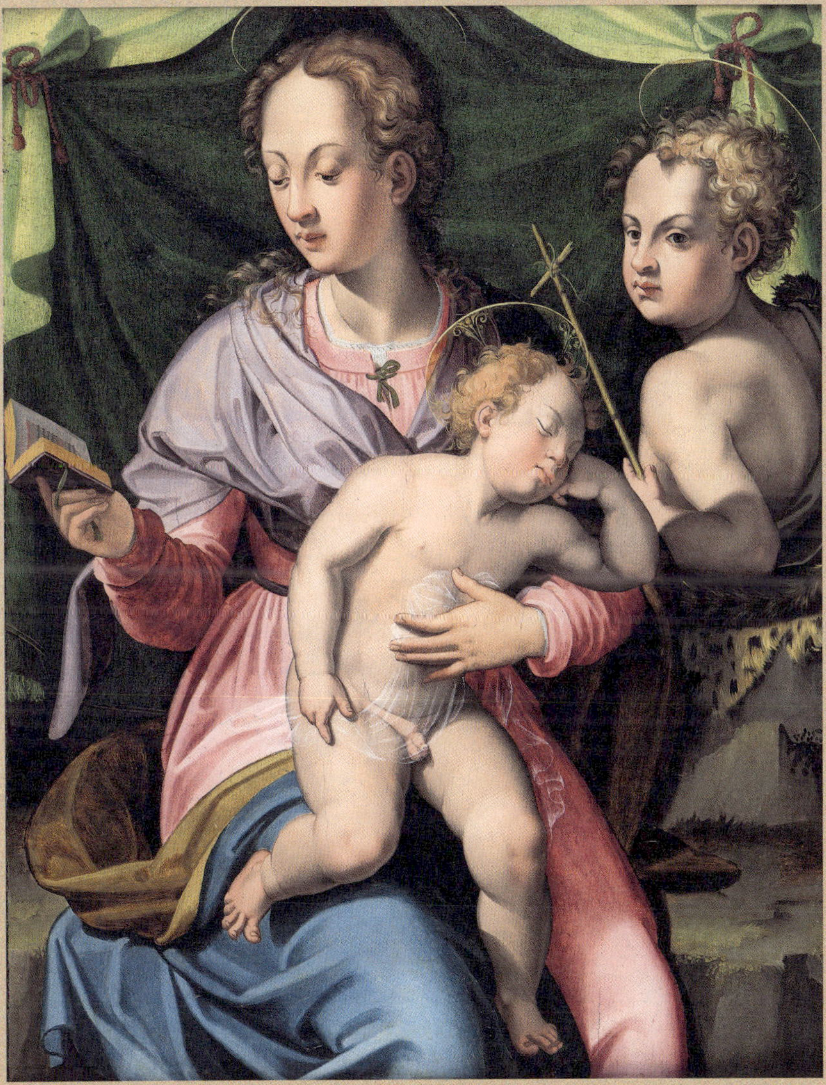

Carlo Portelli, *The Virgin Mary and Jesus with a young Saint Jean Baptiste*, ca. 1535, oil on panel, 111.5 x 92 x 6 cm (framed), inv. 1975.47. Donated by Pascal Greppe, 1906. Musée municipal Paul Dini, Villefranche-sur-Saône.

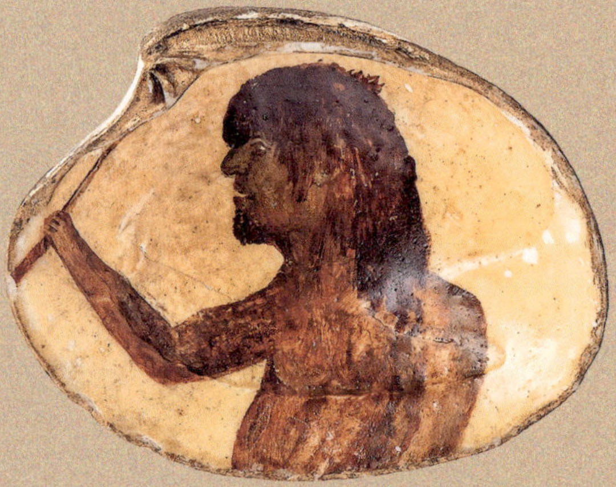

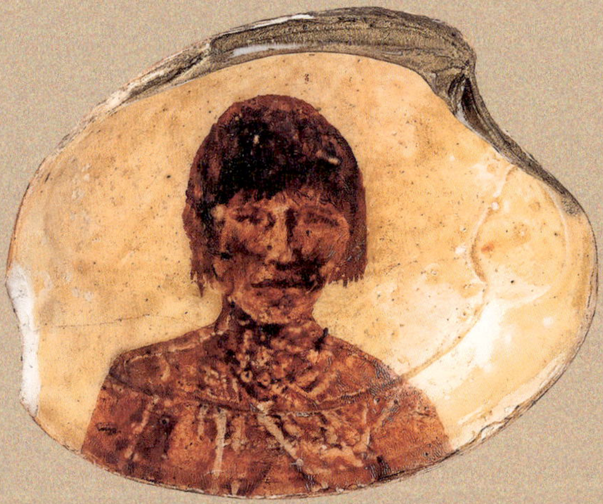

Painted shells, Tierra del Fuego

These two shells, painted with figurative portraits, were brought back from Tierra del Fuego by the missionaries of the Œuvre de la Propagation de la Foi society. The island, which is found at the southernmost tip of the Americas, is home to abundant molluscs – the source of the painting surfaces. The texture of the subjects' hair and the raised relief of their bodies are rendered through different concentrations of red pigment.

Tierra del Fuego (Argentina), painted shells, 19th century, shells and pigment, on loan by Œuvres Pontificales Missionnaires – 1979, inv. D979-3-1279 and D979-3-1280. Musées des Confluences.

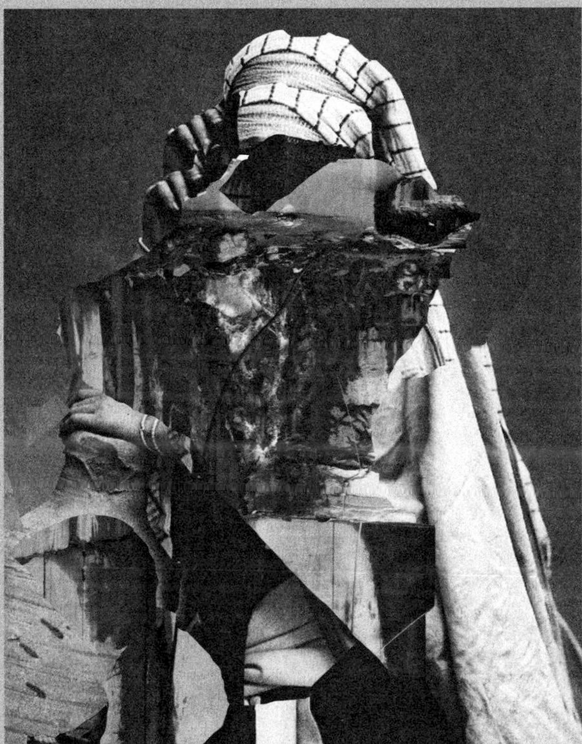

Ailbhe Ní Bhriain, *The Muses III*, 2018, pigment print on bamboo paper. Courtesy the artist and domobaal, London.

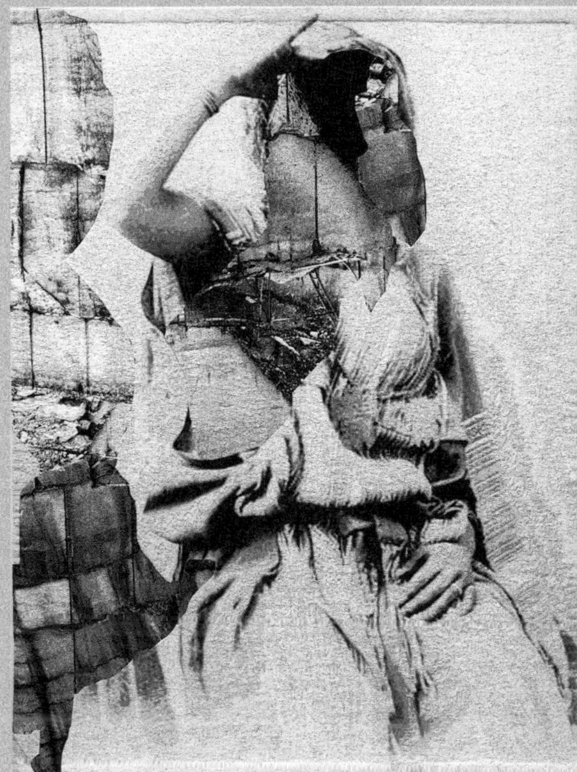

Ailbhe Ní Bhriain, *The Muses I*, 2018, jacquard tapestry, wool, cotton. Exhibition view, Irish Museum of Modern Art, 2022. Courtesy the artist and domobaal, London. Photo: Ros Kavanagh.

Fragile Expectations

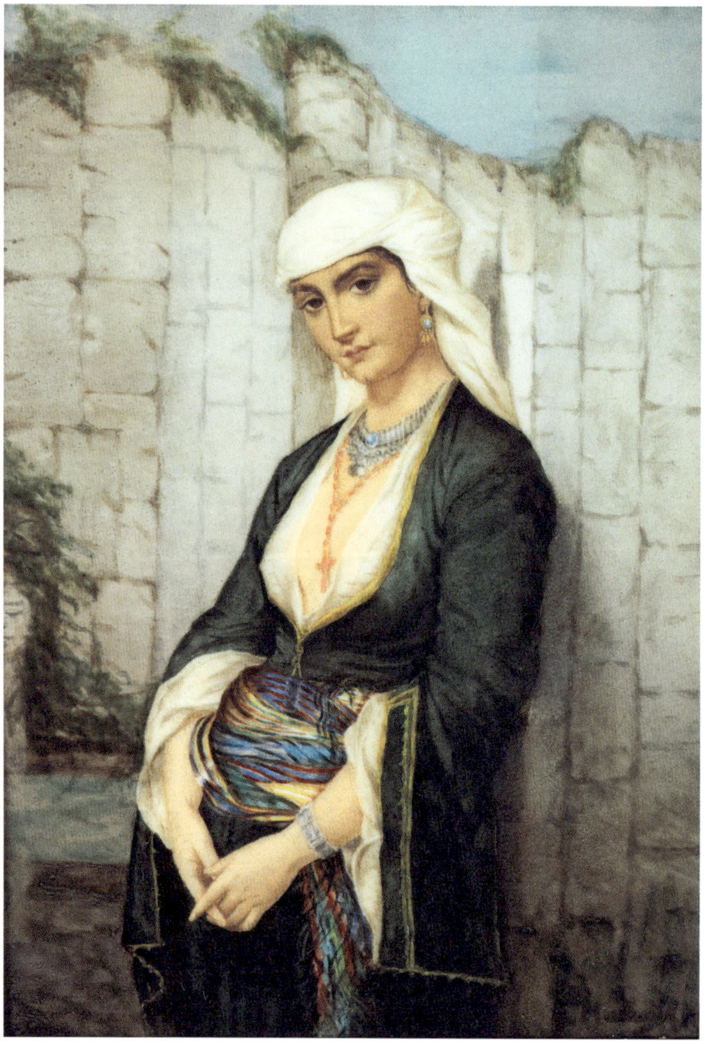

Louise Brunet 07

The streets of Beirut's port district are buzzing with excitement, especially down by the docks where crowds have been gathering since the early morning hours. It is not surprising for this old part of town to be teeming with activity at this time of day, yet something about the frenzied atmosphere feels out of sync with the usual daily hustle.

It is 16 August 1860. Louise Brunet leans against an old wall in the courtyard of the silk factory where she has been working for the last four years. She is wondering whether she should join the other girls who left for the waterfront a little earlier – the superintendent of the factory had even given them an exceptional permission to leave their basins and participate in the current fanfare. Within the hour, a large naval fleet would arrive, a contingent sent by the French to intervene in and quell the hostilities that had erupted last May between the local Druze and Christians.

In announcing the special permission, the superintendent had declared it "a great day for the natives of this land, and for France." Louise is still trying to wrap her head around this absurd statement. She understands how, considering the events of late, some would think that the local Christians might need protection. But are they at such a risk that France needs to intervene with 6,000 soldiers? Or is it that France senses in these skirmishes an opportunity to safeguard its economic interests and maintain its dominance over the local silk industry? In the past years, raw silk has become an increasingly lucrative commodity on the global market and accounts for almost 60 percent of all exports from this otherwise unassuming port. Mulberry trees, the favoured food source for the silkworks necessary for the production of raw silk, have long ago replaced the grains and cereals that used to be the pride of Mount Lebanon's farmers, Louise's family included. The demand for silk cocoons among the largely Lyon-based French silk merchants has become so great that in a few years mulberry trees will occupy nearly 80 percent of all cultivated lands.

Anonymous, after Émile Vernet-Lecomte, *Maronite woman*, 19th century, oil on porcelain, 25 x 18 cm. Philippe Jabre Art Collection.

Louise finally decides to head down to the waterfront. After all, it is not every day that a military fleet headed by a general sails into such a small port. Louise descends the main road, which, normally brimming with bustling shops, brokers' stands, peddlers' carriages and street vendors, is eerily empty. But she hears the cheering crowds in the distance and picks up the pace. Her heartbeat is accelerating. The last house is now behind her. She makes a left turn, and her feet finally touch the sand. A spectacular scene emerges: Charles Marie Napoléon de Beaufort d'Hautpoul is perched on his studded white horse. His arm is stretched before him, his white gloves glistening in the light as he charges through the dazzled onlookers with a dense column of troops behind him. Upon departing from Marseille, d'Hautpoul and his troops were addressed by Napoleon II himself, who declared, "Wherever the French flag is seen to pass, nations know that a great cause precedes it, and a great people follows it." Louise notes the tricolore flag rising out from within the crowd. Women throw themselves at the General's feet and lift their babies up to him as if to seek his blessing. "Is he a soldier or a prophet?" Louise wonders in disbelief. It is a spectacle that will be carved in Louise's memory forever.

Some of Beirut's elites look over the proceedings from a distance: the Khazens, the Sursocks, the Bassoulis and other reputable families who made their fortunes in the silk industry. Amongst them are many French factory owners, almost all of them from Lyon, including her boss. Louise recognises the Portalis brothers, owners of the factories in Btetir; Monsieur Figon and his wife from Palluat et Testenoire in 'Ain Hamadeh; and Monsieur Croizat, the broker of the Guerin family. They were all regulars at the factory. Louise is certain that while she can recognise all of them, they most probably had no recollection of her at all, or her name: Mahboubeh, Arabic for "the loved one". The thought of being so anonymous and inconsequential to these people makes her at once furious and desperate.

Perhaps Louise's indignation today is too irrational, even ill-founded. But there will be times in the not-so-distant future when others will also feel Louise's rage and desperation. Her despair will be shared by the entire populace when the great famine hits during World War II as hundreds of thousands of people perish from hunger with nothing left to eat but the leaves of mulberry trees. They will understand her rage when they hear the words of Louis Pradel, president of the Lyon Chamber of Commerce, when he says "that here in Lyon, Lebanon is considered to be a colony". The Lyon Chamber of Commerce will raise more than a million francs in 1920 to support the French Mandate in Lebanon, which will last until 1943. They will welcome General Gouraud, the first High Commissioner of France, who on 1 September 1920 will declare the founding of Great Lebanon. In his speech, he will make a point to praise the significance of this budding nation's port. Many years later, the French will come back after a terrible explosion hits that same port mentioned by Gouraud, where Louise Brunet stands today, witnessing history being made. But this will happen a long time from now and will be witnessed by other Louises in the future.

Louise feels someone yanking her arm, pulling her away from her musings. She turns around. It's her friend from the factory Amal, whose name is the Arabic word for hope. "There you are", she says, "we have been waiting for you." Louise feigns excitement. Amal pulls her sleeve. "Follow me. We can have a better view from the other side." Louise disappears into the feverish scene while the crowds cheer: "The French have come to save us!"

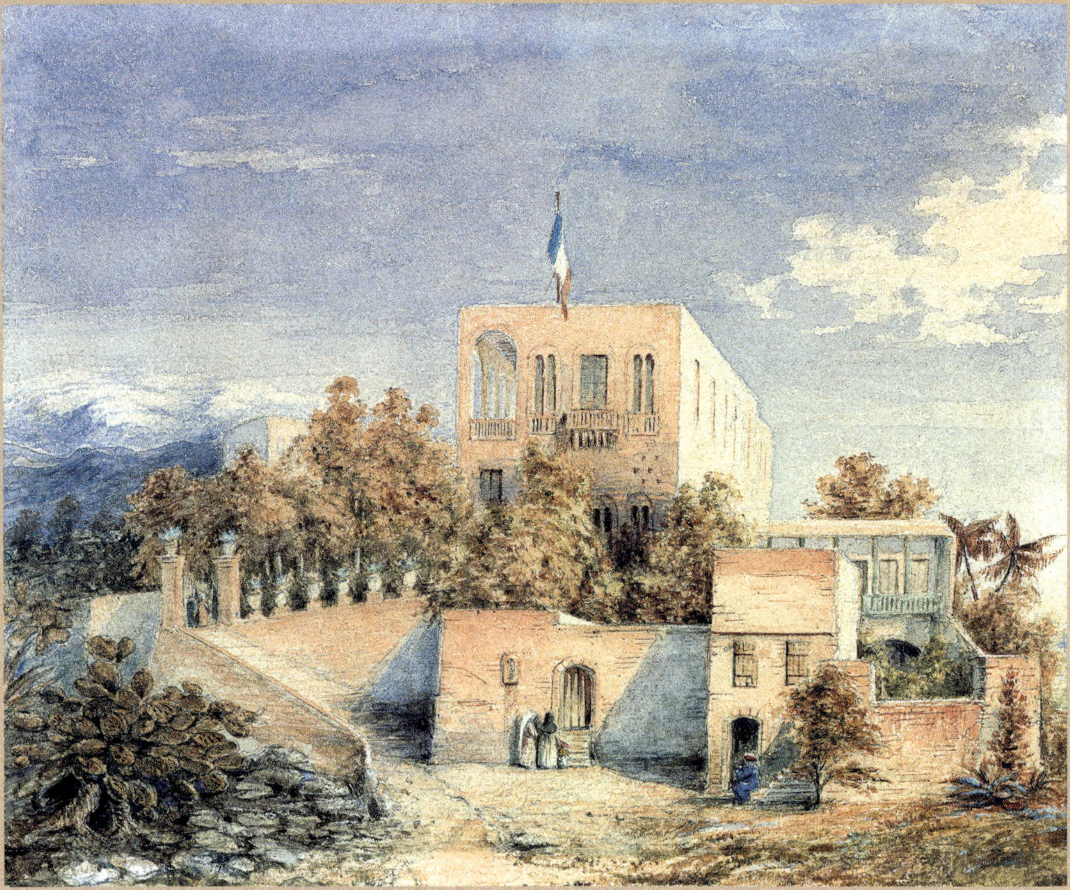

William de Niewkerque, *French Consulate in Beirut*, 1850, watercolour on carton, 21.4 x 26.3 cm. Philippe Jabre Art Collection.

The French Consulate in Beirut

The French Consulate was established around the time that Lyon expatriates arrived in Lebanon in the 17th century and established a more permanent presence in the early 19th century. From the 1830s onward, it was tasked with assisting the reform of Syria and particularly to defend French nationals in Lebanon. Thanks to the consulate, French spinning mill owners were exempt from the taxes levied on their Lebanese counterparts, and they won every trial against the latter thanks to consulate support. This watercolour by William de Niewkerque depicts the Jeday Palace, the seat of the political authorities; another building in the port area that is no longer standing, it was devoted to commercial activities.

The French Army Entering Beirut, Led by General d'Hautpoul

In August 1860, Napoleon III ordered a French expedition to Syria commanded by Charles Marie Napoléon de Beaufort d'Hautpoul (1804–1890), in response to the political and religious unrest that had shaken Lebanon since March of that year due to clashes between the Druze and Maronite populations. After France's intervention, an autonomous Christian government was appointed on 9 June 1861, which helped to free the people of Lebanon from Ottoman control but left the interfaith conflicts unresolved.

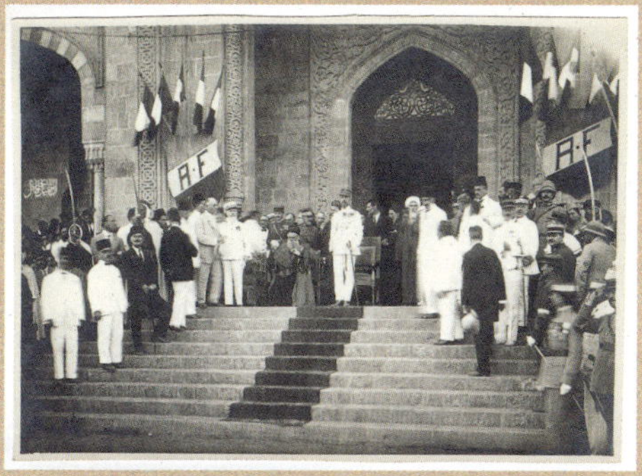

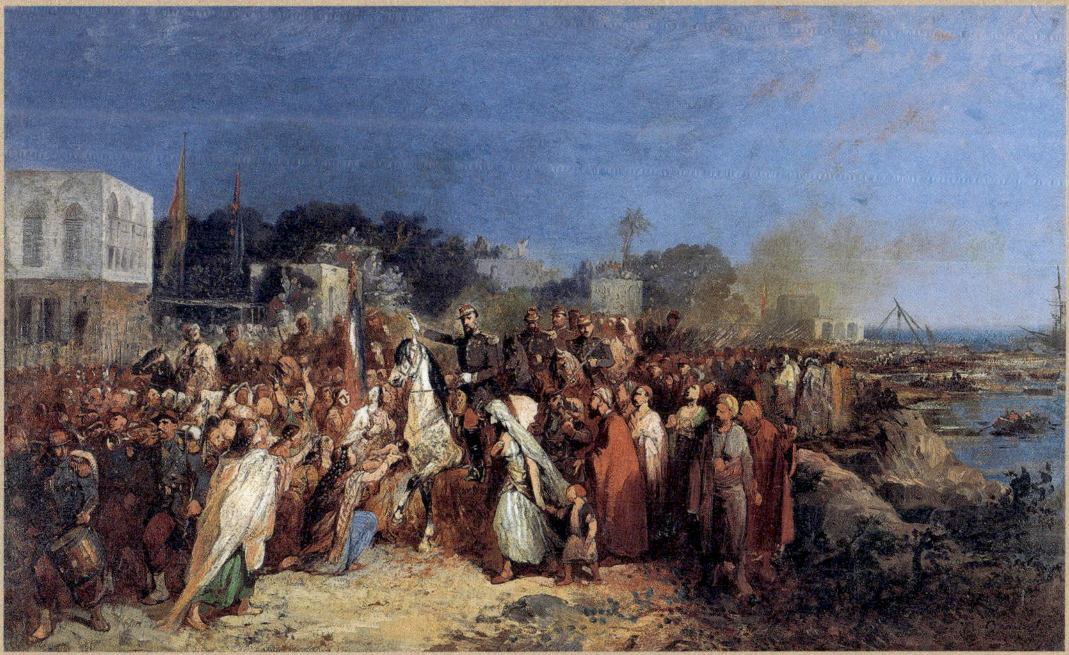

Jean-Adolphe Beaucé, *Entry of the French army in Beirut with General d'Hautpoul at the helm*, 19th century (undated), oil on canvas, 63 x 100 cm. Philippe Jabre Art Collection.

Declaration of Greater Lebanon by General Gouraud on the porch of the Résidence des Pins Palace, Beirut, 1 September 1920, inv. A005221. Archives du Ministère de l'Europe et des Affaires Etrangères – La Courneuve / Collection Gouraud.

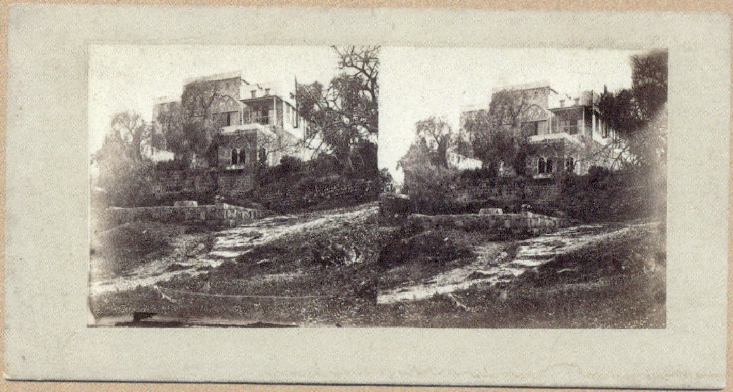

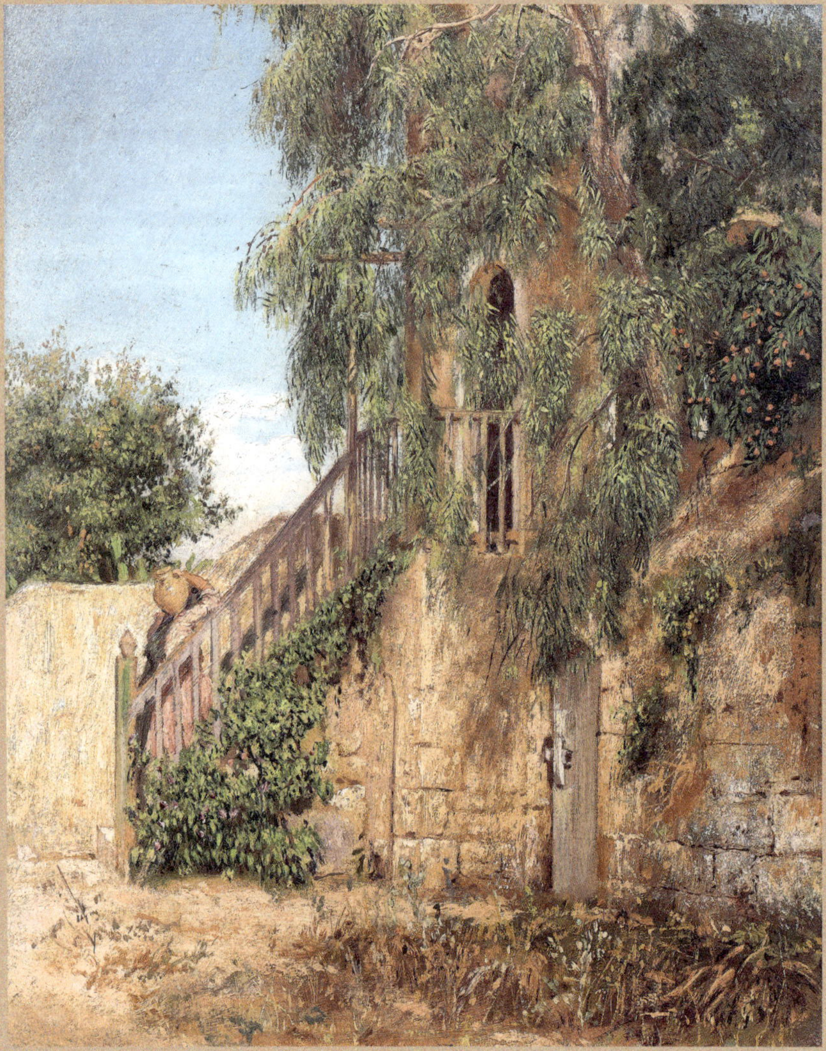

Countryside Where the Comte de Laferté Lived and Main House of the Comte de Laferté in Ras Beirut

The Comte de la Ferté is thought to have been the first citizen of Lyon to establish a spinning mill in Lebanon, in 1836. His business, located in the Beirut area, prospered thanks to the labour of hundreds of Lebanese who were paid a pittance and worked in appalling conditions. To expand his mill, the count readily impounded all the village's water sources for his sole benefit, forcing the villagers to make long journeys to fetch water. His disputes with the country's customs authorities and the diminishing competitiveness of silk from Beirut put an end to his business.

Top Anonymous, *Main Residence of Comte de Laferté in Ras Beirut*, ca. 1865, stereoscopic view, 6.3 x 13.3cm (framed: 8.5 x 16.8 cm). Gabriel El Daher Collection.

Bottom Johann Ludwig Rudolph Durheim, *Comte de Laferté's country home in Ras Beirut*, ca. 1865, oil on panel, 25 x 20 cm. Ronald et Berthe Chagoury Collection.

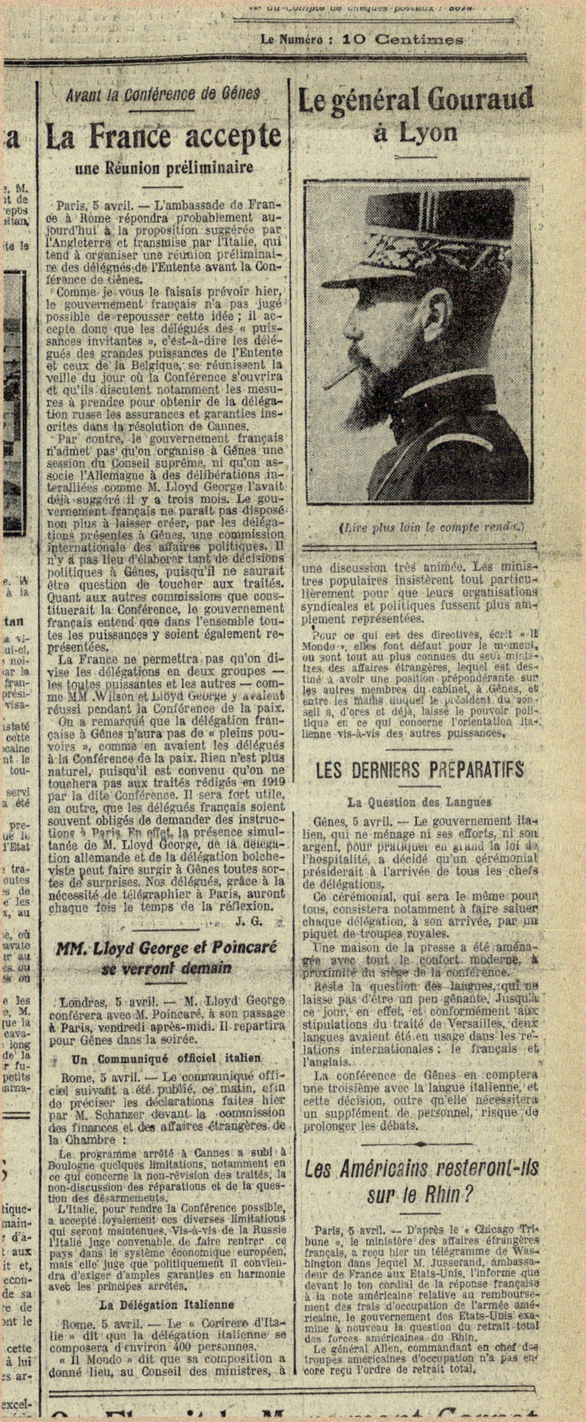

Le Numéro : 10 Centimes

Avant la Conférence de Gênes

La France accepte

une Réunion préliminaire

Paris, 5 avril. — L'ambassade de France à Rome répondra probablement aujourd'hui à la proposition suggérée par l'Angleterre et transmise par l'Italie, qui tend à organiser une réunion préliminaire des délégués de l'Entente avant la Conférence de Gênes.

Comme je vous le faisais prévoir hier, le gouvernement français n'a pas jugé possible de repousser cette idée ; il accepte donc que les délégués des « puissances invitantes », c'est-à-dire les délégués des grandes puissances de l'Entente et ceux de la Belgique, se réunissent la veille du jour où la Conférence s'ouvrira et qu'ils discutent notamment les mesures à prendre pour obtenir de la délégation russe les assurances et garanties inscrites dans la résolution de Cannes.

Par contre, le gouvernement français n'admet pas qu'on organise à Gênes une session du Conseil suprême, ni qu'on associe l'Allemagne à des délibérations interalliées comme M. Lloyd George l'avait déjà suggéré il y a trois mois. Le gouvernement français ne paraît pas disposé non plus à laisser créer, par les délégations présentes à Gênes, une commission internationale des affaires politiques. Il n'y a pas lieu d'élaborer tant de décisions politiques à Gênes, puisqu'il ne saurait être question de toucher aux traités. Quant aux autres commissions que constituerait la Conférence, le gouvernement français entend que dans l'ensemble toutes les puissances y soient également représentées.

La France ne permettra pas qu'on divise les délégations en deux groupes — les toutes puissantes et les autres — comme MM. Wilson et Lloyd George y avaient réussi pendant la Conférence de la paix.

On a remarqué que la délégation française à Gênes n'aura pas de « pleins pouvoirs », comme en avaient les délégués à la Conférence de la paix. Rien n'est plus naturel, puisqu'il est convenu qu'on ne touchera pas aux traités rédigés en 1919 par la dite Conférence. Il sera fort utile, en outre, que les délégués français soient souvent obligés de demander des instructions à Paris. En effet, la présence simultanée de M. Lloyd George, de la délégation allemande et de la délégation bolcheviste peut faire surgir à Gênes toutes sortes de surprises. Nos délégués, grâce à la nécessité de télégraphier à Paris, auront chaque fois le temps de la réflexion.

J. G.

MM. Lloyd George et Poincaré se verront demain

Londres, 5 avril. — M. Lloyd George conférera avec M. Poincaré, à son passage à Paris, vendredi après-midi. Il repartira pour Gênes dans la soirée.

Un Communiqué officiel italien

Rome, 5 avril. — Le communiqué officiel suivant a été publié, ce matin, afin de préciser les déclarations faites hier par M. Schanzer devant la commission des finances et des affaires étrangères de la Chambre :

Le programme arrêté à Cannes a subi à Boulogne quelques limitations, notamment en ce qui concerne la non-révision des traités, la non-discussion des réparations et de la question des désarmements.

L'Italie, pour rendre la Conférence possible, a accepté loyalement ces diverses limitations qui seront maintenues. Vis-à-vis de la Russie l'Italie juge convenable de faire rentrer ce pays dans le système économique européen, mais elle juge que politiquement il conviendra d'exiger d'amples garanties en harmonie avec les principes arrêtés.

La Délégation Italienne

Rome, 5 avril. — Le « Corirere d'Italie » dit que la délégation italienne se composera d'environ 400 personnes.

« Il Mondo » dit que sa composition a donné lieu, au Conseil des ministres, à une discussion très animée. Les ministres populaires insistèrent tout particulièrement pour que leurs organisations syndicales et politiques fussent plus amplement représentées.

Pour ce qui est des directives, écrit « Il Mondo », elles font défaut pour le moment, ou sont tout au plus connues du seul ministre des affaires étrangères, lequel est destiné à avoir une position prépondérante sur les autres membres du cabinet, à Gênes, et entre les mains duquel le président du conseil a, d'ores et déjà, laissé le pouvoir politique en ce qui concerne l'orientation italienne vis-à-vis des autres puissances.

Le général Gouraud à Lyon

(Lire plus loin le compte rendu.)

LES DERNIERS PRÉPARATIFS

La Question des Langues

Gênes, 5 avril. — Le gouvernement italien, qui ne ménage ni ses efforts, ni son argent, pour pratiquer en grand la loi de l'hospitalité, a décidé qu'un cérémonial présiderait à l'arrivée de tous les chefs de délégations.

Ce cérémonial, qui sera le même pour tous, consistera notamment à faire saluer chaque délégation, à son arrivée, par un piquet de troupes royales.

Une maison de la presse a été aménagée avec tout le confort moderne, à proximité du siège de la conférence.

Reste la question des langues, qui ne laisse pas d'être un peu gênante. Jusqu'à ce jour, en effet, et conformément aux stipulations du traité de Versailles, deux langues avaient été en usage dans les relations internationales : le français et l'anglais.

La conférence de Gênes en comptera une troisième avec la langue italienne, et cette décision, outre qu'elle nécessitera un supplément de personnel, risque de prolonger les débats.

Les Américains resteront-ils sur le Rhin?

Paris, 5 avril. — D'après le « Chicago Tribune », le ministère des affaires étrangères français, a reçu hier un télégramme de Washington dans lequel M. Jusserand, ambassadeur de France aux Etats-Unis, l'informe que devant le ton cordial de la réponse française à la note américaine relative au remboursement des frais d'occupation de l'armée américaine, le gouvernement des Etats-Unis examine à nouveau la question du retrait total des forces américaines du Rhin.

Le général Allen, commandant en chef des troupes américaines d'occupation n'a pas encore reçu l'ordre de retrait total.

"Le général Gouraud à Lyon [General Gouraud in Lyon]", *Lyon Républicain*, 6 April 1922, inv. LR19220406. Courtesy Bibliothèque municipale de Lyon.

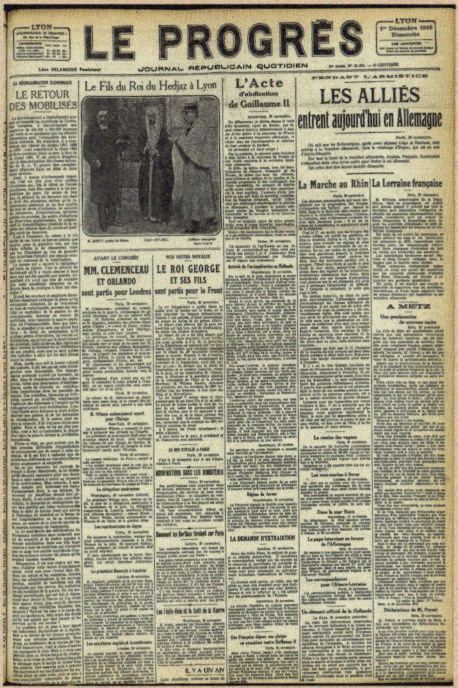

LE PROGRÈS

JOURNAL RÉPUBLICAIN QUOTIDIEN

LE RETOUR DES MOBILISÉS

Le Fils du Roi du Hedjaz à Lyon

L'Acte d'abdication de Guillaume II

LES ALLIÉS entrent aujourd'hui en Allemagne

MM. CLEMENCEAU ET ORLANDO sont partis pour Londres

LE ROI GEORGE ET SES FILS sont partis pour le Front

La Marche au Rhin

La Lorraine française

A METZ

"Le Fils du Roi du Hedjaz à Lyon [The son of the monarch of Hijaz in Lyon]", *Le Progrès* (Lyon), 1 December 1918. Courtesy Bibliothèque municipale de Lyon.

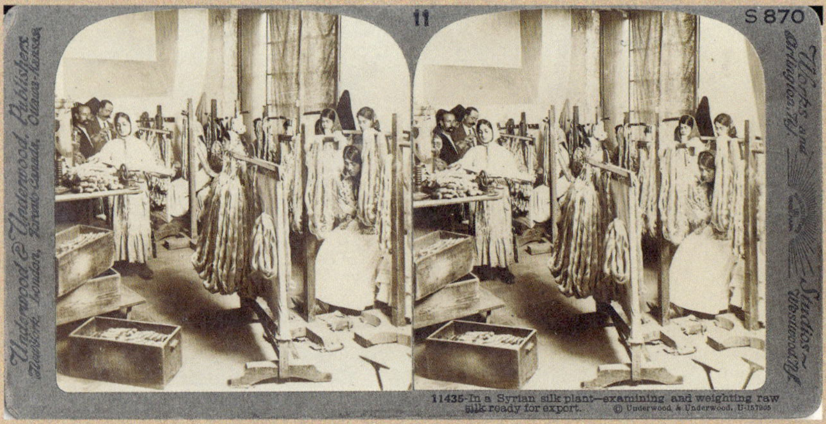

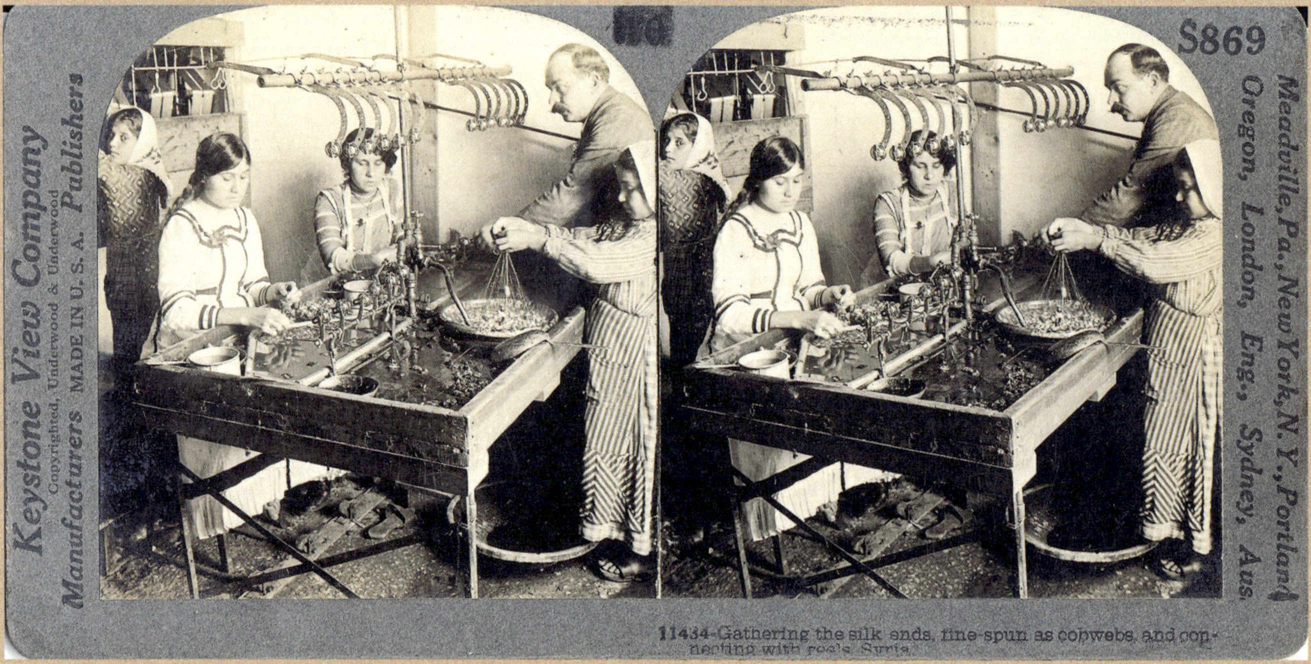

Top Underwood & Underwood (publisher), "In a Syrian silk plant-examining and weighting raw silk ready for export", Syria, 19th century, stereoscopic view, 8.6 x 17.7 cm, inv. 11435 / U157905.

Bottom Keystone View Company (publisher), "Gathering the silk-ends, fine-spun as cobwebs, and connecting with reels", Syria, 19th century, stereoscopic view, 8.6 x 17.7 cm, inv. 11434. Courtesy Philippe Jabre Art Collection.

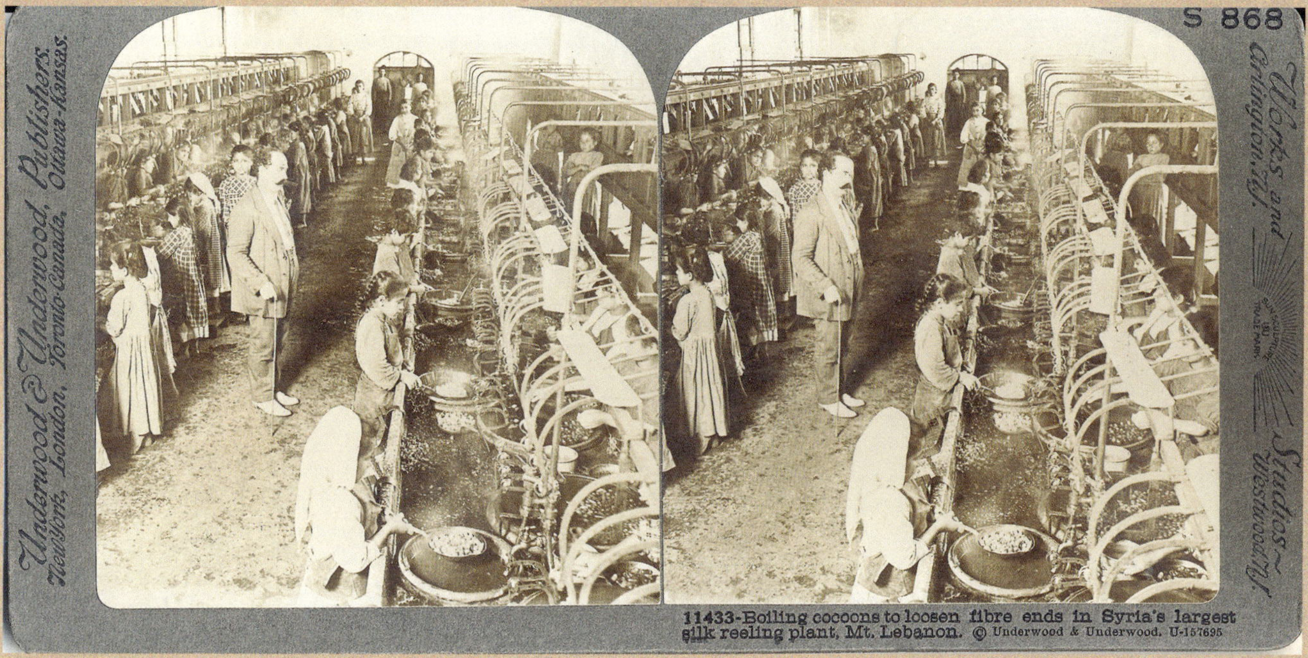

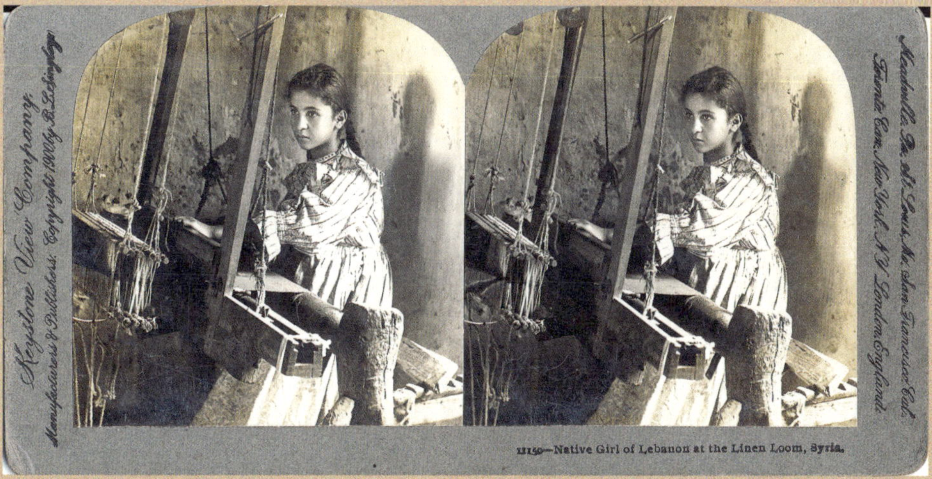

Top Underwood & Underwood (publisher), “Boiling cocoons to loosen fibre ends in Syria's largest silk reeling plant – Mt. Lebanon”, 19th century, stereoscopic view, 8.6 x 17.7 cm, inv. 11433 / U-157695. Courtesy Philippe Jabre Art Collection.

Bottom Keystone View Company (publisher), “Native Girl of Lebanon at the Linen Loom – Syria”, 19th century, stereoscopic view, 8.6 x 17.7 cm, inv. 11150. Courtesy Philippe Jabre Art Collection.

A Chronology of the Historical Events *1625–1943*

Julia Etournay-Lemay

1625

French Jesuit missionaries began their first expedition to the Persian Gulf region, arriving in Aleppo.

1831

The "restored" Society of Jesus was permanently established in Mount Lebanon, with the charge of the Jesuit mission assigned to the province of Lyon. The mission continued to expand further into Syria and the surrounding region.

1836

The first silk spinning mill in Beirut owned by a Lyonnais entrepreneur was founded by the Comte de Laferté.

1838

The Portalis family, in partnership with commercial partners in Lyon, moved their business interests from Alexandria, Egypt, to Mount Lebanon, opening a silk mill in the village of Btetir.

1840

Drômoise female spinners, recruited by the Portalis brothers to work as experienced labourers in their silk mills, arrived in Mount Lebanon.

1842

After sustained clashes between the Druze and Maronite Christians, and under pressure from the French, a "double" qaymaqamate was established in the Mount Lebanon region along sectarian lines.

1853

Jesuit priest Joseph Gemayel founded the Sisters of the Immaculate Conception, known in French as the Mariamettes, for the education of young Lebanese women. It was the first Maronite congregation with an active apostolate.

1860

Escalating violent clashes between Christian and Druze communities precipitated a French intervention ordered by Napoleon III and led by General d'Hautpoul. The autonomous province of Mount Lebanon was founded as a direct result of these events.

1875

The University of Saint Joseph was founded after the Jesuit seminary in Ghazir, founded in 1843 to train local Maronite clergy, was transferred to Beirut.

1902

An observatory, the first in the region, was established in Ksara in the Beqaa Valley by Jesuit monks to monitor rainfall and seismic activity in the region.

1910

Chekri Ganem premiered his play *Antar* at the Théâtre nationale de l'Odéon, which was turned into an opera by Gabriel Dupont in 1921.

Chabrières, Morel et Cie. brought a suit against G. Malpertuy, director of the company's spinning mill, accusing him of theft and bankruptcy.

1914–1918

First World War

The outbreak of the First World War precipitated what became known as the Great Famine of Mount Lebanon (1915–1918), which led to numerous deaths and a significant wave of immigration; almost 30 percent of the population left the country, particularly for North and South America. It also catalysed the fall of the Ottoman Empire, which had governed Lebanon since 1516.

1918

Establishment of the Lyonnais Committee for French Interests in Syria

The Committee originally included 15 members from various French institutions in Lebanon who were also eminent figures from the city of Lyon, including politicians like Edouard Herriot, silk mill owners like Ennemond Morel, academics and clergymen like the Jesuit historian Paul Huvelin, industrialists like Joseph Gillet, and representatives of the Chamber of Commerce – Jean Coignet, in particular. In 1919, the Committee organised a Congress on Syria in partnership with the Chamber of Commerce of Marseille.

1919

Investigative mission to Syria

A mission financed by the Chambers of Commerce of Lyon and Marseille was initiated to "explore [the virgin lands] and undertake a methodical exploration of Syria, from both an economic and scientific perspective".

1919–1922

High-Commissionership of General Henri Gouraud

8 March 1920 Emir Faisal was declared constitutional king of the Arab Kingdom of Syria by the Syrian National Congress government led by Hashim al-Atassi.

1 September 1920 With the French Mandate awarded by the League of Nations, French General Henri Gouraud proclaimed the establishment of the State of Greater Lebanon, beginning the mandate system of government.

1923

The League of Nations extended the further administration of Syria and Alexandretta, including territories of present-day Lebanon, to the French Mandate.

1939–1945

Second World War

1943 After the election of Bechara al-Khoury as president, the Constitution of Lebanon was amended to abolish the French Mandate, leading to the unilateral declaration of Lebanon's independence.

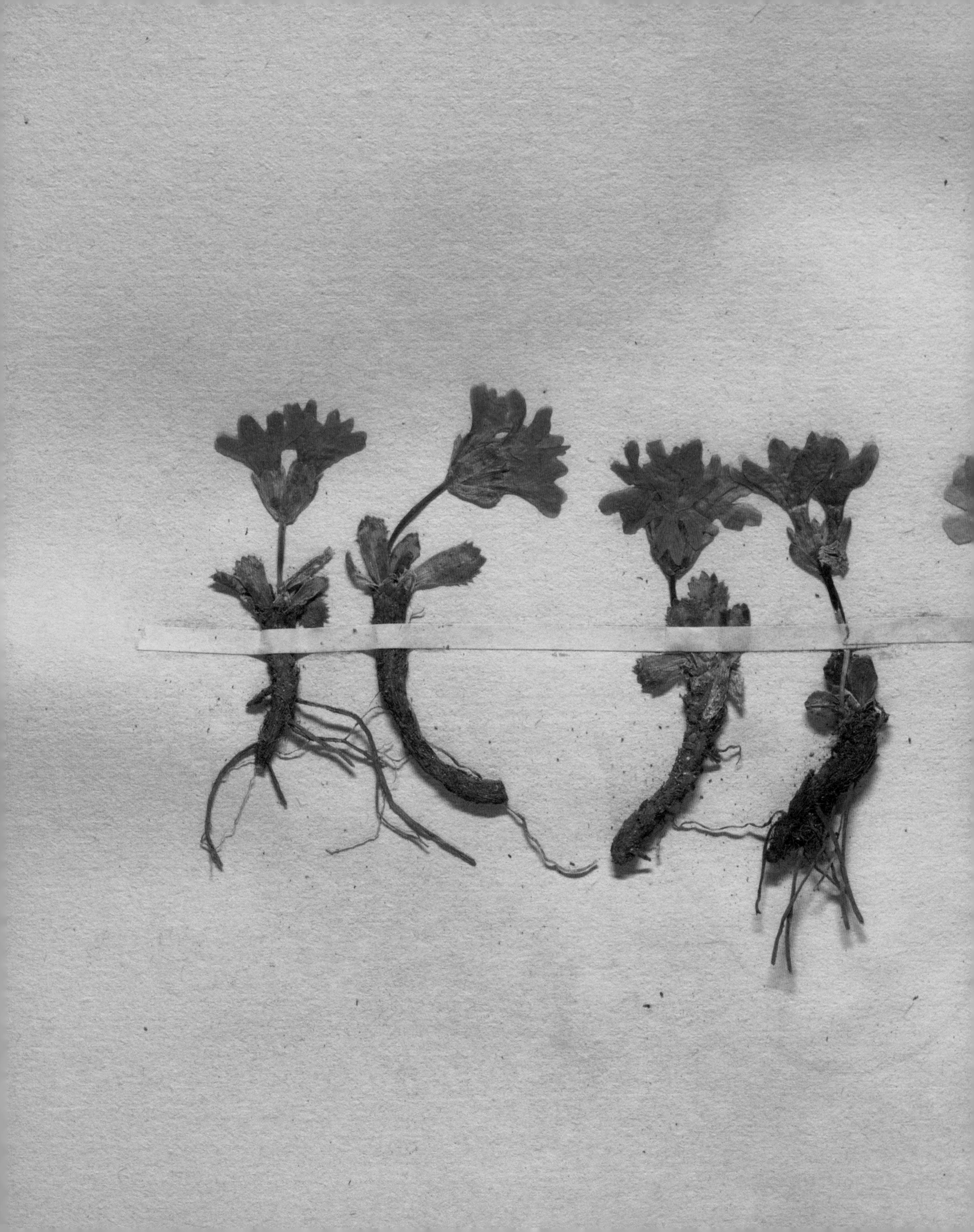

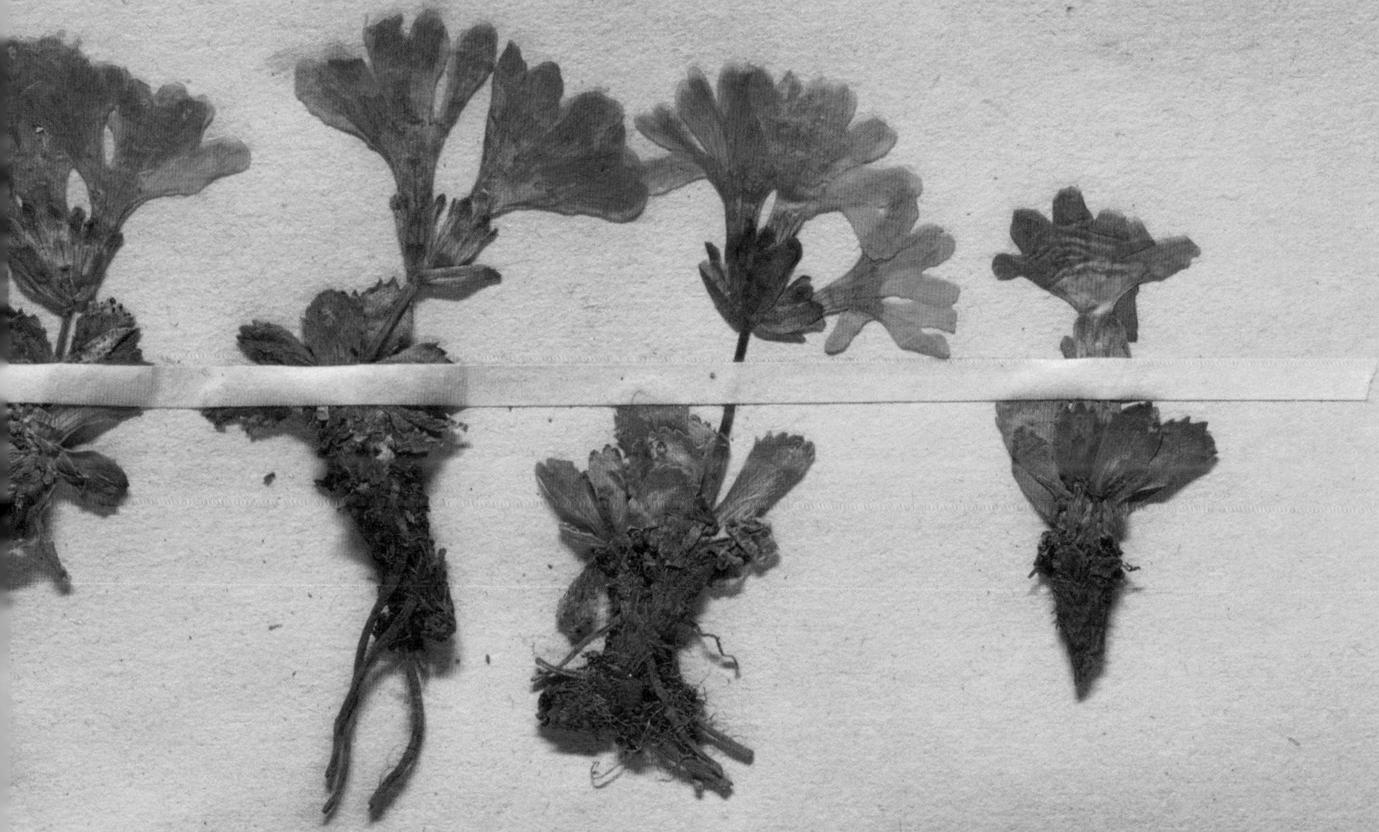

Hanging on a Silk Thread

Recollection(s) of Lebanon

Text by
Julia Etournay-Lemay

1 September 1920 is a day that the Lebanese have awaited eagerly for years – and which the newspapers have announced with great pomp. People are finally speaking of Lebanon, independent from Syria. People are even speaking of Greater Lebanon. How could this not be a proud moment? How could it be helped, giving hopes over to the winds of change? After all, these words seem to reflect reality. To celebrate the event, General Gouraud has gone above and beyond what is customary. He wears his formal white suit reserved for important occasions. He has reviewed the seating plan over and over again. The tables are decorated with floral centrepieces, and Residence des Pins smells entirely clean and fresh. The General's conscience is more at peace than ever. Earlier in the day, he delivered a speech that would mark not only his career but the history of an entire country, he is sure of it. He was encircled by Beirut's most influential journalists and surrounded by important French and Lebanese elites. The intonation of his voice when he said, "The great day has come," had quite the effect! And: "the warm heart of this country beats in Lebanon and its mountains" – what a choice of words! He had not come up with that one himself, of course, but the delivery was his; he had made it his own. No doubt about it, his High Commissionership will be one for the history books.

Tonight the only thing coming out of the residence's Salon de Provence is the hearty laughter of the guests: exultant, perhaps simply drunk, but filled in any event with the sensation of having made history. Like all important historical events, this one too is made up of smaller stories: tales my grandmother told me when I was a child. Where did she get them? I never found out. But I would like to think that she was Madame Gouraud's chambermaid, and she heard it all from her privileged observation post. If you are not afraid of the clouds of cigar smoke, let's put on our evening wear and step inside the General's residence to hear the snippets of these accounts more clearly.

The predominant voice in the sitting room belongs to Father Cattin. An incorrigible chatterbox and a renowned Jesuit priest, he is the rector of the University of Saint Joseph – the most prestigious university in Beirut – and delights in recounting how the origin of the French presence in Lebanon is both Jesuit and Lyonnais. The fellow proudly recalls how a small number of missionaries from Lyon departed to evangelise Lebanon and Syria beginning in the 17th century. Was it a desire for adventure? Encounters with a new place and people? The prospect of rapid conversions? Or perhaps the sincere drive of a boundless faith? It is certain that they set off from Marseille in 1625 and founded several institutions in Mount Lebanon where their flocks in need of evangelisation resided. It was also the place best suited for Europeans accustomed to the temperate French climate. But these pioneers did not have the time to settle down permanently. The hostility directed at them by the local populations and, more importantly, problems within the Jesuit order itself sent them back to France.

Father Cattin has brought with him a young priest with a bright future who is looking to take his first steps out into the wider world. Though, unfortunately for him, none of the guests seem to have bothered to ask for his name, the young man is a veritable fount of knowledge:

> "In the early 19th century, Lebanon's appeal was still very real in France. The Lazarists had been the first to renew the attempted religious conquest of Lebanon with the support of the French government. They often took over our old, abandoned Jesuit institutions. We, or our illustrious predecessors, soon followed these Lazarists, though we did not benefit from the same outright political support. Nevertheless, we founded six seminaries in Bikfaya, Ghazir, Zahlé, Deir al-Qamar, Sidon and lastly Beirut. The Company then sought to delegate the foreign missions to its regional branches, which was a golden opportunity for Fourvière, headquarters of the Jesuit province of Lyon. In 1834, Lyon officially found itself in charge of the Syrian mission."

Father Cattin interrupts, maybe afraid of being outshined by his protégé:

> "The Jesuits were quickly accepted by the Lebanese and Syrian populations, it's a fact! Our success was the result of offering increasingly diversified services that were specifically suited to each territory: from orphanages for poor children to seminaries designed for a privileged audience seeking to open doors to prestigious posts in the local administration. We even founded

> institutions for girls! And, given that our great open-mindedness is proverbial, you must know that, more than any others, we welcomed the vocations of Lebanese women desirous of taking holy orders by creating "indigenous" branches. The Mariamettes are our greatest success. Did you know that some were refused admission due to an overabundance of candidates? Not so common, nowadays! They opened one structure after another, though this was not always to the liking of the still very masculine – and European – Jesuit administration."

Madame Gouraud greatly enjoyed this final barb, and her eyes, if I'm not mistaken, seemed to gaze at our Reverend Father with great tenderness.

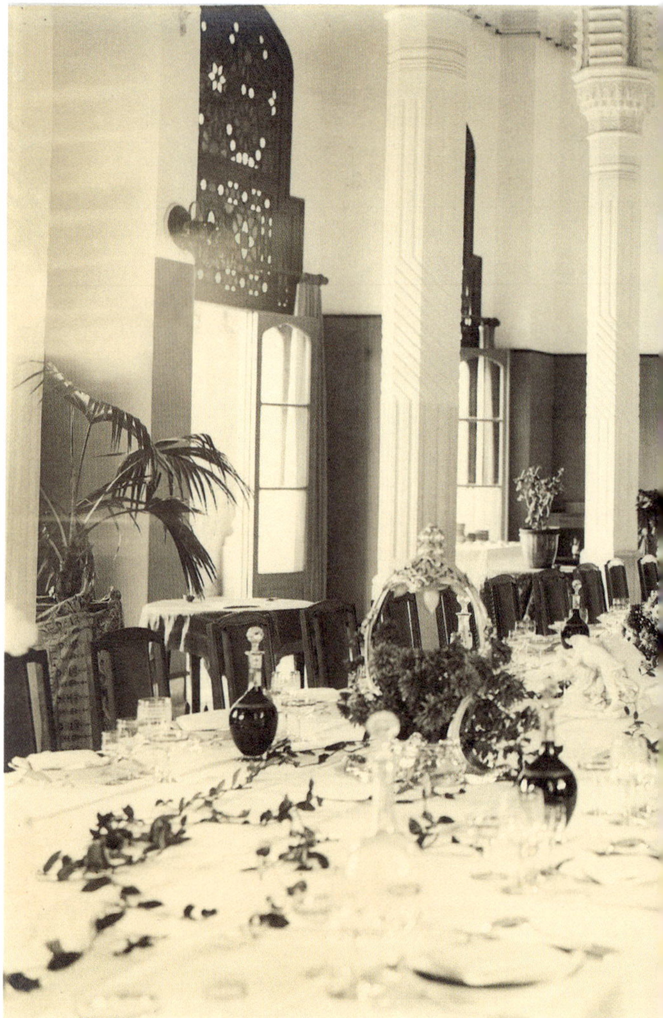

Monsignor Hoyek is also following the conversation with great interest. A skilful politician himself, he is not a friend of Gouraud. The host was forced to invite him this evening because he is an indispensable ally. And for good reason. He is the head of the Maronite Church that championed the foundation of a State of Greater Lebanon. Despite his piercing stare and long, intimidating beard, he is known to all the Christians of Lebanon and elsewhere for his unshakable optimism. Here is his reaction to Father Cattin's words:

> "What most impressed the Arabs was the Jesuits' heroic conduct during the various anti-Christian revolts in Mount Lebanon. The entire period from 1842 to 1860 was marked by exceptional violence! Thanks be to God that your priests opened their doors and took in our poor Christian disciples, who had been chased off their lands."

Monsignor Hoyek knew these events well. In 1860, he was 17 years old. He had entered the Ghazir seminary the year before and remembered the distraught faces of the women collapsing from panic and fatigue on the institution's front steps. He also recalled the arrival of the French, gleaming on horseback in the middle of August. Despite the heat, the populations had gathered around the port to witness their arrival. The fighting had, of course, already ceased by this time, which led some to doubt the humanitarian motivations of the French and accuse them of coming merely to reaffirm their economic interests. Convinced of the goodness of their hearts, Hoyek had defended them and blamed the rough seas for delaying the expedition's arrival through no fault of their own.

Monsignor Hoyek is suddenly wrested from his thoughts by Albert Potton, Vice-Consul of France in Antioch, who weighs in. Secretly anti-clerical like his mother, he cannot bear such a lengthy intervention by the churchmen and is eager to remind everyone that if the French were here in Lebanon, it was because some illustrious ancestors – Lyonnais, it's true, but absolutely secular – had the good sense to see the potential of this beautiful country:

"It was a real opportunity. The silkworm harvests were excellent. And it wasn't like it is now, labour was much cheaper! The Portalis brothers from Marseille were among the first to come. The youngest of them seemed to have been no less brilliant than the eldest. That is what people said, anyhow. I myself never had the chance to be introduced to them. Beginning in 1838, Fortuné's letters, which were preserved at the Consulate, requested the French consul's protection in the establishment of a silk mill. Once this was in place, Portalis set about looking for low-wage workers who were sufficiently experienced to begin production immediately, as well as to train the rest of the workforce. It was then that he had an idea: to bring in female spinners from Lyon and its surrounding region. The idea was a good one on paper, but it didn't take into account the character of the girl recruits. One of them was a real troublemaker, but I just can't remember her name. Lucie? Lise?"

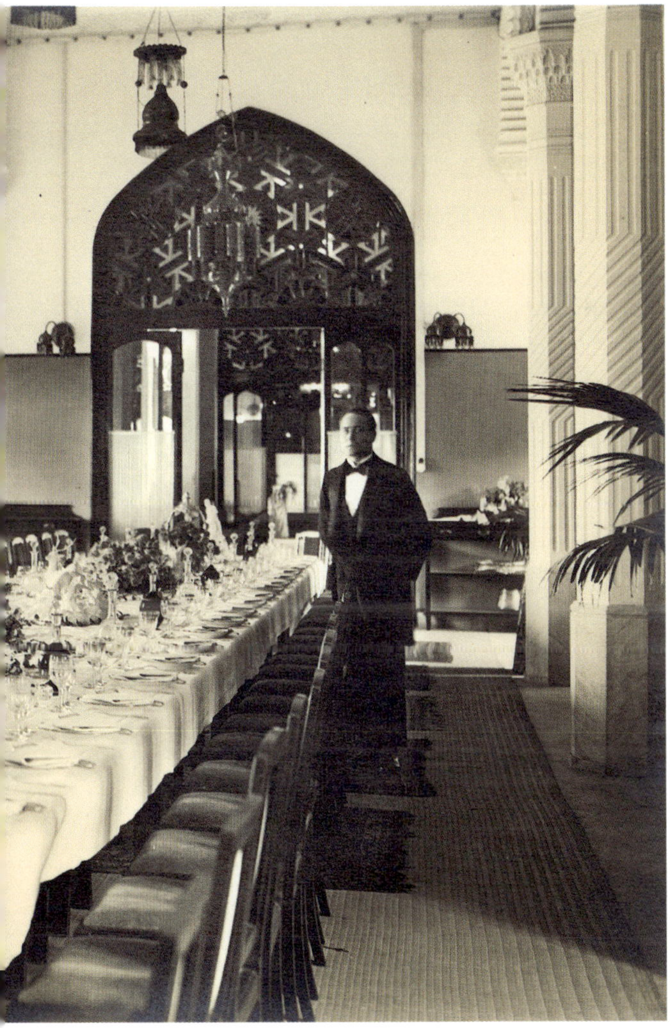

Beirut: Dining hall of the northeast salon, Résidence des Pins, 1 January 1920, inv. A004967. Gouraud collection. Centre des Archives diplomatiques de La Courneuve.

"Louise. Louise Brunet," says a voice from the other side of the sitting room. It belongs to Charles Croizat: director of the renowned Veuve Guérin et Fils spinning mill in al-Qrayye, member of the Chamber of Commerce of Lyon and privileged confidante of all of Mount Lebanon's Lyonnais mill owners. His talents as an orator and schemer made him the go-to man for sensitive negotiations and other assorted swindles among all the Frenchmen in Lebanon. Thus, he is well-versed in his colleagues' secrets. The story of Louise Brunet had left a particular mark on him, because it allowed him to poke fun at Portalis, his great rival.

Madame Gouraud quickly throws him a better one: "Since you have interrupted our friend Albert and seem familiar with the story, do share it with us. You've piqued my curiosity."

"I'll try my best to satisfy you, Madame," replies Charles Croizat, standing up, adjusting his suit and clearing his throat, well aware that all eyes were fixed on him:

"Among these Drômois spinners was Louise Brunet, a young woman of eighteen with a well-tempered character. In 1839, when she had just been released from prison – probably due to her involvement in the silk workers' revolt – she crossed paths with a certain Clément Dreveton, whose daughter, I believe, is one of your friends, Madame Gouraud, is she not? No? What a pity. The fact remains that Dreveton, appointed by one of the Portalis brothers, promised the girl heaven and earth in Lebanon: a stable situation, assured income, lodgings and a complete change of scenery. She didn't hesitate for long. Ultimately, she knew she'd exposed herself too much in the silk workers' revolts to ever find work again in France, and at any rate, she hoped to find better working and living conditions. So she followed Clément Dreveton to Marseille, recruiting other spinners from the Drôme region en route."

"But problems weren't long in coming," Potton interrupts, and continues:

> "The embarkation on the *Héliopolis*, the brig that was to take them from Marseille to Beirut, had its hiccups. Two of the women had brought their children, which didn't go over well with the captain. Complicating things further, the latter was seduced by Louise, whose scandalous behaviour throughout the journey I won't get into. If you could only imagine the obscenities I chanced to read in the legal documents conserved at the Consulate! Indeed, Portalis was obliged to file suit against his henchman when the latter had a great deal of difficulty prying Louise away from the captain."

Charles Croizat, who certainly knows the importance of tugging on heartstrings to liven up a story and win over his audience, chimes in with further details:

> "My friends, you must imagine what this journey represented for these girls in an extremely precarious situation! Dreveton shamelessly exploited their state of wanting to "make a deal" with them. He sold them clothing and articles of personal hygiene, as well as the materials necessary for their work as silk spinners: bobbins of thread, pins, needles, skeins of silk, an apron, ribbons, Mulhouse Indian-style fabric, slippers, even combs. While Clotilde Damar, one of the spinners, was eventually able to pay Dreveton back, this was not the case for her co-worker Marie Gay, so young and fragile, who died from the plague before managing to settle her debts after just a few months in Lebanon."

Charles takes a long dramatic pause, during which his sombre expression takes in each and every member of his audience. Everyone was hanging on his every word. Nevertheless, he has yet to arouse the empathy of these men who believe they saw in Dreveton an innate sense of business rather than any sort of cruelty. Yet he didn't give up, determined to present an accurate picture of the situation of these girls whom, in the last analysis, he admired, though he would never admit it. He continued:

> "The girls were put up in a large dormitory within the spinning mill itself. But Louise Brunet soon grew disillusioned with a situation she had fantasised over – the naïvete of youth! The working conditions were, it must be said, deplorable, and hygiene was completely lacking. They were required to work thirteen hours a day in summer and winter, in poorly lit rooms with no air circulation that were far too small for the 70 to 80 spinners. It was suffocatingly hot. All day long the girls plunged their bare hands into the boiling water made more caustic through the use of corrosives. The smell of dead larvae mixed with chemical products certainly overwhelmed the fragrance of the surrounding pine forests."

"Didn't I hear that the old Portalis was quite the scoundrel?" ventured Madame Gouraud, who seemed to be the only one moved by these words.

"What do you expect? Business is business!" interjects Potton, garnering the

General's look of approval, going on:

> "A climate of fear reigned in the Portalis mill, and our Drômoise spinners bore the consequences of it, as well as the young recruits from the orphanage adjacent to the mill—"

"Who were mostly under the age of eight," Charles interrupts, engaged in a relentless struggle for the success of his story, and continues:

> "The conditions were so bad that the heads of the orphanage regularly helped the young girls escape! Imagine yourself under constant surveillance by men crouching in the shadows, ready to leap up at the tiniest broken thread and confiscate your entire day's salary – and with no mercy, for this is how they made their living! And I won't even get into the nocturnal intrusions of ill-intentioned men in the dormitories."

"Yet back then, this system aroused the admiration of all European spinning mill owners, pointing to it to explain the production's quality," Potton adds.

"Our dear colleague Ennemond Morel, who visited the mill several years ago, said himself that such very low salaries would no longer be acceptable, neither there nor anywhere else," adds General Gouraud without looking up from the pipe he carefully lights.

The more attentive guests might have heard Madame Gouraud swearing to herself after all these revelations that she would never again wear her blue silk dress out of solidarity. A heavy silence falls on the other members of the gathering. It is unclear if it is caused by Charles Croizat's stirring account or by the whiskey the guests are sipping. A book in Madame Gouraud's library in the next room happens to provide further insight into the Lyonnais spinning mills in Lebanon and is worth a look during this momentary pause. The following passage is of particular interest:

> "Competition was stiff among the spinning mills established in Mount Lebanon. To assure the stability of his personnel, but also to impede acts of rebellion, Portalis chose to recruit only girls of around seven whom he trained and kept at his Btetir mill, bound by contracts that could only be broken by marriage, which often occurred around age 16, or through the payment of an enormous indemnity, which he knew these young girls' families could not afford. During the first year, the girls helped with more menial tasks at the mill, collecting rainwater or snow to fill the tubs and observing the work of their older colleagues. Eventually they worked at a reduced spinning speed in a "drying-room school" under the supervision of a veteran spinner. Portalis thus made sure that the silk they created was of the highest quality despite the young girls' lack of experience.
>
> "In other mills, the majority of the children came from adjacent orphanages, such as the one run by Sister Gélas, a Lyon native affiliated with the Lazarists, where the girls worked for free. At the boarding school of the Sisters of

Charity, located near the Veuve Guérin et Fils mill in al-Qrayye, the system was even more perverse. The girls received a salary that was intentionally kept far below the price of their room and board. Families thus could not remove their young daughters without having to settle a debt that increased with each passing day. If a family found out about the swindle and tried to reclaim their child, mill owners did not hesitate to use immoral means, kidnapping the young girls or destroying account books to get rid of evidence. Escape was therefore the only solution; assisted by the Mariamette Sisters, who were Lebanese Jesuits, many young spinners disappeared during Sunday strolls.

"All resistance was generally kept in check. Nevertheless, a certain Louise Brunet, a native of the Drôme region, supposedly fomented a revolt in the Portalis mill before running off. Such outright opposition to the European spinning mill system was unique, but just because she was the only one to claim her right to dignity loud and clear does not mean that other attempts did not take place – at least for those who know how to spot them. From lawsuits by spinners who weren't paid by mill owners to direct confrontations that degenerated into violent clashes, it is certain that the spinners did not hold their tongues or their hands. However, the mill owners were powerful and protected by the French Consulate, and they always prevailed. A man like Culty, whose employees had the audacity to cast doubt on his morality, pushed this deviousness to the point of taking them to court for defamation.

"Spinners needed to be clever to turn the situation to their advantage. Since there were no written contracts, many fled from their mills and joined others offering higher wages, and returned when the situation was no longer as favourable. This created a genuine market of supply and demand. When the mill owners became privy to this strategy, they hurried to demand regulations from the French Consulate to protect their interests, leading to the introduction of written contracts. These agreements provided that in cases of flight, fugitive spinners would be punished and not the mill owners who needed to attract new workers for their factories."

But let's put down this book before we lose track of the time. I hear the party starting up again in Monsieur Gouraud's sitting room and we should hurry back.

General Gouraud's friends have been waiting for this moment the whole evening: the guest of honour, Monsieur Chekri Ganem, has sat down at the piano. The most prominent man in Paris's artistic milieux for the last ten years, Ganem is a master at seducing his audience. He is also an ardent defender of Lebanese autonomy against the Turkish authorities. This struggle has earned him the admiration of his fellow citizens and the not disinterested friendship of French dignitaries. Born in Beirut, he was exiled at the beginning of the war. This evening marks his long-awaited return as an artist. He has prepared a special piece for the occasion: his tragedy *Antar*, which was adapted as an opera by the famous composer Gabriel Dupont six years earlier, and was never performed. Yet Chekri adores the candour of the emotions that each cadence produces and the discreet oriental colour that the vocal exercises and choruses provide. The excerpts he has chosen to play this evening are tender, fragile tunes, so fragile that, upon contact with the tympanum, you almost fear they might break, like the health of his friend Gabriel, whose death has forced the composer to live in isolation. The power of the music cannot be translated into words, but the assembled guests, who sink slowly into the velvet of the armchairs, seem completely enthralled by the journey.

The music appears to have aroused the guests' nostalgia – or could it be one of the rare subjects that can unite such diverse personalities? Whatever the case, our friends, as soon as the applause has finished, cannot help invoking their glorious pasts:

> "Ah, we never got bored back in the old days! And there was a solidarity that's lacking now. Yes sir, in the milieu – the silk manufacturing milieu, of course – we were like a family! It made us stronger. Take Portalis, since you mentioned him earlier: His sister was married to the Count de La Ferté, and his daughter to Bataille, two of our most illustrious predecessors."

"What made us strong most of all was our fathers' integration in local life!" chimes in a small man, Tabet, a Lebanese mill owner who works closely with the French, who continues:

> "Your famous Portalis made generous donations for the construction of the European hospital of Beirut, serving French interests first and foremost. He also lent a hand in the reconstruction of the city after the bombardment of 1840."

It should be noted that the greatest power of the mill owners, at least from my perspective, was their positions as judge-assessors or legal experts in judicial matters, which made them the masters of verdicts affecting their colleagues. This was true even when, at the same time, they had been indicted in other cases, notably for fraud.

General Gouraud, who seemed amused by the previous exchanges, decides that it is nevertheless time to remind these men that they would be nothing without his help. Without the aid of the Consulate, that is. But when it comes right down to it, what's the difference? He explains that the silk merchants even back then, received significant support from the French Consulate. He tells how the latter was the sole interlocutor capable of standing up to the Sublime Porte, which would have loved to restrict the French mill owners' privileges. He recalls:

> "On numerous occasions the Turks tried taxing our mill owners, unsuccessfully, even though the Lebanese themselves were taxed. It was a relentless struggle, and an endless one at that."

An outside observer might find this mention of the conflict between the Lebanese and French authorities profoundly ironic, especially at a dinner celebrating the collaboration that led to the foundation of a new state. Fortunately, such soirées only bring together the converts of a single faith, without a chuckle escaping our guests.

Gouraud continues his sermon. Since the 1840s, he recounts, the situation in Mount Lebanon has grown tense – he wasn't there, but he must have studied the files of his predecessors quite closely. Despite the arrest of some of the leaders, the Europeans were no longer welcome. The customs office carried out constant searches, raids and inventories in the spinning mills, while the city governors and the pashas obstructed any attempt to modernise these facilities. The General was particularly struck by the customs office's habit of sequestering European imports; for someone like him who ate nothing but dried Drôme apricots for breakfast, this would have been extremely bothersome!

Henri Pharaon, seated right in front of him, has had all the apricots he can stomach. The product of an incredibly rich Lebanese family that built its fortune in banking since the Middle Ages, and more recently through the sale of silk cocoons on behalf of European silk manufacturers, he has never wanted for anything. Come to think of it, there was one thing: he dreams of being a member of the exclusive group of these European mill owners. His father raised him with an awareness for hierarchy and passed on to him this maxim: He who wishes to command must pass himself off as submissive. Nonsense! Henri would like to enjoy the same honours, which is why he did not hesitate for a second to come this evening, even if he knew that his father would have looked down on him for it. Henri promised himself not to get agitated no matter what the French said about the "Arabs" and that he would model his own behaviour on that of his neighbours. At this point in the evening, the observational period has finished and he feels ready to imitate them:

> "I remember a time when the situation was particularly delicate in the 1850s, or sometime then, and up to the eve of the First World War. The conflict focused on the tithe applied to fresh cocoons. The customs office sequestered all the silk from mills that had not paid this tax, and we all know how inflexible the schedule is for sending silk to Europe. The entire production could have been squandered! The mill owners rose up. They wrote that they hadn't paid this tithe for 40 years—"

Approving shouts of "That's exactly right!" and "Well said!" escape some of the guests.

> "—and that they had no intention of starting now."

Henri is proud of his little gesture, but it doesn't last. General Gouraud is rolling his eyes. *What ingrates!* he thinks to himself. *Ingrates who only act out of self-interest and never remember all the help I gave them.* He calls an end to this generalised outpouring of nostalgia: "But in the end the French Consulate succeeded in negotiating the silk's departure by underlining the economic repercussions for Lebanon."

Henri does not concede defeat so easily:

> "With your permission, General, it cannot be denied that the Ottomans would not have accepted the silk's departure without the intervention of Europe's merchants, who showed the extent to which their personal interests were at stake. What is more, even they could not make the Ottomans renounce

the strict conditions on this cleared export. Mill owners had to be able to provide a certificate confirming the Lebanese origin of the silk. This made it nearly impossible for mill owners who had been trading contraband, who then had to lower their production costs with foreign silks of poor quality."

So far, Henri's plan is unfolding perfectly. But he has become carried away and, despite himself, adds a mischievous remark, gazing at the other guests with sparkling eyes:

"Merchants like yourselves certainly did try to circumvent the law time and time again. Mourgue d'Algue and Ladreyt, for example, among your predecessors, embezzled and speculated on the privileges that the customs office granted them. You should have seen them – the customs office was furious! Others attempted to load their silk onto ships in secret without paying their duties. They certainly didn't lack imagination. But Rostand's attempt was not soon forgotten. A customs officer had been shot, after all. No one was joking about that at the time, let me assure you. This dramatic episode gave rise to dispatches condemning the European merchants and calling for the destruction of all the spinning mills!"

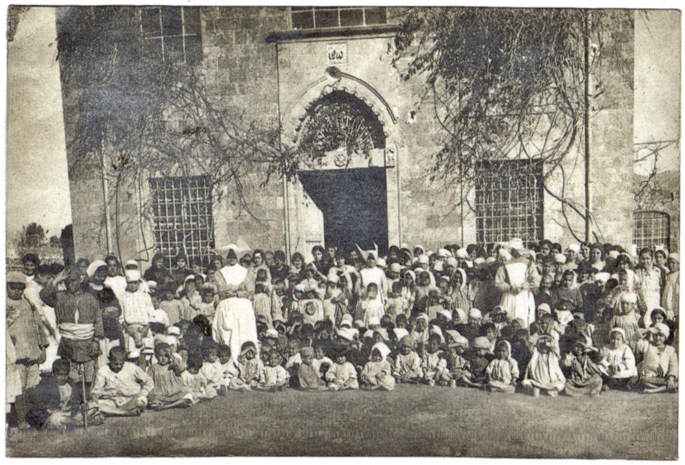

"When it comes right down to it, my friend, the fraud of French mill owners pales in comparison to the fraud of the Arabs!" Potton replies, and continues:

"Do you remember Toubia and Asfar? Those two Lebanese sold their cocoons to all the French mill owners, asking for advances. But they were using this money to run their own spinning mill! They never delivered the promised cocoons and, in debt up to their necks, continued doing business as though nothing had happened."

Ennemond Morel agrees, speaking as heir to the great Chabrières, Morel et Cie, the successors of Arlès Dufour. "We ourselves paid the price for this Arab mentality, going on ten years ago now," he says gravely and goes on:

"Our old partner Guillaume Malpertuy had French blood, exclusively, but it seems clear that being born under the sun and pines was enough to turn him into a thief! This despicable individual represented us in Lebanon and we trusted him entirely. We provided him with the money necessary for the purchase of cocoons, the functioning of the heating tubs and the spinning, as well as the relations with the brokers in Lebanon! Now, you might say that we shouldn't have given him so much responsibility, but it happened gradually over time. First, he grew vague in the details he gave us, responding to our dispatches only periodically. Do you know what we eventually discovered?

Mount Lebanon, *The famine in Lebanon*, ca. 1915–1918, photograph taken by the French army, inv. A004575. Courtesy Archives du Ministère de l'Europe et des Affaires Etrangères.

> He used all the funds we sent him for his own mill! You have no idea what turmoil we faced for the many long months of this affair. Never again shall we repeat the mistake of trusting the natives of this country."

All the guests nod approvingly, scandalised. Among them is Henri Pharaon, his cheeks blushing.

The silence that follows is nonetheless quickly broken by our dear fount of knowledge, the young Jesuit who was among the first to speak this evening, and who is finding it difficult to keep silent for much longer. After an inner struggle to restrain the flood of knowledge burning his lips, he cries out despite himself. "The economic stakes are nothing compared to science!" he exclaims. With all the looks searching for the source of this voice, given that everyone had forgotten his presence, he comes up with something that everyone can agree on:

> "What I mean to say is that they go hand in hand. The Chamber of Commerce and Industry of Lyon drives the advance of science. It was, correct me if I'm wrong, at the forefront of all scholarly studies on Lebanese silkworms. The latter's vitality was so highly reputed that samples were taken to try to introduce its cultivation in France's African colonies. The Prefecture of Ardèche even appealed to the Chamber of Commerce to help obtain enough specimens in the goal of improving the French races."

At this point Father Cattin finds a perfect transition to direct the conversation back to the Jesuits' work:

> "You forgot to mention the observatory of Ksara! Yes, yet another of our creations. It was long one of the most powerful in Europe. They would calculate the weather for weeks in advance, observing the sky every night before it became a telecommunications antenna, because yes, one must adapt to one's time. This is also what we've done with the University of Saint Joseph, which is why it still stands today and, I might add, at the centre of Lebanese higher education. I'm not sure if people still know, but it arose from the transfer of the Ghazir seminary in 1875. This university meets the demand for the education of the children of the Lebanese elite, but it also successfully competes with the American influence, increasing its number of students as well as its educational offerings. The seminary has turned into a veritable university with a growing number of faculties: the Faculty of Theology, of course, but also that of Medicine, which owes its creation to the University of Lyon and provides the chance for a true collaboration. Lyonnais professors come to teach in Beirut, while Lebanese students can complete part of their curriculum in Lyon. Next came the Faculty of Oriental Studies, an institution unique to Saint Joseph's. Then, a few years ago, the Faculties of Law and Engineering opened and once again showed the decisive contributions of Lyon. Their creation required the foundation of an association – the Lyonnais Association for the Development Abroad of Higher and Technical Education – at the head of which we once again find our friends, the silk mill owners. What is more, we have not forgotten our

compatriots: the children of French functionaries, including your own, benefit from advantages, such as admission without application and a preferential tuition rate. In doing so we aim to express our thanks."

If you think Father Cattin would have made a better head of propaganda than a warm-up act, you are absolutely right. I even saw Madame Gouraud fight back a yawn, and the members of the Committee have begun talking more or less discreetly among themselves. In fact, as at all dinner parties where not all guests know each other, groups have formed. Gouraud shines at the centre. Father Cattin and the young Jesuit speak on the side, reacting every now and then to the exchanges of the university's eminent professors who remain within earshot. The Lebanese sheikhs and notables converse in low voices. Lastly, a rather heterogeneous group attracts our attention: the "Committee", as its members call it. Its full name is the Lyonnais Committee for French Interests in Syria, and it was founded in 1919 to safeguard French commercial and political interests following the First World War in Syria and especially in Lebanon. Presiding over it is Ennemond Morel, one of the guests at this prestigious dinner, who comes from a great Lyonnais family of mill owners, a detail revealing much about the Committee's ambitions. Also among its members are Henri Terrail, mill owner and president of the Union of Silk Merchants, as well as Guérin and Mourgue d'Algue. But there are also professors from the Universities of Lyon and Saint Joseph like Paul Huvelin and Jean Lépine – who didn't join them this evening, and the indispensable Auguste Isaac and Édouard Herriot, to name only a few.

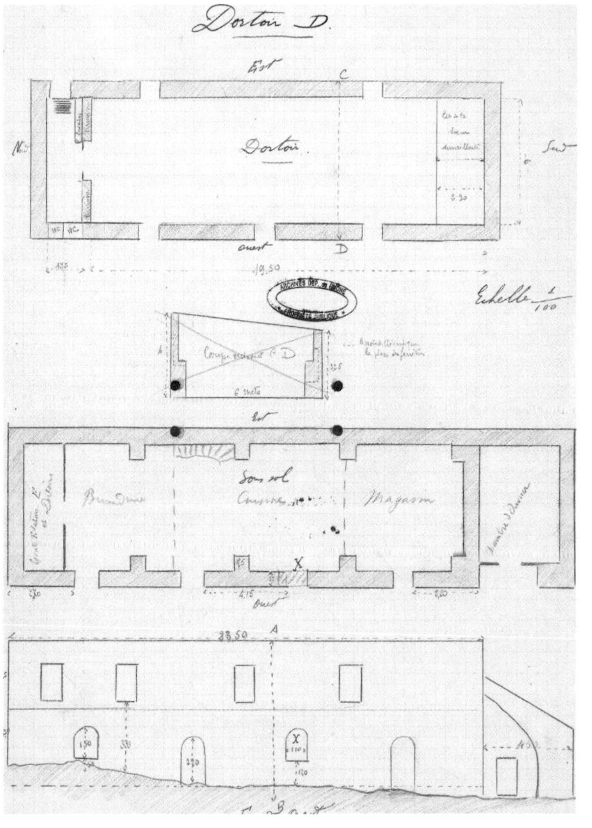

General Gouraud's reception seems to mirror these bonds that united Lebanon and the capital of the Gauls – the Lyonnais were certainly well represented among the guests. Whether he is trying to please them or is sincerely nostalgic, the Parisian General suddenly waxes poetic on the beauty of the city of Lyon, remarking, "Those red roofs, those shades of ochre on the facades, the great Tête d'Or Park… You can't help being seduced by the 'City of Scamps'!"

"Have you travelled there often, General?" asks Father Cattin.

Gouraud replies:

"I've actually just returned, dear friend! I was admirably welcomed last November by the Chamber of Commerce and Lyon's most eminent figures. At the time, we discussed the Syrian problem at length, and I believe I can humbly affirm before you that I resolved it. I had promised to work with all my heart and soul for French commerce in Syria and its perpetuity, and look where we are today – is it not fantastic?"

Veuve Guérin et Fils, Floor plan, cross-section and elevation of dormitory D of the factory at al-Qrayye, ca. 1909. Arch. dép. Rhône, 145J169.

Cattin offers:

> "General, I must tell you that your voice still resonates in me. Your speech about the indomitable courage of the Frenchman in Syria was truly moving. Unlike this supposed Prince of the Hejaz – you know the one, who claims to be the defender of all Arabia. Please! He came one year before you with nothing more than his colourful costumes and princely title to attract attention. Fortunately, all the craze surrounding him is now over and done with. That will teach him to court the English over our France, which has done so much for the Middle East."
>
> "Are you referring to Emir Faisal?" Potton cuts in, adding:
>
> "When I think that we gave him every honour. The Prefect of the Rhone made the trip in person to accompany him to visit the silk mills and military factories. Yet Faisal preferred to stay in his room rather than attend the exhibitions of the aeroplanes and machine guns. These Arabs have no sense of priorities. All they care about is entertainment – ridiculous! – to spend the evening at the opera with his retinue in boxes decorated in the colours of his country. There is no shortage of volunteers! General, I can only thank you for getting rid of him. Today, this joke of an *emir-midon* is surely selling peanuts on the café terraces."

Gouraud cracks a smile at this witticism. He is already dreaming of his next triumphant entrance into the thousand-year-old city. The speeches he would give about his victory in Syria already seem to be materialising before him. He will meet with the CCI , but also with the Union of Combatants and even with the banks. He will make himself indispensable, advancing elegantly between the sky-blue rows formed by the officers' uniforms beneath the lofting strains of the "Marseillaise". The memory of the glorious Faisal, and with it the risk of being overshadowed by him, would finally be no more.

Let's leave the General to his sweet dreams. I cannot help noting an omission on this day of celebration: discussion of the war. Is the memory perhaps still too fresh? All the privations and fears seemed to have branded the foreheads of the Lebanese. As foreigners, the missionaries were forced to return to Beirut. Once there, the army commandeered their convents and colleges. Many fathers were arrested and imprisoned, though not for long as the orders were unclear. Schools that charged tuition were closed, and only some elementary schools and orphanages managed to stay open. The lay population were also deeply affected: letters show that every family, even the wealthiest, suffered. Inventories of private homes and monasteries were used to confiscate provisions, clothes and especially bedding. Precious objects were taken as well, naturally. And when those questioned refused to cooperate, they were severely threatened. The Jesuits were greatly impacted by the pillaging of the Faculty of Medicine; all their instruments were carried off to Damascus. Nothing was left of the library and its oriental manuscripts, which had been the pride of Beirut. The offices of the military postal service occupied these spaces. From this dark era, lists detail the precious objects and works of art that were seized, abandoned or even hidden in the cracks of walls behind furniture or buried in private gardens – grist for the mill of treasure hunters' imaginations.

But let's not ruin the party with these old stories, we should let our companions bid each other adieu on good terms. At the end of the evening, hope is essential! Hope for the friends of the General to see French interests endure in this beautiful land, while the population dreams of independence.

Did this notion of "Greater Lebanon" constitute the promise of a brighter future? What power do these words hold? And how exactly did Lebanon suddenly become "Greater"? Could General Gouraud's dinner reception have been the first step towards Lebanese independence? I ask you. For though I am convinced of the importance of proclaiming this name – Lebanon – loud and clear (and with such pride!) I do fear that in the mouth of Gouraud and others, this "greater" was intoned with a lowercase "g". It is an adjective describing its borders perhaps, or an appeal for support. It certainly did not mark the end of the French Mandate in Lebanon, and it would be another 23 years until the Lebanese achieved true independence.

I have transcribed this story for you just as it was told to me by my grandmother during the long summer evenings I spent each year at her house in Beirut. I am completely fascinated by these figures who haunt Lyon with the names they have bequeathed to its streets. Truth be told, I was more intrigued by my grandmother. What a crazy life she lived! I did not have to wait 23 years to find out the end of the story. I saw so many photos at exhibitions and concerts that ceaselessly animated the Beirut of the 1950s and 60s, a utopian time when everything seemed possible: Religious reconciliation, peace, splendour and luxury for all. The brand-new logos of the banks that you ran into on every street corner, the oranges you ate at the bay of Zeitouneh while watching buildings literally rise up before you, the white buses with a red stripe. Then, the civil war destroyed everything. People saw Beirut's monstrous face, monstrously real. Last week, as I watched over my grandchildren playing with a ball near the marina of the new Confluences neighbourhood in Lyon, I saw a Transport Commun Lyonnais bus pass by, and it reminded me of the disfigured face that is once again the Beirut of today after the explosion in the city's port on that August afternoon in 2020. I thought back to the tearful face of Emmanuel Macron, whether genuine or feigned, as he embraced entire families, just as France had embraced all of Lebanese life a century earlier. It was now no longer a question of fascination. I wanted to understand.

This text is freely inspired by the archives of the Consulate of France in Beirut[1] *and those of the Lyonnais silk companies,*[2] *as well as the Lyonnais press of the time.*[3] *It is the result of numerous months of research that unearthed an immense quantity of these micro-histories which, here and there, cross paths with History.*

Julia Etournay-Lemay

1. CADN, Nantes

2. Departmental and Metropolitan Archives of the Rhône, Lyon

3. Municipal Library of Lyon

Colophon

This catalogue is published in conjunction with the exhibition *manifesto of fragility: The Many Lives and Deaths of Louise Brunet*, 14 September – 31 December 2022. macLYON, Lyon.

CATALOGUE

Editors
Sam Bardaouil and Till Fellrath

Coordinating Editor
Natasha Gasparian

Authors
Sam Bardaouil and Till Fellrath
Isabelle Bertolotti
Julia Etournay-Lemay
Franny Tachon

Graphic Designers
Studio Safar

EXHIBITION

Curators
Sam Bardaouil and Till Fellrath

Artistic Director
Isabelle Bertolotti

Research assistant
Julia Etournay-Lemay

Exhibition Coordination
Frédérique Gautier
Franny Tachon

Exhibition Designer
Olivier Goethals

Technical Managers
Olivier Emeraud, Pascale Guinet

Exhibition Registrars
Pomme Harbonnier, Yuna Le Rudelier, Lauriane Vatin

With the help of Bérangère Amblard, Janelle Beau, Lucie Colleu, Charles-Olivier Gohy, Muriel Jaby, Marilou Laneuville, Auregann Le Bouffant, Matthieu Lelièvre, Julien Nemoz, Elise Vion-Delphin and the entire Biennale de Lyon and macLYON teams

The curators wish to thank all the artists, collectors, foundations, galleries and institutions for their collaboration and support:
Mohamad Abdouni; Gabriel Abrantes; Ann Agee; Julio Anaya Cabanding; Giulia Andreani; Olivier Bathellier; Joachim Bandau; Sarah Betite; Luc Berthet; Bernard Berthod; Armelle Bonneau-Alix; Phoebe Boswell; Sylvain Bouteille; Sarah Brahim; Delphine Cano; Georges Cardoso; Sylvie Carlier; Berthe et Ronald Chagoury; David Cizeron; Jean Claracq; Nicolas Daubanes; Karine Delerba; Anaïs Desrieux; Laurent Deverriere; Michaël Douvegheant; François Dubois; Julie Duprat; Şirin Ediger; Gabriel El Daher; Buck Ellison; Léo Fourdrinier; Geneviève Galliano; Nicki Green; Léa Herlet; Marie-Paule Imberti; Claire Iselin; Philippe Jabre; Merja Laukia; Hélène Lafont Couturier; Sophie Leconte; Richard Learoyd; Hannah Levy; Charlotte Maday; Lucy Mc Rae; Luc Requier; Marion Ménard; Jesse Mockrin; Esclarmonde Monteil; Ailbhe Ní Bhriain; Jeanne Orlé; Stéphane Paccoud; Cécile Parigot; Alain Peyrot; Sergueï Piotrovitch d'Orlik; Joanna Piotrowska; Christina Quarles; Sylvie Ramond; Manuelle-Anne Renault; Paul Ripoche; Erin M. Riley; Ugo Schiavi; Markus Schinwald; Sylvie Selig; Xavier de la Selle; Maria Serrano; Jeremy Shaw; Kim Simonsson; Anne-Laure Sounac; Maxime Tonnerre; Salman Toor; Guy Tosatto; Isabelle Varloteaux; Ludmila Virassamynaiken; Munem Wasif; Zhang Yunyao and Agnès de Zolt.

Archives départementales du Rhône et de la métropole de Lyon; Archives jésuites; Archives nationales; Bibliothèque municipale de Lyon; Bibliothèque historique de la ville de Paris; Bibliothèque nationale de France; Casey Kaplan, New York; domobaal, London; Don Gallery; Double V Gallery; Estate of Semiha Berksoy; Galeria Jacqueline Martins; Galerie Max Hetzler Berlin|Paris|London; Galerist; Gallery Isabelle van den Eynde; Hauser & Wirth, London; König Galerie Berlin/Seoul/Vienna; Ministère de l'Europe et des Affaires étrangères - Centre des Archives diplomatiques de Nantes (CADN) and Centre des Archives diplomatiques de La Courneuve; mother's tankstation ; Musée des Beaux-Arts, Lyon; Musée des Confluences, Lyon; Musée de Grenoble; Fondation Fourvière / Musée d'Art Religieux de Fourvière; Musée d'Histoire de Lyon - Gadagne; Musée des Hospices Civils, Lyon; Musée des Moulages; Lugdunum - Musée & théatres romains, Lyon; Musée municipal Paul-Dini, Villefranche-sur-Saône; Night Gallery; Œuvres Pontificales Missionnaires - Maison de Lorette; Pace Gallery, New York; The Peter Hujar Archives LLC; The Philippe Jabre Art Collection; Pilar Corrias, London; P-P-O-W Gallery; Staatliche Kunstsammlungen Dresden; Southard Reid.

LA BIENNALE DE LYON

SILVANA EDITORIALE

ISBN 9788836652983

Direction
Dario Cimorelli

Art Director
Giacomo Merli

Editorial Coordinator
Sergio Di Stefano, Giulia Mercanti

Copy Editing
Jackie Ricciardi

Production Coordinator
Antonio Micelli

Translations
Scriptum S.r.l

Photo Editor
Silvia Sala

Press Office
Alessandra Olivari
press@silvanaeditoriale.it

MIX
Paper from responsible sources
FSC® C127663
FSC
www.fsc.org

Silvana Editoriale S.p.A.
via dei Lavoratori, 78
20092 Cinisello Balsamo, Milano
tel. 02 453 951 01
www.silvanaeditoriale.it

Reproductions, printing and binding in Italy

Printed October 2022